Essays & Sketches

Essays & Sketches

OBERLIN

1904-1934

BY

Kemper Fullerton

Essay Index Reprint Series

Originally published for
OBERLIN COLLEGE
by
YALE UNIVERSITY PRESS

BOOKS FOR LIBRARIES PRESS
FREEPORT, NEW YORK

INTERNATIONAL STANDARD BOOK NUMBER:
0-8369-2361-8

LIBRARY OF CONGRESS CATALOG CARD NUMBER:
70-156644

PRINTED IN THE UNITED STATES OF AMERICA

TO

MY DEAR WIFE

In memory of the many happy years
that we have spent together

CONTENTS

The Arboretum—November

FOREWORD

IT is with considerable hesitation that I offer to the public the following selection of essays and sketches, most of which are definitely connected with the noon-hour chapel service in Oberlin College. I doubt if I ever should have had the courage to publish them but for my dear friend, Howard Doust, of the class of 1931, who came to me early in his senior year to extend to me a formal invitation from his class to give their commencement address. It was very pleasant to be so honored, and I yielded, though with grave doubts, to Howard's persuasion. The kindly reception later given that address was one of the happy experiences of my life. Accordingly, when Howard came to me again in the summer of 1937 with the suggestion that I publish a selection of my chapel talks in which the student audiences had shown an interest, I consented without delay. But in the midst of our maturing plans came Howard's untimely death. I cannot refrain from expressing at this point my deep sorrow at the death of one who had shown himself in every way to be a true friend. Without his encouragement and unfailing faith in what I was trying to do, this book would never have been offered for public inspection.

My warm thanks are also due to my friend and colleague, Professor Louis Lord, who took up the plans for publication which Howard's death had left unfinished and brought them, with some necessary changes, to completion, with characteristic willingness to spend any amount of time and labor to aid a friend.

I should like to say a word about the collection of essays and sketches as a whole. At first sight they seem to lack any principle of unity whatever. They were given at various times and with no thought, originally, of any possible relationship among them. But they may be grouped as follows without undue artificiality:

Part I contains the more or less informal talks given in the College Chapel. The first sixteen of these talks, it is hoped, may either awaken or strengthen student interest in some of the fundamental problems of religion and ethics which an educated man should be willing to consider as an organic part of life. As such they should have an interest for students outside the Oberlin circle as well as for those who like to breathe in an Oberlin atmosphere.

The three addresses on the Genius of Oberlin in Part II reflect the special religious and ethical interests to which Oberlin dedicated itself at the beginning of its history. While these, again, have Oberlin chiefly in mind, there are incidental suggestions in them which may be of interest to colleges and universities which, like Oberlin, were founded primarily in the interest of religion, but which, unlike it, have subsequently become thoroughly secularized. The memorials on Dr. Bosworth and Dr. Currier may be regarded as illustrating, in their persons and teachings, the strength with which the early convictions of Oberlin were still held in the generation immediately preceding my own, though in Dr. Bosworth's case there was a very definite tendency to turn from older methods of solving ancient problems to newer ones.*

Parts III and IV are admittedly much more heterogeneous in character. The material in Part III has a loose connection with the preceding essays through the fact that the experiences recounted in it are very definitely the results of my connection with Oberlin during my sabbatical year. A section of the second chapter was also given in chapel and the third was written for the *Oberlin Literary Magazine* (prede-

* At this point a full appraisal of Dr. King's great work would be in order. But it has been the particular privilege of others, notably of Professor Wager, to fill out the hiatus left in my collection of essays (*see* the *Alumni Magazine* for April, 1934). Further, no paper of mine in the present miscellany was originally written for this collection.

cessor of the *Olympian*) at the request of Elizabeth Martin of the class of 1916. Two of these chapters are disproportionate in length as compared with other sections of the book and their interest is of an entirely different kind. It so happened that we were among the very few Americans who were in Jerusalem during the early stages of the World War, and it is possible that our wartime experiences may be even yet of sufficient historical interest to warrant preserving an account of them in permanent form. Their frankly autobiographical character also fits, without undue difficulty, with the thinly veiled autobiographical character of much of the preceding material.

The sketches, "Shreds and Patches" and "Some Problems of Liberal Protestantism," in Part IV have special claims to appear in this volume. The latter is more theological in character than the other sections of the book but it is a by-product of many years of hard work and has, I trust, a contribution to make to the solution of some of the burning religious problems of our times. The somewhat unconventional mingling, in "Shreds and Patches" and elsewhere in these sketches, of what was spoken in all seriousness with what was said in lighter vein may be justified by the fact that our College chapel service has often presented in my time similar combinations of grave and gay. Though my book is primarily designed for the Oberlin constituency and indulges in not a few localisms, I cherish the hope that a larger circle of readers may also find in it incidental suggestions here and there which may prove helpful in starting fresh trains of thought on subjects new and old. Finally, I may add that the inclusion of "Jonah" in the book is due solely to my love for this little tract which has filtered down to us out of an immemorial past like some sweet perfume.

I wish to make acknowledgments to the *Christian Herald* for permission to use the material in an article of mine, "When the War came to Jerusalem," published May 22,

1918; to the *Survey Graphic* for the poem "Runnin' Wild" which appeared in an article on Jazz by Mr. J. A. Rogers in the issue of March, 1925; to *The Journal of Religion* for permission to reprint my article, "Some Problems of Liberal Protestantism," in Vol. XVI, July, 1936; to *Harper's Magazine* for the court scene from "The Pacifist Bogey," Oct., 1930; to *The Modern Temper* by Joseph Wood Krutch (Harcourt, Brace, 1929); and to *The Idea of Progress* by J. B. Bury (Macmillan and Company, 1920).

K. F.

Oberlin, September, 1938

PART I
MISCELLANEOUS CHAPEL TALKS

THE CHURCH

All Saints' Day, Jerusalem, 1914

ALL Saints' Day falls on November 1. It is introduced by Halloween on the evening of October 31. Until 1914 I never fully realized the connection between the two celebrations. My associations with Halloween were the usual ones—ringing doorbells, pumpkin faces, ducking for apples, and as much noise as possible. Halloween was originally a pagan festival which was later grafted on to the Church festival of All Saints. The latter seems to have originated in the ninth century and was itself a Christian substitute for more ancient observances connected with the cult of the dead. The origin of the customs connected with Halloween goes back to remote antiquity, to the Druids and to the feast of Pomona, the Roman goddess of fruit trees (hence the prominence of apples and nuts in our celebration). I would not begrudge the historic right to celebrate Halloween in the traditional way, the right to disguise yourselves in masks in order to make yourselves unrecognizable by the goblins who prowl abroad at that time and who "might get you if you didn't watch out," or to make all the noise you can to frighten off any ghosts or demons who may chance to be out racketeering on this particular evening. These customs are among the vested interests of youth which I hope the growing opposition to vested interests in general will still permit.

But sixteen years ago I had an experience which has ever since led me to think less of Halloween and more of All Saints' Day. It was an experience difficult to put into words, but I will try for I believe something was involved in it which has always been helpful to me and may be helpful to you. Sixteen years ago this week I was in Jerusalem. To the tourist in normal times the city rarely discloses itself. Its surface aspect, at least in those days, was not inviting, and travelers usually come away disappointed. Its numerous rubbish heaps seem to obliterate the past and to make the present ugly. It is difficult, at first, to realize that in those streets the prophets of ancient Judah and Jesus himself once walked and taught. But we were there not in normal but in abnormal times. The Great War which had engulfed so much of the world was gradually sucking Jerusalem, the world city, down into its terrible vortex. The tourists had all fled. The city was left to itself as it had not been for over fifteen hundred years. At that time I saw the real Jerusalem emerge, the city of perhaps a longer continuous history than any other in the world, a city of tragedy, yet which has always been to Jew and Christian alike a symbol of hope. Its aspect befitted its history. It was gray with age and stern looking, almost forbiddingly so. Only its wonderful walls served to soften at times the harsh impression which it made, as they turned golden-brown in the afternoon sunshine or soft gray-green in the twilight. This ancient capital, solemn and stern, yet with a certain mellowness imparted to it by its encircling walls, seemed to me to be a symbol of the bereavement and sorrow of the world, an epitome of the tragedy of human life, but of tragedy heroically endured.

On October 31 we learned that Turkey had entered the war. There was no frolic that Halloween in Jerusalem. I shall never forget as long as I live the strange sensations I had as I walked through the city's streets that autumnal afternoon. Scarcely a soul was to be seen. The day happened to be both a Jewish and a Mohammedan sacred day, and the usually crowded markets and bazaars were all closed. The stillness was almost uncanny. It seemed as if the city which knew, as few cities have known, what bloodshed and the terror of war meant, had withdrawn within itself to meditate upon the meaning of this new chapter in its history which was now about to unfold. Yet, strangely enough, a kind of calm settled down upon us. There seemed to be expectancy but not nervousness in the air. It was as if this world city recognized that it must take its place in the World War as a matter of course. The city which stood as a symbol of the tragedy of human life seemed to be facing the new crisis like an aged man who has come to understand that sorrow is a necessary part of life but is not daunted by the thought. It was as if we were entering into the sweep of the great world agony in the one place on the earth where its meaning would be fully understood. There was a certain solemn exaltation in the thought.

That same week I had received the news of the death of a very dear friend. He was a man just my own age and one whom I had known and loved from early boyhood. He was rapidly attaining a position of national prominence. One evening, as he was crossing the street in front of his own home to mail a letter to his mother, he was struck down and killed by a young girl, speeding in an automobile. At the funeral service his coffin had been borne aloft on the shoulders of young men through the aisles of the cathedral in which he had exercised the office of a Bishop, in order to symbolize the challenge which his life of Christian faith threw down to his untimely death. Rarely in my life have I realized so keenly the solemnity of human existence as I did in the last week of October, 1914. But was that all of it? Was there nothing more in human life than sorrow and tragedy?

In that year All Saints' Day fell on a Sunday and we went to Vesper service at the Anglican Cathedral of St. George's. Most of the English residents of Jerusalem who could get away had left weeks before. Of the Cathedral chapter only the canon and the head master of the boys' school remained behind. But the choir of young Syrian lads had not yet been disbanded, and the canon had thus far managed to continue the full service of the church without interruption. That Sunday afternoon there were only seven of us in the congregation to join in the responses—my own family, a retired English army officer and his son, and two others. I recollect very distinctly the feeling that came over me as we sat, a small handful of us, in the nave of the great church in the growing dusk, while the storm of world conflict was swirling all about us and beginning to beat against the walls of Jerusalem. That beautiful cathedral in the city where the Christian faith was born, with the stately music sounding through its aisles and the words of comfort and re-assurance issuing from its pulpit, became for me a symbol of the Christian faith and an embodiment of the Christian Church. In spite of all the anxiety, the world-agony, the per-sonal sorrow of the time, there was a sense of security in that service, a majesty and serenity that appealed to something much deeper than the aesthetic sense. The Church of Christ stood tranquil in the midst of the uproar. The calmness of the ancient city and the calmness of the service seemed to join in a great antiphonal:

> Our lives through varying scenes are drawn
> And vexed with trifling cares;
> But thine eternal thought moves on
> Its undisturbed affairs.

It may be objected that all this was only a sentimental reac-tion to a very unusual situation. This is undoubtedly a pos-sible explanation. Yet I prefer to believe that now and then there come crises in the lives of all of us in which we catch a glimpse of a deeper meaning in existence than at other times and are confronted with profounder realities than those of our ordinary daily life. What I have described may be thought by many to be only moonshine. Yet moonshine may also be thought of as the reflection of the most tremendous reality in our solar system, the sun itself. In the present instance, city, church, and sacred day seemed to suggest that the consciousness of an immemorial past and of an unhorizoned future is of great value to one who would pass through his brief segment of life with dignity and calm. For All Saints' Day is the day on which the Church looks back upon the saints, apostles, prophets, martyrs of its heroic past and thinks of them not as dead but as living in the blessed future. In that feast a mystical union is effected between the past, the present and the future, and the glorious memories of the Church are merged into yet more glorious hopes.

And in that cathedral service at Jerusalem it seemed as if the eternal world had for a moment disclosed itself and the invisible had become visible. Somehow the thought of death and the other life did not come with the shock and strangeness with which it often meets us. That other life seemed to surround the present life protectingly as the walls of Jerusalem surround the sorrowful city, to fill it with a solemn and majestic beauty like the beauty of the cathedral service. Security, nobility and beauty—it is these qualities which the realization of the unseen world, whither the saints have gone, should impress upon our lives. Security, as against the nervousness and anxiety of a life without faith. Nobility, as against all that is mean and vulgar. Beauty, as against the rubbish that clutters up the pathways of the soul. This realization is an achievement of faith. The unseen world cannot be demonstrated to exist by logic or by science. If it could, it would probably lose its religious value. Nor can its reality be felt with equal vividness at all times. But as the inexorable years advance upon us and the time of our departure is at hand, may the truth that seemed to me to be unfolded, if only for the moment, in the Vesper service on All Saints' Day in Jerusalem become ever less shadowy and more substantial, and may we increasingly realize the essen-

tial thing in that expectant vision of the writer of the Epistle
to the Hebrews:

But ye are come unto Mount Zion and unto the city of the living
God, the heavenly Jerusalem, and to the innumerable hosts of angels,
and to the general assembly and church of the first born who are en-
rolled in heaven, and to God the judge of all . . . and to Jesus the
Mediator of a new covenant . . .

THE CHURCH

"Nie wieder Krieg," Berlin, 1922

SUNDAY, July 30, was a bright, warm day in Berlin. Again, as on that tragic day eight years earlier, crowds were gathering in the square before the same royal Palace, from the balcony of which the Kaiser made his famous speech announcing war. We watched them assemble, quiet, orderly, all of them, as far as we could judge, belonging to the working classes. Weaving in and out among the people were processions of young men and women, bare legged, with wreathes on their heads, led by players on violins and guitars, the representatives, at that time, of the youth movement in Germany. Two young boys at the risk of their lives climbed the tall equestrian statue of Frederick William III and waved the flag of the Republic in the face of this representative of the Hohenzollerns.

The scene was impressive in the extreme. Here was a vast demonstration against war by representative workingmen of the world, most of whom had themselves known war at first hand. *Nie wieder Krieg* sounded on every side. There was a genuine religious fervor in it all, a great moral protest against the blood and agony and folly of the preceding years. As we watched the strange sight, we felt that we were seeing something new under the sun, that here was a great tide welling up out of the life of the common people of the world and bearing us on to new continents of truth to be explored and made fruitful for the needs of man.*

The formal exercises were to begin at twelve o'clock. While waiting for them to commence I chanced to look across the square to the Church of the Apostles, the court

---

* The fulfilment of these fond hopes has been sadly postponed, but it is to be hoped only postponed.

church of Berlin in former days. Architecturally it was hideous—huge, aggressive, arrogant. But over the main portal there were written two passages of Scripture that caught my eye. "Come unto me all ye that labor and are heavy laden, and I will give you rest. . . . This is the victory that overcometh the world, even our faith." At eleven o'clock the regular services of the church were over. The few members of the congregation had straggled out. The great doors under the Scripture texts had swung to. At noon, thirty representatives of those who had labored and were heavy laden mounted thirty different speakers' stands and simultaneously denounced war with Apostolic fervor though not in the name of the Apostles, and then the augmented band of the laboring men stood on the steps before the fast-closed doors of the Church of the Apostles and played, not a choral of the ancient faith but the "International"! I confess, to one like me whose life had largely revolved around the Church, those closed doors, the vast throng intent upon its great ethical protest but utterly oblivious of church and texts, and the strains of the "International" sounding through the spaces where, only a few years before, one of the most powerful absolute monarchies in the world had ruled, were a baffling, a staggering experience. Was it an omen that those spiritual forces identified with the Christian Church, which had been an integral part of Western culture for two thousand years, were at last played out? Is the Christian Church to take its place with the hierarchies of the Babylonian Pantheon and the cult of Jupiter Capitolinus? Is its spirit unequal to the rigorous demands of the present day? Are our exercises in Oberlin, our chapel hour, our Y.M. and Y.W. activities, our church services on Sunday, just automatic motions, muscular contractions of an organism that is already dead, or at least just about to die?

These are serious questions, not to be lightly brushed aside, and for my part I do not believe that any young man

or woman who aspires to live the Christian life can expect to
do so without the sound sense of his choice being fiercely and
aggressively challenged from every quarter. Nevertheless,
though these "fears and scruples" at times force themselves
upon my mind as they must upon the mind of every thought-
ful person who seriously confronts the facts of life today, I
feel I can honestly say that in the bottom of my soul I believe that the Church's course is not yet run, its power for
good is not yet spent. When I think of the spiritual significance of the invitation and the faith inscribed over the portal of the castle-church in Berlin, I believe there is a power
there which will force those doors open again. I believe that
at the heart of the Church's life, obscured though it often is,
there is the noblest form of idealism yet revealed to man, an
idealism capable of almost endless varieties of expression
and therefore adaptable in a marvelous degree to the changing needs of man. It was this idealism which accomplished
perhaps the most remarkable feat in the history of civilization, when in three short centuries it hurled from the throne
"the antique sovereign intellect" embodied in the Roman
Empire—that most compact and powerful organization ever
formed by man. It is no accident that the chronology of
world history falls into just two periods, the ages before
Christ and the ages subsequent. It was this idealism which
showed its striking power of self-renewal at the time of the
Reformation and in company with Humanism introduced
our modern era. I believe this power of self-renewal is constant in the Church. Its idealism will not suffer itself to be
covered over for any length of time with mere conventions
and pretenses, adopted by a spiritually lazy generation which
regards the demands of idealism as too strenuous, or by selfish people who wish to use the Christian Church for their
own unworthy ends. Sooner or later it is bound to break
through. I grant that when one sees some weak and strug-
gling congregation presided over by some inefficient parson

who understands neither the essence of his own religion nor
the needs of human nature, it is hard to realize the great life
that lies behind such a futile phenomenon. But the vast momentum of the Christian Church, due to the accumulated experiences of the noblest of men in every country and every
clime for the past two thousand years cannot be ignored.

And in what does this idealism consist? I believe it consists, essentially, in a spiritual view of life, springing out of
Jesus' doctrine of God and of man as the son of God, more
refined, more noble, more beautiful, more benign than is con-
ceived in any other religion or philosophy. I realize, young
men and young women, that this is the expression of my convictions, not necessarily of your convictions. But as students
of history you are confronted with the Christian Church as
an historical phenomenon that has entered into the very
warp and woof of the civilization of which you yourselves
are a part. As educated persons, it is not only your privilege
but your duty to consider how far its claims and ideals
should enter into your life's plans and ambitions.

I have spoken thus far of the Christian religion and the
Christian Church as if they were one and the same thing.
But this is not quite accurate. It is truer to say that the idealism of the Christian religion embodies itself in an organization, the Christian Church. No ideal can live an unembodied
life. An ideal without some organization to incorporate it
and spread it is only a daydream, a fancy unattached to reality. An ideal, as distinguished from a daydream, has some
point of attachment to reality. The real always falls below
the ideal, the Christian Church as an organization below the
Christian religion as an ideal. But is the fact that the Church
as an organization necessarily falls short in some degree of
the ideals for which it stands a reason for neglecting or
scouting it? If you are at all interested in the idealism of the
Christian religion, there is every reason why you should
identify yourself with that great historic organization by

which this idealism has been propagated. And now I come to the practical application of this.

The college student leads in some respects a very abnormal life. He lives largely apart from the ordinary obligations of home and community. He has his own circle of social obligations, to be sure, but he is usually no organic part of the community in which, for four years, he happens to live. Now the various churches are important factors in the community life. Their interests and their supporters are mainly found in the homes of the community. College students, even Christian college students, are therefore apt to take very lightly any obligations connected with community churches. Hence, special church services are often provided by the colleges themselves. Oberlin has never felt that this was a satisfactory solution of the problem. The normal life and activities of the Church cannot be developed in a purely college church. Oberlin has accordingly always considered the community churches to be the best instruments for supplying the religious needs of the students and avoiding the danger of their becoming detached from the normal life of the Church during the four years of their college course. Too often it happens that religious activities solely confined to the students divert their interest from church life, an interest seldom or never regained in after years.

May I in a closing word suggest what the Church has to offer. It does not offer a good time. Other facilities which need not be mentioned provide that. It offers something more necessary than that. This is perhaps the most restless, the most self-conscious, the most dissatisfied era in the history of the world. As has often been pointed out, our mechanical mastery over nature has outstripped our moral development. We have acquired vast powers which we have not yet learned how to apply to moral and spiritual ends. What is the consequence? A divided self, nervous instability. The experience of the war and postwar years may be regarded, pathologically, as an attack of nerves on a cosmic scale—first, hysteria increasing to homicidal mania, and then prostration. I venture to say that there is scarcely a young person among you, however strongly the hot blood of youth may pulse in his veins, however seemingly contented with merely a good time he may be, who does not at times feel distraught, confused, dissatisfied, who does not feel the lack of something in his life which he finds it difficult to define. It is quite possible to crush out these struggles against the spirit which was born in you and which protests for a time against its starvation, and to effect a unified life on a low plane, the plane, for example, of a successful, heavy-jowled man or woman of the world perfectly content to sit on the porch of a summer hotel after a heavy breakfast and before a heavy dinner and to enjoy the vulgarities of the comic Sunday supplement. This is a possible culmination for the lives of many of you. But in that very culmination you condemn yourselves to the life of an animal.

There is another possible way to achieve a unified life. On quiet Sunday mornings, to sit awhile in a place dedicated to the collective expression of a faith in the reality and importance of the unseen world, to listen to the gentle singing of the inner spirit, to grow into the consciousness that you belong to two worlds which can be brought into unity not by the gradual cancellation of the higher world but by a gradual sublimation of the lower one. The Church offers the opportunity of a unified life on a high plane. The Church offers not a good time but peace. "Unfold ye portals everlasting. Come unto me all ye that labor and are heavy laden and I will give you rest. . . . This is the victory that overcometh the world, even our faith."

THE OLD TESTAMENT

I HAVE been asked to speak briefly to you about the Old Testament. What I have to say will mean little to you unless I can assume two things, first, that you have some interest in religion as one of the chief factors in the cultural development of the race, and secondly, that you have some interest in religion as an important factor in your own personal life. If you have no such interest I may be permitted to pity you, and you may be permitted to turn a deaf ear to me, and we are quits.

What we call the Old Testament is a collection of documents which cover a period of just about a thousand years, from, say 1150 B.C., the approximate date of the Song of Deborah, one of the greatest battle odes of the world, to 165 B.C., the date of the Book of Daniel. Both these documents come out of great national crises and are direct products of these crises. In this respect they are typical of the Old Testament literature as a whole. It is preëminently a national literature, intimately connected with the experiences of one of the most gifted peoples that has ever lived and suffered. About halfway along this period of a thousand years, say 600 B.C., this people endured a terrible national calamity. The flower of the nation was bodily deported hundreds of miles across the Syrian desert to the plains of Babylonia. Other nations had been similarly deported by the Assyrian and Babylonian kings and become lost forever in the surrounding populations. The Jews were the only nation of antiquity to survive such a catastrophe. After some seventy years they returned to Jerusalem.

On their arrival they set to work to do two things. The first was to build a church. The religious significance of their return was more prominent in their minds than its political significance. This religious interest persisted. For the next four hundred years they were, for the most part, politically insignificant, a petty province under Persian, Greek, and Roman rulers. It was their absorption in religion that impressed Greek travelers.

The second thing they did was to collect what they could find of their ancient literature that had survived the vicissitudes of the Exile. This literature consisted of some of the most wonderful story-writing to be found in antiquity, legends about the origin of their nation and their early kings, devotional poetry connected with the temple service, laws, principally regulating the temple worship, and above all, the words of their great prophets or religious leaders. This literature existed in a very fragmentary and confused form which makes it undoubtedly difficult to understand, but it nevertheless represents one of the most priceless legacies of the race.

Now the important thing about these fragments is that their interest is almost exclusively religious. Where this was not the case, the collectors who reverently gathered them together surrounded them with a framework which sought to impart to them a religious meaning. These collections of earlier fragments were supplemented in the course of the next four hundred years with still other compositions, historical memoranda, religious tracts, poems, hymns, sermons, many of them, also, preserved only in fragmentary form, until the collection of the Old Testament as we now have it was completed. All of this supplemental work was done with the same religious interest which animated the earlier writers and collectors.

The Old Testament is thus a literary phenomenon unique in the history of the world. It is the reflection of the history of a people who had once possessed a very strong sense of nationality; who had, at times in their earlier history, exercised considerable political control over their neighbors, who had suffered and survived a national calamity such as no other nation had been able to survive; who then sought to reconstruct their national life on a distinctively religious basis; and who, finally, developed a national literature that was also distinctively religious. The Old Testament is thus the reflection, almost exclusively, of the religious experience of Israel and Judah for a thousand years, from its primitive and even barbaric beginnings to its culmination in the purest form of religion and ethics to be found anywhere in antiquity. It does not reflect the intellectual or aesthetic or social or political life of the people except incidentally. Its emphasis is upon the religious life.

But you may very naturally ask: What has this to do with me? The Old Testament might be of interest to a student of the history or philosophy of religion, but why should I concern myself with it? If this were all that is to be said about the Old Testament, this objection might have some measure of justification. But it is not all.

When the collection of Old Testament documents was practically complete, there arose among this peculiar people the last and greatest of their prophets, who at the same time was destined to become the greatest religious leader of mankind. All his life he fed upon the religious literature of his people. His soul was steeped in its ideas. He said that he came not to destroy the Law and the Prophets but to fulfil them. The Old Testament was his Bible and the Bible of his earliest followers. Thus, through the example and teaching of Jesus and his Apostles, the Old Testament came to be in turn the first part of the Christian Bible. And now a strange thing happened. When this literature of the Jews moved out of its provincial confines into the larger world of Graeco-Roman civilization the impression it made was a very mixed one. People could read it only in a poor and inelegant Greek translation. In such a form it had little to commend it, from a literary point of view, to men alive to the exquisite beauty of Greek literature. It seemed formless, raw, common. It also had originated in the alien Semitic civilization and contained many primitive concepts the key to whose meaning had been lost. Even the morals of parts of it as distinct from its total effect seemed defective to those familiar with the advanced philosophical and ethical systems of Greece.

To many converts to Christianity who had been philosophically trained the Old Testament became a positive offense. About 150 A.D. a movement sprang up within the Christian Church, led by a remarkable man named Marcion, to exclude the Old Testament from the Christian Bible. The conflict was a hot one. For a time it threatened to wreck the Church. It was finally decided in favor of the Old Testament, and from that day to this the Old Testament has been one of the controlling factors in the religious life of Europe and, later, of America.

This decision was of supreme importance. By it the Church refused to cut its tap root, and established for the regulation of its own development one of the most fundamental principles for the life of any great organized movement in society, the principle of historical continuity. By it the Church associated itself with spiritual experience rather than with philosophical speculation, with life rather than with doctrine. It connected itself definitely with the experience of the past, and provided a proof that the Christian religion is a great unfolding movement in the history of the human race, which, beginning in the primitive experiences of mankind, and expanding, purifying and ennobling itself as time went on, reaches down to our present and becomes an integral factor of our civilization. Thus, through the Old Testament we become spiritually linked with primeval man in a very definite and tangible way. We become part of a sequence of spiritual experience covering a period of at least three thousand years.

Does the existence of such a body of religious experience

have no significance for you? Is there no support for you in your spiritual struggles in the thought that you are part and parcel of a vast, continuous, spiritual movement, that you stand in a long succession of godly men and women? Perhaps this mystical union with the past, reënforced through the Old Testament as a part of our religious inheritance, means nothing to you. In that case I am sorry, for it is only to the hopelessly Philistine that the mystical, the spiritual, poetry, art, religion, mean nothing.

I have dwelt thus long on the importance of the Old Testament as an integral factor in the Christian experience which we have inherited because this fact is seldom discussed. I have left myself time for only one illustration of the Old Testament's inherent spiritual power, which explains the profound influence it has exerted.

In 745 B.C. one of the great conquerors of the earth came upon the stage. His name was Tiglath-pileser and he was a king of Assyria. Syria and Palestine trembled at his name. And well they might. His chronicles are a dreary repetition of how he "conquered, plundered and burned with fire" the capitals of the wretched little Kingdoms of the West-land. But the sands of the desert finally buried Tiglath-pileser and his chronicles and his capital, and only in the last fifty years have his mutilated records been recovered and deciphered by scholars working with enduring patience in their studies, remote from the notice of the majority of men. And why is there today any interest in this mighty warrior? Six years after he came to the throne, in the small fortress-capital of Jerusalem, hidden away in rough mountain country off the beaten line of the world's traffic, a Jewish citizen, Isaiah, the son of Amoz, received his call to a prophetic career. His life was spent in the attempt to guide his country through the terrible crisis precipitated by Tiglath-pileser and his immediate successors. Everyone in Syria and Palestine knew the name of Tiglath-pileser. Few if any outside of his fellow countrymen ever heard of Isaiah and most of his fellow citizens bitterly disliked him. But from that day to this the fragments of Isaiah's utterances which have been preserved have been a source of spiritual refreshment to countless numbers of men, and the main interest of the records of the Assyrian king, when they were at last dug out of the rubbish heaps of Nineveh, was the fact that they threw a flood of light upon the words of the Hebrew prophet. Above the dull reiteration of Tiglath-pileser's atrocities—"I conquered, plundered and burned with fire"—sound to our day Isaiah's words, "In returning and rest ye shall be saved, in quietness and confidence your strength shall be." The Old Testament deals in the final analysis not with the noisy conquests of arms and the pageantries of power but with the conquests of the human spirit and the quiet triumphs of the inner life—with the things unseen and eternal.

THE BIBLE

MANY years ago, in 1871 to be exact, my father
made his first trip to Europe. The journey in those
days was not the ordinary event which it has since
become, and when father chanced to meet a fellow passenger
who had already made it six or eight times, he was duly impressed. But he was still more astonished when this traveled
friend confessed to him that he had lived all his life so near
to Niagara Falls that when the wind was in the right direction he could hear the roar of the cataract, and yet he had
never seen it. Wonders that are accessible do not usually
allure. We are too apt to take them for granted. Thus, the
wonder of the Bible has ceased to impress us. Its very acces-
sibility has tended to dull our interest in it. There was once a
time when this was not the case, when the acquisition of a
copy of the Bible marked an epoch in a man's life. Luther
tells us in his *Table Talk* that he was twenty years old before he saw a Bible. Though printing at that time had been
practiced for more than sixty years, and the Bible was among
the first books to be printed, yet the cost of printing was still
so great that the ordinary man rarely owned a copy. A mar-
ginal reference in a Bible of 1499 states that it had been
bought for nine gulden, three times the price of a fat ox in
the contemporary market. But today the little spring that
bubbled forth with the publication of the Psalter in 1457
(the first printed book which has a certain date attached to
it) has become a flood, a veritable Niagara pouring from the
presses of the world at the rate of millions of copies annu-
ally. As it flows past us in ever increasing volume what
thoughts does it awaken in our minds?

A great river makes a wonderful appeal to the imagination. We think of its tiny sources far off in cool and shady

forests or among the snows of lofty mountaintops. We think of the quiet brooks or boisterous mountain torrents which seem to have no aim in life except to run or tumble about and gather wild flowers. By and by they settle down to business. They turn a wheel to cut the trees or grind the corn which their own moisture has ripened. As they unite in a gathering volume they begin to bear up steamers, prescribe routes of trade, determine the sites of great cities, till we find their rolling tide fertilizing and draining vast areas of land— a prime factor in the development of a continent. Some people are able to stand on the bank of such a river and never raise the question whence it comes or whither it goes or what is its significance. They who live upon its banks have seen it so often that it has lost its suggestiveness for them. They take it for granted.

To my mind the Bible is such a river. If you have been accustomed to look at it with a vacant, lusterless eye, and without the kindling interest of an explorer, may I ask you for just a few minutes to stretch the wings of your imagination, as old Heinrich Hudson stretched the wings of his small craft, and venture up this ancient river and catch something of the wonder and beauty of its course.

The wise old son of Sirach once compared the Mosaic Law to the four rivers of Paradise. There was a deeper truth in this comparison than he himself may have been aware of. Did you ever sufficiently realize that the sources of our Bible are in the remotest uplands of history? The Bible is the strongest link between us of the twentieth century and the men of the elder world. Many of the ideas and speculations beneath its surface are those of men at the dawn of history. I do not mean that the literary sources of the Bible are so ancient. Probably the oldest document of any length, the Battle Ode of Deborah, goes back only to the twelfth century B.C. I am speaking here of its thoughts. In his Bible the

Christian clasps hands across the centuries with men who lived when history was still young.

Again, when we look at the Old Testament as a whole, we see the ancient springs now united into a great river that has drained antiquity for us, more especially Semitic antiquity. I think it is no merely partisan claim, but a claim which can be safely subjected to the severest tests of historical criticism, that the Old Testament is the supreme literary and religious product of the Semitic world. As we learn more accurately the many points of contact between the Old Testament and the literatures of Egypt, Syria, Assyria, and Babylonia, we realize with increasing distinctness the astonishing superiority of Hebrew thought and literary expression.

But there was another great basin through which our river was to flow. To ignore the tributary streams that entered it from Persia, there were the sparkling waters of Greece. The Old Testament was translated from Hebrew into Greek, from a language belonging to one family (the Semitic) into a language belonging to an entirely different family (the Indo-Germanic)—at the time a prodigious literary accomplishment. Turned into this new channel, the stream became colored, as every river does, by the new soil through which it made its way. And then the turning point in its course was reached. It suddenly expanded and deepened into a current which seemed so different that even a new name was given to it—the New Testament. Not only did the increasing volume of waters still flow from the old sources, but fresh new springs seemed to be feeding them. The New Testament was, on the one hand, still Semitic, Oriental in its spirit. But it was originally written in the greatest language of the West, one of the finest media of human thought yet devised, the Greek language, and by men who not only spoke Greek but were, to some extent at least, influenced by Greek civilization. Here was, indeed, a marvelous combination—the

supreme intellectual and spiritual product of Semitic culture
(the Old Testament) canalized into the New Testament
which was written in the intellectually most stimulating language of the West.

It is said of Alexander the Great that he thought the Upper Nile and the Indus were one and the same river. May I
take advantage of so distinguished a precedent and speak of
the river which we have been exploring as changing its course
from Asia into Europe. The Oriental book was now adopted
by the West and made its own. Again the lands through
which it flowed colored the stream. Greek thought interpreted it; Latin thought interpreted it. Germanic and English thought interpreted it. Wherever it went, it brought fer-
tility along with it. New harvests of piety and spiritual
power were constantly springing up along its banks. The
Bible did not dry up by any means so completely in the
Middle Ages as has often been supposed. At least it continued, like some streams in the South, as a great underground river, bursting forth at intervals with new power.
Dante drew from it when he sought in his *Essay on Monarchy* to wash away the stains upon the civilization of his
day. Roger Bacon, reputedly the first to catch a glimpse of
the modern world, wrote an Epistle to Clement IV *In Praise
of Holy Scripture*. The followers of Wycliffe and John
Huss and all those parched souls who might otherwise have
perished in the deserts of ecclesiastical abuses slaked their
thirst at this perennial stream, until, at the Reformation, it
became confluent with that other tide of thought and experience which we call the Renaissance, and out of the mighty
flood thus formed the modern world emerged as the earth at
its creation emerged from the Deep.

For four hundred years the Bible has occupied a central
place in Western culture. The political upheavals which accompanied the Reformation had a biblical background. Civil
liberties and religious liberties now became inextricably in-

terwoven, and in this struggle for the liberation of human thought, for liberty of conscience and for freedom of the individual, the Bible has been a chief factor. Humanism by itself would have been unable to achieve the complete independence of the individual. It did not have the moral courage for the bloody struggles that at that time seemed to be necessary. Witness the result of Humanism in Italy where we find it in its purest development. It is true, as Burckhardt points out, that it produced a very interesting form of individualism and found expression in a glorious art that has gladdened the world ever since. But ethically, the Italian Renaissance was largely ineffective. It was the German Reformation which assured to the individual soul its rights as the religious unit over against the Church. In this the German Reformation was essentially biblical. Luther could never have composed his great reforming *Address to the German Nobility* or his even greater tract on *The Freedom of a Christian Man* if he had not first secured himself against the authority of the Church by reasserting the authority of Scripture. And in all the long and agonizing struggle that ensued the Bible was the battle flag that led the advance, till every page of it seems to have been splashed with the blood of martyrs and scorched with the fires of burning men from Spain to Smithfield.

And ever since those terrible days the commanding position of the Bible has been maintained. In literature and dogma, in politics and science, in individual reform and social betterment, the story is the same. In Milton, the greatest poet of Humanism, as Symonds calls him, the Bible is a dominant factor. His political tracts, especially his *Defense in Behalf of the English People*, in which the great principles of democracy are laid down against the contentions of James I (who sought to bolster up his regal claims by appealing to the same authority), derive an important premise in their argument from the Bible.

We cannot picture the Puritan without a Bible in his hands, and what the Puritan has meant and still means to the best life of the modern world we may at least dimly appreciate when we see on every side of us the hideous consequences of a morally relaxed civilization. On the other hand, it is interesting to notice how the great awakening of the social conscience that has characterized the opening decades of the twentieth century, has taken on, almost unconsciously, a biblical form (witness Tolstoy). And Kipling's death reminds us of the hold which biblical phraseology and allusion still have upon our English literary tradition, even in a writer in whom one would least expect to find it. Take for example the following stanza from "A Song of the English":

> Fair is our lot—Oh, goodly is our heritage!
> (Humble ye, my people, and be fearful in your mirth!)
> For the Lord our God Most High,
> He hath made the deep as dry,
> He hath smote for us a pathway to the ends of all the Earth!

There is not a phrase in it that does not show indebtedness to the Bible. I cannot forbear recalling also the testimony of Edmund Gosse, the English literary critic, who tells how, when a boy of only eight years, he listened to his father reading the magnificent first chapter of the Epistle to the Hebrews and was introduced thereby into "the magic of literature."

But we have yet to catch one more brief glimpse of a great bend in the course of our noble river where it finally rolls out into the sea. The nineteenth century saw the expansion of foreign missions, the most remarkable development in many ways, in the history of the Christian Church after its first three centuries and after the epoch of the Reformation. In foreign missions the Eastern book, interpreted by the West, is given back to the East again. The ancients had the idea of a world ocean that flowed around the earth. Our Bible, whose sources we have found in the uplands of the prehistoric, and whose gathering volume we have watched spreading from Asia into Europe, we now see expanding into innumerable delta streams in the five hundred languages and dialects into which it has been translated, until it finally enters into a world ocean encircling the globe. But its waters are unlike the dark, tempestuous waters of the primeval chaos of the ancients which threatened destruction to all that was beautiful and pure. The river of which I speak is, rather, like the crystal river, described in the Book of Revelation, which proceeds from the throne of God and of the Lamb. "And on this side of the river and on that side is the Tree of Life bearing twelve manner of fruits, yielding its fruits every month. And the leaves of the tree are for the healing of the nations."

Young men and young women, what I wish you to realize by the help of my overtaxed metaphor is that the Bible is a world book. I wish you to realize that

> Slowly the Bible of the human race was writ,
> And not on paper leaves or leaves of stone;
> Each age, each kindred adds a verse to it,
> Texts of despair or hope, of joy or moan;
> While swings the sea, while mists the mountains shroud.
> While thunders' surges burst on cliffs of cloud;
> Still at the Prophets' feet the nations sit.

It is true that in these lines Lowell was opposing the old hard-and-fast dogmatic idea of the Bible as a written law book and the thought that outside the sacred enclosure of the canon the breath of God did not whisper into the souls of men. But if our Bible is rightly understood, his words may be applied to it. Our Bible is the product of a world process. In the mere bulk of its circulation, in the vast area of its distribution, in its history that parallels and to a marked degree controls the history of what we know as civilization, the Bible is an absolutely unique phenomenon. It is a literary phenomenon that no educated man or woman can afford to ignore. It is a religious phenomenon that no one interested in the deeper problems of life may overlook. In its strange, eventful history the Bible bears striking testimony to the fact—the all important fact—that religion is one of the chief of mankind's concerns. The Bible has become a world book because it reflects most accurately and at the same time satisfies most adequately the great world needs.*

* It is this book which Herr Rosenberg and his neo-pagans would banish from the German schools in favor of Teutonic mythology as interpreted in Wagnerian opera! Was there ever a greater tragedy in the history of European civilization!

FIRE IN THE BONES*

I HAVE always been plagued by the Bible. I grew up in a very conservative atmosphere. I was told that the Bible was a divine book, and that if I believed every word of it I should get to heaven. I set myself to do this with great assiduity and for a long time succeeded in believing every word of Scripture though I did not get to heaven. Then I began to teach it and ran into Balaam's talking ass. I remembered there were good people in ancient times who had managed to swallow a camel. Why couldn't I swallow an ass? Were not piety and salvability dependent upon the capacity of one's gullet to swallow ungainly beasts? But I could not manage it, at least not all at once. It was years before I found out that I did not have to swallow a talking ass in order to be a Christian.

After that there was peace for a time. The Bible became for me the subject for harmless but absorbing antiquarian studies. Was Sennacherib's invasion of Palestine in 701 B.C. successful or wasn't it? What does the eating of butter and honey referred to in Isaiah 7.15 signify?—questions like those! Then came the war with all its problems. What are the ethics of war anyway? What is the relationship of the individual to the state? What is the meaning of liberty? What is democracy? Have we made the world safe for it by fighting? I began to notice that some people were becoming awfully excited about the Bible, that harmless old thesaurus of antiquarian lore. A Congregational minister ridiculed at length in a reputable and widely read magazine a passage in Isaiah that I had come to regard as religious poetry of a rather high order:

* The date of this chapel talk, about the time of the Palmer raids shortly after the end of the War, may account for its somewhat explosive character.

> In returning and rest shall ye be saved,
> In quietness and confidence shall be your strength.

What was the matter with that? Why was he so opposed to it? He called it "a Gospel of the Lotus Leaves."

A poor creature up in Winnipeg, in a moment of inadvertence, had quoted another verse from Isaiah as applicable to the present situation and was indicted for treason. There must be something in the book that did not fit our times and needs. Then there was the whole tribe of conscientious objectors and pacifists. They began to quote Scripture by the yard and were jailed. It worried me. One of our political ancestors, James Madison, once said in discussing war powers of the government: "It is in vain to oppose constitutional barriers to the impulse of self-preservation." That seemed to fit the case exactly until I recalled that this was essentially the principle which the Germans applied to the sinking of the *Lusitania*. Having got rid of most of the theological difficulties that centered in the Bible, I found myself confronted with political and social problems which centered in the same place. I began to lose taste for my essays on butter and honey. I began to wake up to the fact that there has never been a government for the last two thousand years which did not sooner or later lock people up for quoting the Bible. I began to see that the Scripture was as audacious as Ibsen and as seditious as the Declaration of Independence. Why was this, I asked myself. I came to the conclusion that it was because the Bible was written by men with fire in their bones. One of these fools (I use the word contemporaries applied to Jeremiah) describes the really impossible state of mind he was in at one crisis in his life.

O Lord, . . . thou art stronger than I and hast prevailed. For as often as I speak I cry out. . . . Violence and destruction; because the word of the Lord is made a reproach unto me and a derision, all the day. And if I say I will not make mention of him or speak any more in his name, then there is in my heart as it were a burning fire shut up in my bones. I cannot endure it or bear up (Jeremiah 20.7–9).

Some would say a fellow with such a high temperature as that ought to be placed in quarantine, and all these other cranks who are quoting Jeremiah today ought to be shut up along with him. Then I lighted upon a Bible passage which gave me great ease of mind. The contemporaries of Jeremy thought just as I did about him. The "fool" *would* be pro-Babylonian when the all-powerful Court party was pro-Egyptian and international relationships were very strained "down in Judee." Here is what happened to him:

Then Shephatiah the son of Mattan and Gedaliah the son of Pashur and several others heard the words that Jeremiah said unto all the people, to wit: Thus saith the Lord, he that abideth in his city shall die by the sword, by the famine, and by the pestilence. But he that goeth forth to the Babylonians shall live. Thus saith the Lord, This city shall surely be given into the hand of the army of the king of Babylon and he shall take it. Then the princes said unto the king, Let this man be put to death because he weakeneth the hands of the men of war and the hands of all the people in speaking such words to them. And Zedekiah, the king, said, Behold, he is in your hand; for the king is not he that can do anything against you. Then they took Jeremiah and cast him into the dungeon of Malchiah, the king's son, and they let down Jeremiah with cords. And in the dungeon there was no water but mire and Jeremiah sank in the mire (Jeremiah 38. 1–6).

The only trouble was, Jeremy did not stay put. Some poverty-stricken friends of his took up a collection of old rags and pieces of shirt, tied them together and called down to him as he paddled around in the mud to put them under his arms, which he did and they pulled him out.

MORAL

The Bible appears to be most of the time and for most people a burnt-out coal. But it was once ignited by men with fire in their bones. The danger is that when fanned by the winds which are just now blowing so hard about the world this piece of old slag may become a white-hot, live coal again. It is well for those who do not wish to get burnt to handle it with tongs.

WHAT THE SANDS OF EGYPT TRIED
TO HIDE

EGYPT is above all other countries the wonderland of the world. The contrasts in its scenery are astonishing, the amber-colored desert sands, the mighty sweep of the golden Nile, and between desert and river the ribbon of green wheat fields stretching away for five hundred miles to the first great cataract. At sunset the atmosphere takes up the various colors into itself, blends them with other richer hues, and the air about you seems for a time to bloom out into some gorgeous flower. All this above the desert sands.

And beneath them—what lies there? The remains of one of the most finished and beautiful civilizations that has ever graced our planet. For ages this civilization has been buried almost out of sight except for a few gigantic monuments such as the pyramids and larger temples. But in our day it is beginning to emerge from its long burial; and on the walls of tombs and temples, in beautiful reliefs, we see all the life of ancient Egypt enacted again before our eyes.

Until a short time ago the chief interest of excavator and tourist has been in these reliefs and the inscriptions that accompany them. But quite recently, particularly within the last thirty years, these memorials carved in stone have had to share their interest with the papyri. Thousands and thousands of sheets of this apparently fragile material have been preserved in the antiseptic sands of Egypt, and now we can read on the papyri what the people pictured on the reliefs actually wrote about themselves. Most of the papyri have been found in the rubbish heaps of the buried cities. They do not often contain books. They do not belong to literature in the technical sense of this term. They were mostly used for letter-writing or for diaries or schoolbooks, and especially in the practice of the law and in business. A very considerable portion of those that have been discovered and are now in the various museums of Europe and America date from the first centuries of the Christian era and are in Greek. And of these, some very precious fragments are of special interest for the history of early Christianity in Egypt.

A few years ago I was shown a kind of laboratory in the University of Michigan for which a large number of these papyri had been secured. Many of them were badly disintegrated. There were hundreds and hundreds, perhaps thousands of fragments, some not larger than one's fingernail, which were being sorted out by Dr. Sanders and his assistants and put together as one would put together a jigsaw puzzle. Some of the work was so delicate that it had to be done with the aid of a microscope. And what may come of all this painstaking work? Today Oberlin, for example, has in its library a copy of what is, perhaps, the oldest extant edition of the Minor Prophets, going back possibly to the second century of our era, all pieced together by Dr. Sanders from these bits of papyrus leaves. But there was one small fragment in the laboratory of Ann Arbor that interested me more even than this edition of the prophets. It was a legal document—a *libellus* or certificate—written in two different hands. The first sentence was in the hand of a man accused of treason to the Roman emperors and read as follows:

It was always our practice to sacrifice to the gods, and now, in your presence and in accordance with the order, we have sacrificed and made libations and have tasted the offerings. And we request you to certify this. Adieu.

Then follows in another hand the certification of the legal witnesses:

We, Aurelius Severus and Hermas, saw you sacrificing.

Finally the date is affixed, in the hand of the accused again:

The first year of the Emperor, Caesar Gaius Messius Quintus Trajanus Decius, Pius Felix Augustus (that is, 250 A.D.).

Here, after nearly two thousand years, there is revealed to us the shame of a man who was not true to his colors. I neglected to copy his name. But perhaps it is more merciful to forget it. This libellus is one of forty or fifty similar certificates that are known to exist. It comes out of the terrible persecution of the Christians by the Emperor Decius. The test presented by the Romans to the Christians was whether they would sacrifice to the Caesar or not. The man who was accused in this little papyrus sheet yielded to the pressure and sacrificed. We have the testimony of Aurelius and Hermas: *We saw you sacrificing.*

I have often wondered about this poor recreant to his faith. What turmoil of mind may he have been in the night before or the morning of the day of his trial. Could he sleep before that recantation? Of course he may have been hardboiled, in which case his experience is not interesting. But by 250 A.D. Christianity had not yet produced many hardboiled or simply conventional Christians. I venture to say that our poor friend had a terrible night before he tasted the sacrifice and poured the libation. Was he an old man, I wonder? Then one might suppose he would have been more courageous. If he had only a few years yet to live, why not die now like a man instead of being untrue? But old men probably cling more desperately to life than young men do. The years are so few and so very precious that old men grow miserly of time. Was he a young man and did the fair promises of life beckon him so invitingly that he yielded? Was he married? Did he have children? And did he say to himself: "For my family's sake I must sacrifice? How will they get along without me if I am killed?" Did his wife say

to him as he stood hesitating at the door of his home while
the officers of the law waited for him outside: "My dear,
dear husband, what is the difference if you do pour out a few
drops of wine and taste a little of the sacrifice. You know
that there is only one God and you can worship him in your
heart while you partake. It is only an outward rite after all
and means nothing. Did not the prophet Elisha permit Naa-
man, the Syrian, to bow down in the temple of Rimmon?"
Alas! how many avenues of escape we can find for ourselves
from the obligation to strict integrity of heart and mind!

But how did he feel when he returned home that evening
from the hall of justice, a freed but beaten man? He had
the libellus in his moneybag and he was now safe. I can see
him taking the little papyrus sheet out of his bag and reading it over greedily to make doubly sure. Yes, there was his
guarantee for life, liberty, and the pursuit of happiness.
Happiness! Was there any happiness left for him? Those
words—we, Aurelius Severus and Hermas, saw you sacrificing—would they not sear his conscience like a hot iron?
Egypt's gorgeous sunset flower was now blooming all about
him. Could he enjoy its colors? Or did the landscape seem
to him now all drab and lusterless? He had inflicted upon
himself a grievous wound. Did it ever heal over in the following years? Did its ugly scar ever disappear from his
soul? Poor fellow! I cannot feel indignant at his betrayal of
his noblest ideals, for should I have been more courageous
than he? I can only feel sorry for him and almost tremble
when I think of the tragedy of such a shame, a shame that
was buried by the sands of Egypt for nearly twenty centuries only to be revealed to us today. Can the influence of
any evil deed or any good deed be permanently obliterated?

There were other men in that Decian persecution who
stood the test. Martyrs for the love of Christ, men with fire
in their bones, exalted above their ordinary selves, transfigured.

Remember what a martyr said,
On the rude tablet overhead!
"I was born sickly, poor and mean,
A slave; no misery could screen
The holders of the pearl of price
From Caesar's envy; therefore, twice
I fought with beasts, and three times saw
My children suffer by his law;
At last my own release was earned:
I was some time in being burned,
But at the close a Hand came through
The fire above my head, and drew
My soul to Christ, whom now I see.
Sergius, a brother, writes for me
This testimony on the wall—
For me, *I have forgot it all.*"

Amid the heavenly splendors, the fiery gateway through which he entered into them is a forgotten thing. Old things are passed away, behold all things have become new.

TRADITION AND CONSCIENCE

THE last time it was my privilege to visit the fair land of Italy a shadow rested upon its loveliness— the shadow of Mussolini. Perhaps it is more correct to say that his shadow rested upon *me*. For one who had been a member of the Oberlin Liberal Club in its heyday, when it was "as terrible as an army with banners" to the Administration and to all good and respectable citizens of Oberlin, it was an ordeal to be obliged to keep his mouth shut for five weeks in Italy. My dumb mortification reached its climax when I saw my children, younger then than they are now, parading the streets of Florence on the anniversary of the beginning of the Fascist movement, wearing Fascist pins and singing with great gusto *Viva il Duce!* Everywhere we went we saw these same words scrawled on walls or over gateways. They were irritatingly inescapable.

But in those sorrowful days there was one moment when hope bubbled up within me. As we sailed along the shores of beautiful Lake Garda one balmy spring afternoon, we passed the picturesque little city of Malcesine crowned by a castle that belonged to the famous family of the Scaligers. There, on one of the city walls, were inscribed in huge characters the words *Viva la Libertà! Viva Mazzini!*—a hail to that greatest of Italian Liberals.

I was reminded of that encouraging inscription by a quotation from Mazzini which I later chanced upon and which I should like to pass on to you. It is this: "Truth lies at the point of intersection between the lines of Tradition and Conscience." This is not the word of a Radical. It is the word of a Liberal, and it is the expression of a great truth that is often overlooked, especially by the young. It recognizes, in the first place, the right and the duty of the conscience to assert itself. Conscience has a line of its own. Perhaps in nothing is our modern day so distinguished from antiquity as just in this matter of the supreme importance now attached to the individual and to his conscience.* The Declaration of Independence and the Constitution of the United States are the classic political expressions of this idea. Now it is true that what constitutes you you and me me is quantitatively almost infinitesimal and very difficult to come at through all the wrappings of inheritance and environment. But it is the most precious possession we have and when we allow it for any reason to become obscured, either through inertia or the timidity of conformity, we are committing spiritual suicide, and in our next incarnation we shall be herded, again, with the docile sheep with whom we belong. Perhaps the greatest tragedy of life is the carelessness with which most of us fritter away the energy that inheres in the ultimate basis of our being—the electron of the self. The self must assert itself or be untrue and ineffectual, and in the determination of truth it must be given freedom of expression. This is one side of the picture, but only one side. It is the side of the picture which young men and young women who think at all, and are not living simply imitative and conforming lives, usually emphasize. It is on the basis of the supreme importance of the individual that revolts are organized against conventions and authorities, against college faculties and supposedly inconvenient marriage laws.

But there is another side of the picture to which I would call attention. Truth lies at the point of intersection between tradition and conscience. Tradition as well as conscience has a line of its own. But what is tradition? What are all these authorities and conventions with which each generation is confronted and which seem to young people so needlessly bothersome and meaningless. Is tradition simply the wastage

* Alas! There are today four mighty nations who are challenging the truth of this assertion!

of the past, to be carted out of the way as quickly and un-
ceremoniously as possible in order that the electron of the
self may have an absolutely free field for its operations? Is
there not a danger here? For example, is all that has been
honestly believed before we appeared upon the scene with
our omniscience mere superstition, and therefore to have no
effect upon our manner of thinking and living? What is superstition? It is simply a belief or practice which is outworn,
which has become an anachronism, in other words has lost
touch with the best thought of any given age. Belief in
witches was not a superstition when it was entertained by the
best-educated and most influential men of the time. It *is* a
superstition today. Much of contemporary religion is rapidly
ceasing to be religious and is speedily disintegrating into superstition before our very eyes. Billy Sunday's revivalism
was an example of religion becoming transmuted into superstition because of its loss of contact with the educated
thought of our times.

But we must not scorn all things in the past as intellectually beneath contempt because we may have got beyond
some of them. Again I ask, what is this tradition in its largest sense, this inheritance of ours from the past? Is it not the
product of other personal electrons like ourselves reacting
upon life? And does it not furnish the atmosphere in which
we breathe? We cannot think or act in a vacuum. Tradition,
history, surrounds us as the atmosphere surrounds the earth.
If we could put the present generation into some great bell
jar from which this atmosphere could be sucked out, what
would happen? We would smother both intellectually and
spiritually. Granted that much that mankind formerly believed in has become for us superstition, does that mean that
through all the toiling ages of the past mankind has gained
no experience worthy of consideration, no wisdom by which
we can profit? To pronounce such a judgment upon the past
is to condemn ourselves by anticipation as a lot of fools, for

if this is the final judgment upon our predecessors, as soon as we ourselves belong to the past (and that will be very soon) the same judgment will be rendered against us. A cultivation of a decent respect for the opinions of the past is the only way to secure for ourselves a more lenient judgment by the future.

I think we here in the United States are especially liable to make the mistake of wishing to scrap tradition. Our ancestors came to this continent largely in order to escape its trammels. We rejoiced when we had uprooted ourselves from the supposedly worn-out soil of Europe and had planted ourselves in the rich, virgin soil of the New World. There was, at that time, reason in our madness, but the madness has too often prevailed over the reason and has reached its ultimate and classic expression in Henry Ford's famous dictum that "history is bunk," and in the naïve conclusion of our Babbits that because Henry has made a billion dollars in the manufacture of a democratic automobile, therefore he must be a wise political philosopher—wise as Socrates or Plato or Kant.

"Antiquity," said Jowett, the great Master of Balliol College, who, I think, is a safer guide in these matters than Henry, "has a curious religious power, stronger, perhaps, than belief in a future life." There is a mystical connection established through tradition between ourselves as creative wills today and all the creative wills of the past which it is fatal to truth and intelligent progress to ignore. For truth is an organic thing. It is not arrived at purely by logical processes, but by life. And the life of the past and the life of the present enter into its constitution. Truth lies at the point of intersection between the lines of tradition and conscience, between the grouped experience of the past and the individualistic experience of the present. As our present gradually merges into the past our future will, in turn, become the present, and the organic development of truth will be con-

tinued endlessly. It is this great fact that Bolshevism ignores.
It would substitute logic for history, tradition, a purely rationalized view of life for life's vast variety of experiences.
For this reason, daring as it is, challenging as it is, I cannot
believe that Bolshevism will succeed without serious modifi-
cation. England, with its utilization of tradition rather than
dogmas of abstract political theory, has a better chance at
future power and usefulness than the Russian experiment.

There are three sayings of Jesus which may serve to re-
enforce what I have had in mind in citing this saying of
Mazzini and which may be of aid in the turmoil and threatened disintegration of our thinking, religious as well as political. One day Jesus was asked why the disciples of John
fasted whereas his own did not. His answer was that his disciples and John's belonged to two different eras and that
what was proper for the one was not proper for the other. At
first glance this statement would seem to contradict Mazzini's idea that there is a point at which tradition and conscience intersect and that the truth is to be found at that
point of intersection; Jesus seems to imply a sharp, unbridge-
able distinction between the two eras of the old and the new,
and that the two could never come together. But this is not
the case. In the two famous parables of the patch and the
new wine which immediately follow the saying just quoted,
Jesus provides a qualification of what he has said and at the
same time lays down a general principle for guidance in
times of change and uncertainty. It is folly, he says, to patch
a new, unshrunken piece of cloth upon an old garment for
the tear will only become worse. Similarly, if new wine is
put into old wine skins the ferment of the new wine will
burst the skins. In his first statement Jesus by implication
emphasizes the necessity of change (his system and John's
were radically different and there must be a change from
the one to the other). In the parables he emphasizes its dangers. Patchy systems are of no value. Heterogeneous ele-

ments hurt each other. When new wine is put into old skins not only are the old skins destroyed but the new wine is also lost.

But this is not the most interesting lesson in these two parables. They seem to be given as a kind of excuse for John's disciples. John represents the old; Jesus says that it would be dangerous for John to take just a patch out of Jesus' newer conceptions and put it upon the old system which John still clung to in the main. The new element, when isolated from its proper connections and mechanically attached to the old, would affect the old unfavorably (the garment would be made worse, the skins would be destroyed), and it would also injure the new (the wine also would be lost), for a detached truth is liable to great misconceptions and therefore is dangerous. There is combined in these two parables a theoretical radicalism (the two systems of John and Jesus are quite sharply distinguished) with a practical conservatism (better stay by the old when you do not understand the new).

This last cautious suggestion is taken up and elaborated in a third saying of Jesus which does not appear in the manuscripts upon which our English New Testament is usually based, but is found in one very famous and important text, the so-called Codex Bezae. It runs as follows: On the same day, while watching a man working on the Sabbath Day Jesus said to him: "Man, if you know what you are doing you are blessed, but if you do not know you are accursed and a transgressor of the Law." Here the legitimacy, at times, of a break with the past is admitted. But the commendation of such a break is carefully qualified—if you know what you are doing, only then are you justified in taking the radical step. Undoubtedly there are great crises in the development of civilization in which it seems as if conscience and tradition were arrayed against each other, and a choice must be made. This situation is the most poignant that can arise in the life of the individual or of mankind. It may be remarked in passing that nowhere in literature is the conflict between conscience and tradition more brilliantly formulated than in the Book of Job. But to break with the past, if break we must, is never to be done in a light-hearted and flippant manner. An individualistic radicalism which is unaccompanied by any serious sense of responsibility and a profound devotion to truth is a spurious radicalism. It is only justified when you know what you are doing. When you do not understand what you are doing you are accursed. And here we recur to the dictum of Mazzini. In the long run and as a general principle, truth will be found at the point of intersection between tradition and conscience; between tradition, or the gathered wisdom of the race in times past, and conscience, or the solemn responsibility which rests upon every individual for making his own decisions when confronted by the exigent problems of life. Truth discovered in this way will not have the neatness and precision of formal logic about it, but in it will reside the rugged power of life.

THE FOLLY OF PHYSIOCRACY

AS is well known, the framers of our Constitution were, to a considerable extent, under the influence of French thinkers who immediately preceded the French Revolution. One group of these thinkers was known as the Physiocrats, or those who believed in the rule of Nature. They were the economists of their day. They assumed, according to the paraphrase of their views given by Professor Bury in his very interesting book on *The Idea of Progress*, that the end of society is the attainment of terrestrial happiness.

One of these Physiocrats, Mercier-Larivière, wrote a book in which he sought to discover the law by means of which men may become assured of happiness. But in what does happiness consist? He answers this preliminary question as follows: "Humanly speaking, the greatest happiness possible for us consists in the greatest possible abundance of objects suitable to our enjoyment and in the greatest liberty to profit by them." Liberty, and it is primarily economic, not political liberty, that is in mind, is necessary not only to enjoy but to produce these suitable objects in abundance, since liberty stimulates effort (probably he is thinking of free competition). "Individual property," for Mercier-Larivière, "is the indispensable condition for full enjoyment of the products of human labor."* In other words, you cannot really enjoy what you do not individually own. "Property is the measure of liberty and liberty is the measure of property." By this he seems to mean that you are economically free in proportion to the amount of your property, and on the other hand, the amount of your property will be conditioned by

* The quotations in this paragraph are from *The Idea of Progress* by J. B. Bury.

your economic freedom. "Hence," as Bury points out, "to realize general happiness it is only necessary to maintain property and consequently liberty in all their natural extent. . . . The practical inference [is] that the chief function of government [is] to protect property and that complete freedom should be left to private enterprise to exploit the resources of the earth." The rather frayed modern synonyms for these ideas are "the two-car garage," symbol of abundance, and "rugged individualism," symbol of economic freedom.

Now this physiocratic theory turns up in unexpected places, though in a veiled form. In the Declaration of Independence we are assured that among the unalienable rights of man are life, liberty and not necessarily happiness but the *pursuit* of happiness, though just what happiness is is not defined. In the Fifth and the famous Fourteenth or due-process Amendment to the Constitution we have the phrase of the Declaration changed in a rather significant way to "life, liberty, and property." It is true that the change from "happiness" to "property" is necessitated by the context, for the Constitution is, in these amendments, guaranteeing certain rights *by law*, and it would be silly for the Constitution to guarantee happiness by law. Happiness is an inner frame of mind. This cannot be guaranteed by law, at least not directly. But, on the physiocratic theory, what cannot be accomplished directly may be accomplished indirectly. If happiness consists in the possession of the greatest possible number of objects suitable to our enjoyment—in other words, in the amount of property which we possess—then our Constitution, in seeking to guarantee property, does, in a way, seek to guarantee happiness as well, and happiness undergoes a subtle and significant change from something inward to something outward, and the possession of property becomes one of the great goals of life. I do not set up to be an expert in the history or interpretation of the Constitution. If I have erred here the Political Science Department will very quickly demolish me. Yet I think it is true that the Fourteenth Amendment, which was originally adopted to protect *human* rights, has been largely interpreted by the Supreme Court to protect *property* rights, a fact which has gone far to establish the idea of the immense importance of property in our lives. However this may be, I think it is certain that the physiocratic theory of happiness, wnich unites the idea of happiness with the possession of ample property, whether endorsed by the Constitution or not, has exerted an immense influence upon popular thinking.

This influence was supported by another circumstance. The great era of scientific invention was setting in, and in the nineteenth century it became the dominant factor in our lives. The economic theory which insisted upon the possession of as many objects as possible suitable to our enjoyment now found itself in possession of a tool, namely scientific invention, which could increase the output of these enjoyable objects indefinitely. Thus it came to pass that an economic theory, practically adopted even though it may not have been distinctly formulated, and scientific invention united to impose upon our civilization a thoroughly materialistic conception of happiness. The possession of things, things, in ever and ever greater abundance, became the master passion of men.

The Century of Progress got under way—the century in which man's control over nature in the physiocratic interest of quantity production became ever more accelerated until it reached its symbolic climax at the opening of the Chicago Fair. On the night on which the illumination of the Fair officially began, I listened to the radio broadcast of the episode in the privacy of my own home—a sufficient wonder in itself. You remember the story of that night, how the blind astronomer, Professor Frost, caught, by the power of the inner eye of his imagination, a vision of the way in which to utilize the light from Arcturus in order to start the illumination of the Fair. Forty years ago, at the time of the Chicago World's Fair in 1893, a beam of light from Arcturus had started on its infinitely long journey earthward. Professor Frost proposed to trap this beam of light through the Harvard, Pittsburgh, and Yerkes observatories, amplify it by photoelectric cells, whatever they may be, and convert its energy into the electric spark which was to touch off the general illumination.

On the night on which this daring idea became realized I heard the question of the master of ceremonies: "Are you ready, Harvard?" And almost immediately the broadcaster announced that an answering signal of light had appeared upon the great switchboard ready for the occasion. "Are you ready, Pittsburgh? Are you ready, Yerkes?" And the answering signals were repeated. In a moment there was a whirring sound that grew louder and louder. It was the machine by which the amplified beam from Arcturus became transformed into an electric spark. They called the whir "the voice of Arcturus," and suddenly, at its summons, the Fair burst into radiant light. I confess the impression made upon me was for a moment overwhelming. This was not just a stunt. It transcended the merely bizarre. It was truly awe-inspiring in the illimitable possibilities it opened up to the imagination. Here was no hitching a wagon to a star. It was hitching a star to the network of machinery that man had flung over the earth, commanding those mighty, blazing suns across the infinite stellar spaces to do our bidding, to yield us, *us*, menial service. What an overwhelmingly dramatic symbol of man's control over the vast forces of nature!

And then came a disquieting thought. Just where did this great symbolic episode take place? In Chicago! Notorious even among the wretchedly governed cities of our land for the breakdown of its self-government, for its utter lack of self-control. At the very moment when Chicago commanded Arcturus to do its bidding, its banks were mostly closed, its school children unprovided for, their teachers unpaid, gangsters murdering almost at will in its streets, crime and corruption in unholy alliance, a picture of almost complete moral disintegration.

But Chicago itself is only a grimly ironic symbol of the culmination, during the World War and this postwar period, of the Century of Progress, a progress, a magnificent progress in our control over nature and our ability to produce an infinite number of objects suitable to our enjoyment, but unable to bring us happiness, owing to the catastrophe of our moral collapse. For happiness is not to be found, after all, in the abundance of objects suitable to enjoyment. Ample production is not the sure way to peace and contentment. To-day we are in want in the midst of plenty. Among the many causes for this paradox is there not one that we have overlooked? Is there not a great fallacy at the root of physiocracy, the fallacy that comfort and happiness are identical? During this Century of Progress we have been searching after comforts in the physiocratic delusion that they would guarantee our happiness. But happiness, or joy, which is a word of still deeper meaning, is an inner possession which does not depend, in the last analysis, upon comforts, that is, upon outward circumstance. There is a peace which the world cannot give and which the world cannot take away. The Physiocrats have been too hasty; their philosophy of life is too simple. Happiness cannot be ground out by turning the crank of a machine, even if the crank is propelled by Arcturus, and man is thus relieved of the necessity of earning his bread by the sweat of his brow. The Physiocrats had been warned long ago against staking happiness on the possession of a multiplicity of things. But they ignored the warning. Was not the one who uttered it too uneducated, too inexperienced in the practical affairs of life for a Physiocrat to pay attention to? However that may be, it is possibly a matter of some historic interest to have our attention called, especially at this time, to the warning which physiocracy ignored.

And one of the company said unto the ancient teacher, "Master, speak to my brother that he divide the inheritance with me." And he said unto him, "Man, who made me a judge or divider over you?" And he said unto them, "Take heed and beware of covetousness [that is, the desire always to have more]: for a man's life consisteth not in the abundance of the things which he possesseth" [take notice, ye Physiocrats, ye economists, ancient and modern]. And he spake a parable unto them, saying, "The ground of a certain rich man brought forth plentifully: and he thought within himself, saying, 'What shall I do because I have no room where to bestow my fruits' [a case of temporary overproduction]. And he said, 'This will I do: I will pull down my barns and build greater and there will I bestow all my goods [a case of plowing capital back into the plant]. And I will say to my soul, Soul, thou hast much goods laid up for many years; take thine ease, eat, drink, and be merry.' [He had an abundance of objects suitable, as he supposed, for enjoyment. There was One, however, who thought differently from this eighteenth-century Physiocrat.] But God said unto him, 'Thou fool, this night thy soul shall be required of thee: then whose shall these things be, which thou hast provided?' So is he that layeth up treasure for himself and is not rich toward God."

AMUSEMENT AND THE MUSES

THERE are two forms of intolerance to which we are all more or less exposed—youth's intolerance of age and the elders' intolerance of youth. Youth is apt to regard age as mossback, and age is inclined to look upon youth as silly. I do not propose to attempt any final judgment upon these conflicting opinions, though I am inclined to think the intolerance of youth is more excusable while the intolerance of age has better reasons. I would remind youth of the proverb that "the rolling stone gathers no moss," which certainly implies that the failure to gather moss is in a measure discreditable; and I would also humbly suggest that a bank of soft, green moss is a very lovely thing. On the other hand, for age to be intolerant of youth is less excusable than youth's intolerance of age, because age has once been young and should remember and understand, whereas youth has not yet had the experience of age. How can it, therefore, understand? Further, there is a distinction in silliness which age should keep in mind. Some silliness is simply the expression of sheer stupidity and this is always difficult to put up with. But sometimes age takes that for silliness which is nothing but a gay irresponsibility due to abounding health, and I am inclined to think that hours of silliness in this latter sense are occasionally (with emphasis on the qualifying word) good for us all. All of which is said in the hope that it may ease the way for a word of warning about *amusement*.

I raise the query, which is often raised by those unfortunates who have reached my stage of decrepitude, whether amusement in the student's life is not overdone. I fancy I can hear someone say: "Why is he going to trot out such a spavined old platitude as that? It reminds one of those New

Year's resolutions which are already jaded before January is half over." Well, I will tell you why.

One day, while reading Coleridge's *Aids to Reflection*, I chanced upon an etymology of "amusement" which set me thinking. Amusement—that means away (apart) from the Muses. The Oxford dictionary gives another definition which, I suppose, purports to be more scientific but is not half as nice. Away from the Muses! And who may they be? They are among the loveliest creations of Greek imagination, which is the same as saying that they are among the loveliest creations of human thought, goddesses of song, of poetry, of science, of art, of the dance, nine of them altogether. And what beautiful, liquid names they bear! Clio, the muse of history; Euterpe, the muse of lyric poetry; Thalia, of comedy; Melpomene, of tragedy; Terpsichore, of the choral dance; Erato, of love poetry; Polyhymnia, muse of the sublime hymn or ode; Urania, muse of astronomy which stood for all the wonder of the cosmos, the fair world of order; Calliope, the muse of epic poetry—all children of Mnemosyne, that is, memory. They were the patronesses of all the most beautiful and wonderful things in this beautiful and wonderful world. Amusement, away from all these? Is that what amusement is, and is that what we desire? I think I hear some audacious young person remind me that there is Terpsichore and we certainly still enjoy the worship of her. But do we? Is our mode of dancing a rite which this particular goddess would approve, or is it a rite which she would disapprove, simply amusement, something really apart from her worship? I suggest that when the Greek thought of dancing, he thought of its beauty, the beauty of rhythmic motion, dancing sunshine, dancing leaves on a tree, a dancing wave, dancing youth, all lovely things. When Wordsworth sang

> My heart with pleasure thrills
> And dances with the daffodils

he, too, was worshiping at the shrine of Terpsichore.

Perhaps it will be thought that in speaking in this way I have reached the silliness of second childhood which is more distressing by far than the silliness of youth. But the fact is I am groping after an idea. Amusement, if Coleridge's etymology is accepted, is too often pleasure reduced to the lowest plane, bereft of beauty, of grace, of refinement, of thought. It was Pope who said that "Amusement is the happiness of those who cannot think." It is something, therefore, in which the Muses have no share. For remember that the muse, in Greek, probably means the thinker. We who cultivate the Muses in college are to cultivate the higher forms of pleasure and the only forms which will not finally cloy, the forms in which thought is an element. It is this absence of the ennobling factor of thought in one's life of which Rupert Brooke was thinking when he characterized the American businessman as "one in whose life exhilaration and depression take the place of joy and sorrow." In exhilaration and depression there is no enrichment in life as there is in joy and sorrow. The former sensations are largely physical, not so the latter. These are spiritual.

There is another group of maidens known to Greek mythology. They are the Sirens and the story is told that they once competed with the Muses and came to grief. That will always happen. If you give yourselves over to amusement, to pleasure apart from the Muses, you expose yourselves to the voices of the Sirens, and those who fail to stop their ears with cotton, as the wise Ulysses did, will go upon the rocks.

> Runnin' wild, lost control,
> Runnin' wild, mighty bold;
> Feelin' gay and reckless too,
> Care-free all the time, never blue;
> Always goin' I don't know where,
> Always showin' that I don't care;
> Don't love nobody, it ain't worth while,
> All alone, runnin' wild.

There is the song of one who has listened to the Jazz Siren. How unspeakably sad it is!

> Don't love nobody, it ain't worth while
> All alone, runnin' wild.

But even if you are spared this tragedy and wreck of life, the surest way to become what youth so much despises, a mossback, is to indulge only in those pleasures which are simply amusements, in those pleasures, that is, which have no thought in them, no spiritual elevation, no nourishment for the higher life. What a dismal thing a dull and listless old age is, an old age of boredom! Why insure it by indulging only in amusement when you can secure an ever increasing interest in life by cultivating the Muses? You remember what Wordsworth once said:

> My heart leaps up when I behold a rainbow in the sky,
> So was it when my life began, so is it now I am a man,
> So be it when I shall grow old or let me die.

To preserve the joy and freshness of youth's sensitiveness into old age—that is by no means an unworthy aim in life. But it cannot be accomplished if youth spends all its time and energy in amusement, in a life apart from the Muses. Do not let your natural sense for simple and lovely things become so deadened that Wordsworth's suggestion of the throb of delight to be felt even down to old age on seeing a rainbow becomes meaningless to you. Dare I end with a still more earnest suggestion?

The Hebrews had no such beautiful conception as the Greek conception of the Muses, but they had an equivalent which finds a point of attachment to the Greek idea of the Muses as thinkers and which I would also commend to your attention. Grace and beauty were not the primary characteristics of this Hebrew muse, however. She was somewhat austere of aspect, at least at first glance. They called her Wisdom, but listen to what is said of her.

> At first she will walk with him in crooked ways,
> And bring fear and dread upon him,
> And torment him with her *discipline*,*
> Until she may trust his soul,
> And try him by her judgments.
> Then will she return again the straight way unto him,
> And will gladden him and reveal to him her secrets.

* A word that should be restored to the vocabulary of ethics and education.

THE PROBLEM OF PAIN

A Good Friday Meditation

THIS is Holy Week. It is the culmination of the Lenten Fast and has been set apart by the Christian Church from the earliest centuries as a time in which to meditate upon the solemn facts of sin and suffering. In agreement with the ancient custom of the Church I am venturing to direct your thoughts today to the problem of pain. This is not an easy thing to do before an audience so largely composed of young people. Youth instinctively inclines to shut its eyes to the fact of suffering in life. The joy of life, the beauty of the world—why not dwell on these glad facts alone, especially in the spring when all our senses are responding to blossoming time? And indeed, this beautiful side of life is very real. It cannot and it should not be ignored.

I have a remarkable apple tree in my yard. In its bearing year I never see a fuller-blossomed tree. It is a radiant sight. Its beauty, I am thankful to say, furnishes one of the true premises of life.

Yet there is another side to the picture which is equally real. I cannot forget what happens to those blossoms. Many of them perish without coming to fruitage. Even when the young apples do succeed in forming, they must be sprayed with ill-smelling, poisonous stuff to ward off attacks of evil-minded moths. In spite of all this, suffocating webs are often spun about the branches and must be cut off and burned. Once, with great effort, I had succeeded in raising a fine crop of apples. I looked at them one evening (I remember it well) and admired their polished surfaces, their deep, rich coloring, their rounded ripeness, and said to myself, I will pick them in the morning and win a prize. But that night a higher organism than a moth did its fell work. Intelligent malevolence had stripped the tree. A summer's work was lost. My blossoming apple tree has its sad suggestions of suffering, waste, frustration. These, too, are facts of life. Sometimes I look out upon this chapel audience arrayed in all its springtime splendor of promise and ask myself: What is going to become of you all? What are the disappointments and bereavements, sufferings and diseases that await you? All these things seem to be very remote. It seems platitudinous to talk of them. But when these experiences actually arrive, there is nothing platitudinous about them. They are not formalities but realities, often of the grimmest kind. And if I may be permitted to call your attention to the fact just once (my subject does not allow me to avoid it even though I should like to do so), there is not one person sitting in this chapel at the present moment, enjoying the security and radiance of college blossoming time, who will escape a share in the varying vicissitudes of maturing years. Neither can we count on the Reaper who has reaped for so many thousands of years growing tired or unobservant when our time comes to be gathered in. It is the inevitability of all this that gives such poignancy to our view of life *after* blossoming time. But unless this fact is recognized as a premise of existence equally valid with the premise of life's joy and beauty, we are at best basing our theory of life only on a half-truth. As a matter of fact, the sigh of mankind heaves like a great ground swell through all the tides of human history.

> I advanced in life, I attained unto the allotted span;
> Wherever I have turned it was evil, evil.

Thus mourns an ancient Babylonian sage. And the Israelite peasant answers back out of his sad experience of frustrated labor:

> In the sweat of thy brow shalt thou eat bread,
> Until thou shalt return unto the soil, for from it wast thou taken;
> For dust thou art and unto dust thou shalt return.

Even the terror of death itself at times seems to be a relief as compared with the greater terror of life.

> Death comes to me
> As the sweet odor of myrrh,
> Or as when one sits under a spreading sail on a breezy day,

sings an early Egyptian poet after reviewing his life of suffering. And Job answers back in his agony with these terrible words:

> Why giveth he to the weary one light,
> Or life to the bitter in soul?
> Who wait for death but it cometh not,
> Who dig for it more than for buried treasure,
> Who rejoice with exultation when they find—a grave!

These are not simply poetic fancies. They reflect the actual conditions and feelings of many men today. Think of the thousands of shrieking or desperately silent wounded men on the battlefields of Europe a few short years ago. And the question presses: Why cannot the same power which produces the beauty of blossomtime protect it through maturity? Why are beauty and ugliness, pain and pleasure, joy and sorrow, good and evil so inextricably intermingled?

We are often told that pain and sorrow are retributive in character—punishments for our sins, or that they are disciplinary—whom the Lord loveth he chasteneth. These answers have a measure of truth in them, but they are quite inadequate to solve the problem of pain, and for one simple reason. This problem is not an exclusively moral one for pain is not confined to mankind. The brute creation is involved and terribly involved in suffering. No one has urged this fact with greater force than H. G. Wells in that curious and clever, perhaps more than clever, book, *The Undying Fire*. It is sometimes said that the sin of man has in some mystical fashion implicated the whole of creation in misery. This claim cannot be admitted. The dinosaurs warred sav-

agely upon each other long before man became a moral creature capable of doing and spreading wrong. Again, our
nerves, which can so readily thrill to pleasurable sensations,
can equally throb with the acutest agony. Was this strange,
double-edged nervous system of ours developed only after
man began to violate what he knew to be right? Scarcely.

Still further, as David Hume suggested long ago, many
of our sufferings come from the fact that the laws of nature
are impartial. This impartiality has its advantages, for it
provides a measure of security for the race as a whole; we
can depend upon the unvarying laws of nature. But these
impartial laws are pitilessly indifferent to the needs of the
individual. If I slip on the deck of a steamer in a gale and
fall into the sea, not one of all those multitudinous waves
about me will abate its fury and smooth itself out in kindliness to help me float a little longer. When Mount Pelée blew
its head off some years ago, it did not stop to consider whether
it was situated on a desert island where its irruptive excesses
would do no harm to anybody. It disgorged its hot ashes and
molten lava upon its thousands of victims living in St. Pierre
with absolute indifference, as Vesuvius once did on Pompeii. I
remember reading in the papers at the time of Mount Pelée's
eruption the suggestion that the inhabitants of St. Pierre,
just as the inhabitants of Pompeii, must have been a bad lot.
But to introduce volcanic action into the moral order in this
way did not help me at all. Jesus himself refused to accept
such an explanation when he asked whether the people upon
whom the tower of Siloam fell were wicked above all others.
If he had been acquainted with the Newtonian formulas he
would have said that it was gravitation, taking advantage
of some unintentional architectural defect, not wickedness,
that produced the catastrophe.

No. Pain is not confined to the moral order. It seems to be
a part of the very warp and woof of nature. It might be
thought that we can see a little way into the meaning of it

when we observe how, at times, it seems to be a condition of pleasure. We cannot enjoy a melody to the full if we know nothing of dissonance. We cannot enjoy coolness or warmth if we know nothing of their opposites. But again, such considerations do not get us very far, for why should the ear be deafened by the crash of thunder in order to be able to enjoy a melody of Schubert, or why should coldness have to be exaggerated into freezing cold or warmth into burning fever in order to secure pleasure from coolness or warmth? Why these frightfully exaggerated contrasts in nature which entail so much suffering? Are they necessary in order that we may enjoy? Why should we be blinded by the sun at midday in order to be able to enjoy the sunset at evening time?

The pain of nature in its awful totality remains a mystery, one of the insoluble ultimates of life. Similarly, when we come to the world of intelligence and moral action, we are equally baffled. If we explain pain on the principle of retribution and say "whatsoever a man soweth that shall he also reap" and infer that the infraction of moral law always entails suffering, this explanation is not sufficient. Job long ago exposed the fallacy in the argument when he replied to the charge of Eliphaz the Temanite that he was too impatient under his sufferings:

Oh that my impatience could indeed be weighed,
And my misfortunes placed in the balance against it;
For now the latter would be heavier than the sands of the sea.

In other words the lack of proportion between sin and suffering or the exaggeration of suffering prevents the problem of pain from being solved in the moral sphere any more readily than in the sphere of nature. The fact of the anguish of many saints and of the relative happiness, if judged by externals, of many evil men, prevents us from adopting the easy and fatuous optimism of the Psalmist who said,

I have been young and now am old,
Yet I have not seen the righteous forsaken,
Nor his seed begging bread (Psalms 37.25).

He should have learned more than that by the time he was old. This is the idealization of the world by a man born blind, and the closer observers and profounder thinkers of Israel knew that it was not true. No. The problem of pain can no more be solved than any other ultimate problem of existence. If any further proof of this statement were needed, it would be found in the fact of *cruelty*, that ugliest trait in human nature, which takes pleasure in the infliction of humiliation and pain upon another. What possible rationality can be found in cruelty? Here the darker mystery of evil increases still further the mystery of pain. What purpose, then, is there in discussing it? Why not forget it? I answer, because life will not allow us to forget it, try as hard as we may. The real problem for us is not the speculative one as to the origin of or reason for pain, for which no final answer has been as yet discovered, but the practical one of how we shall meet it when it comes. Can we extract some good out of our suffering?

There is the Buddhist answer which countless millions of our fellowmen have accepted. Buddha, indeed, believed that he had solved the mystery of suffering. It originated, he said, in desire. To destroy suffering one must first kill desire. Peace comes finally only in Nirvana where all desire and sensibility are quenched. In the practice of the Eightfold Way by which desire was to be destroyed many kindly and noble virtues were released. But Buddhism is the way of profound pessimism and logically leads to an asceticism which becomes in the end anticultural. Not along this line is there hope for mankind. It is the way of surrender.

There is the way of challenge, the way of courage. The Stoic attitude is here a typical one. Firmly believing in the final reasonableness of nature, as the Buddhist did not believe, the Stoic proudly challenges suffering as an irrelevance. Within his own soul, itself a part of the Reason in the Universe, he seeks support. Stoicism has also produced many admirable characters. But when with proud disdain it dismisses so large a part of life as an irrelevance, one is somehow left unconvinced. Besides, I doubt whether our age, which leads an externalized life and which is little acquainted with the resources of the life within, would be able to maintain the unimpassioned, rather frigid, even though nobly calm feeling of Stoic superiority to what the Stoic calls irrelevance.

An attitude of courage which would possibly appeal more to a generation dominated as ours is by the mysticism of action rather than by the mysticism of thought is the attitude of adventure which bravely challenges life's vicissitudes. It is the attitude which Browning sums up in the familiar lines from "Rabbi Ben Ezra":

> Then welcome each rebuff,
> Which turns earth's smoothness rough,
> Each sting that bids nor sit nor stand but go;
> Be our joy three parts pain,
> Strive and hold cheap the strain,
> Learn, nor account the pang, dare, never grudge the throe.

Or perhaps an even finer expression of this adventurous attitude toward life is found in an ancient Greek epitaph on a shipwrecked sailor:

> A shipwrecked sailor buried on this coast
> Bids you set sail.
> Full many a bark when we were lost
> Weathered the gale.

In these brave lines the power of the nettle, pain, to sting is, in part at least, overcome by firmly grasping it. Yet I do not believe this courageous optimism of the adventurer as he sets forth on the perilous sea of life, and which has a special appeal to youth, is the final word of advice.

There is also the attitude toward pain of pious acquiescence, not the endurance of the Stoic who is too proud to flinch at an irrelevance, but the endurance of a righteous man who faces life in its totality of joy and misery in humble faith in an unseen power.

> The Lord hath given and the Lord hath taken away,
> Blessed be the name of the Lord.

This is courage, too; the courage, not of adventure, but of piety. But even this is not the last word. Nor is it the distinctively Christian attitude toward pain, though it has been incorporated into that attitude.

The Christian view of pain, and it is this view of it which we commemorate in Holy Week, looks upon pain as affording an opportunity to exhibit a self-surrendering love, the ultimate form of love. Whatever criticism may be passed upon the defects and weaknesses of the Christian Church as manifested in history, whatever reservations may be entertained with respect to much of its theology, in this thought which is the very heart of the Christian message the Christian Church has made the profoundest contribution of all to the practical problem of our attitude toward pain. In the Cross it has won the final triumph over pain by uniting it—strange, ineffable, most moving coincidence—with love.

> O Cross that liftest up my head,
> I dare not ask to fly from thee;
> I lay in dust life's glories dead,
> And from the ground there blossoms red
> Life that shall endless be.

Blossoms red! The radiance of blossomtime returns, though now tinged with the crimson of the sacrificial blood that stains the Cross of the great sufferer.

> In this sign thou shalt conquer.

THE *MYSTERIUM TREMENDUM* OR THE
ESSENCE OF RELIGION

THIS College has never been ashamed to confess its belief that religion is one of the major interests of mankind. The chapel hour is intended to give expression to that conviction. But what is religion? Of course it is impossible, within the limits of a chapel service, to discuss this question with any adequacy, and perhaps that is fortunate for me. If I had all the time I wished, my own confusion as to the correct answer might be more fully revealed than in a fifteen-minute talk. Hiding, therefore, behind the limitations of my time, I should like to make a suggestion or two that I hope may at least stir in your minds a new interest in the subject.

First of all, it is probably needless to say that I do not necessarily identify religion or a religious experience with going to church, helpful and important as I think it is for young men and young women to identify themselves with an organization which has stood during two thousand years, as no other organization has stood, for an idealistic view of life, and which serves as a link to unite us with some of the richest experiences of mankind. Neither would I identify religion or religious experience with subscription to some formal creed or other. Creeds have had their uses in guarding us from intellectual vagaries, but the varying intellectual forms which religion assumes at different times are not to be confounded with religion itself. A very common and rather unfortunate mistake in our day is to confuse religion with morals. We often suppose that to lead a moral life is to lead a religious life. This by no means follows. The origin of our ethical life lies in the sphere of our human relationships, and the ethical life is developed along rational lines. The origin of our religious life is in the sphere of the transcendental, in our relationship, not with our fellowmen, but with what Matthew Arnold calls "a power not ourselves," a power which is felt rather than inferred by processes of reasoning, and which is therefore in a sense suprarational. It is true that religion, in its more highly developed forms, always becomes moralized, and to the degree that it does so the rational, intellectual element is introduced. The "power not ourselves" becomes "the power not ourselves which makes for righteousness." In the religion of Israel and in Christianity the moralization of religion has, as I believe, reached its culmination. Indeed, at the present time and in our thoroughly rationalized and materialized civilization we have often so completely transformed religion into morals that we are in grave danger of forgetting that religion in its essence is something independent of morals, though capable of becoming moralized. That is, it is not morals, but the motive power of morals. And religion is this because it belongs primarily to the suprarational or transcendental sphere. But is this not all just metaphysical abstraction, with no reality behind it, having nothing to do with our daily lives? Yes, it is metaphysical, that is, beyond physics, but it is not for that reason unreal. Perhaps I can make my meaning clearer by asking certain very concrete questions.

When you are working in the biological laboratory and are examining the strange and marvelous processes of life, does the feeling of awe and wonder ever sweep over you? The feeling that you are just a little chip in the great current of life that flows out of the vast depths of the past and is sweeping on into the equally vast depths of the future? Does this feeling inspire in you a certain self-distrust, a desire for a more stable anchorage or a more skilful piloting than you can find within yourself or in the society about you? If so, are you not, whether consciously or unconsciously, reaching out to the transcendental, to that Other which is beyond and above you, and is not this, however undeveloped, a religious experience?

While you are working in the physical or chemical or astronomical laboratories and the terrific exactitudes of nature's laws are illustrated day by day, does the question ever come to you: What if I should fall out of alignment? What if I should fail to adjust myself? How can I escape being crushed by these relentless laws of nature that are powerful enough to hold flaming suns in their orbits and from which the apparently lawless meteors, though traveling for a million miles away from our solar system, cannot escape? How can I achieve an integration with this great universe in which I live and move and have my being and which yet is beyond me, so immeasurably beyond me? Do such questions arise in your mind? Then you are having an essentially religious experience. Are you studying some great poet, a play of Shakespeare, an ode of Wordsworth, "a chorus ending of Euripides," and does a word, a phrase, a couplet, suddenly break in upon your soul and you feel the lift of the poet's imagination and are for a moment carried out beyond yourself into another world, which you cannot perhaps precisely define, but which is, nevertheless, a real world and a glorious one while the experience lasts? Then you are having a truly religious experience, mediated by art. I am not speaking merely sentimental twaddle. Men *do* have these experiences. Remember with what intensity Wordsworth felt the transcendental in nature? I do not claim to have had such experiences often or to have felt them as poignantly as other men have done. Yet I can never forget the feelings I had when I first read Keats' poem, "On first looking into Chapman's Homer," or William Vaughn Moody's "The Death of Eve," or the marvelous close of Sophocles' *Œdipus at Colonus*, marvelous even in an English translation.

Do you never watch the sunset and see the radiance expanding and dying away again, tender and evanescent? Do

you never look up into the sky at night and see what your
fellowmen have seen for thousands of years—the silent, un-
erring march of the stars through the illimitable spaces—
and realize the sacredness of it all, and feel that it would be
a profanation to attempt to use the vast resources of nature's
power and beauty simply to minister to a life of self-indul-
gence? Does not our ordinary life, with its trivial or vulgar
aims, seem at times to be unreal when laid against the life
of nobleness and sanctity? Do you never have a slight shiver
at the possibility of leading a life on a low plane? I trust
you have had such a chill for it is a religious experience, this
time taking on a moral significance. And all these apprehen-
sions mean that for a moment, at least, you perceive where
reality is to be found and long, in your weakness, to lay hold
on it.

There is another variety of religious experience, the
strangest of them all, in which the soul does not look outward upon nature or art, but looks inward into the recesses
of the human heart, there to find the greatest mystery with
which the human mind can grapple, the mystery of sin. Do
you never reflect upon the savage hatreds, the calculated
cruelties, the unbridled lusts and wild debaucheries that
have devastated our modern civilization, writhing across it
like some horrible dragon, and do you never connect the fact
that all these atrocities arise out of the hearts of human beings with the fact that you, also, are a human being? Does
it never make you fear lest sometime the savage beast that is
in every one of us, both men and women, may suddenly
break the weak chains of convention in these unruly times
and devour your better self? Do you never realize that there
are fellow citizens of yours, living just as you do, gossiping,
good-natured, friendly neighbors and happy Nordics just as
you are, who suddenly change into devils as they smell the
singed flesh of a man of another race burning alive before
their frenzied eyes? This thing actually happens in this fair

land of ours and in our day! Have you never been frightened
at yourself, at your own demonic power to do evil? Perhaps
the greatest of all the Negro spirituals, in which a crucified
race expresses in words and music a profound religious insight into the significance of the crucifixion of our Lord, begins with the two lines,

Were you there when they crucified my Lord?
Sometimes it almost makes me tremble, tremble.

This trembling is not at the physical agonies of the crucifixion. It is at the mystery of lawlessness that is within us,
the demonic power which seems at times to seize us all and
once in the past crucified Jesus Christ. Unless you have, on
occasion, trembled at this mysterious potency of evil within
yourself, your religious experience in its moralized form has
been a limited one.

If, on the other hand, you have ever chanced to see an
older man or woman with a demeanor at once benign and
dignified, whose eyes are evidently accustomed to look at
wide horizons and who, therefore, can approach the horizon
of life with a quiet, even a cheerful confidence, in whose
face the soul shines through, and if you have felt in the
presence of such a person the meaning of the purification of
life that sometimes takes place in later years, you are having
a certain measure of religious experience. In such a percep-
tion you, too, may feel that warm, sweet wind, the creative
breath of God, which blows over the chaos in our souls from
the world of spiritual reality.

What is the common element, in a greater or less degree,
in all these experiences which I have tried to describe? It is
the sense of mystery, the mystery of purpose in the world,
the mystery of cosmic law and order, the mystery of human
lawlessness that needs the grace of something higher to save
it from itself, the mystery of beauty, the mystery of serenity
in the midst of confusion. But it is not the sense of mystery

alone which denotes these experiences as religious. It is the feeling of awe that is engendered by them. It is the feeling, to borrow an idea recently formulated by a profound student of religious experience,* that in this universe of ours and in this manifold life there is, indeed, something other than ourselves at work, the *mysterium tremendum*, majestic, august, transcendent, of unbounded energy. The natural reaction to the realization of this power is the feeling of awe, and no experience in which awe in some measure at least is not present can be called a truly religious experience. It is at this point that the religious experience is most clearly differentiated from an ethical one.

I know that there are many today who will say that all this is stuff and nonsense. I know, also, how hard it is for us to believe in its reality, amid the clatter and din of a world in which "things are in the saddle." But I also know that the saints and poets and prophets of mankind have usually confessed their faith in this great overtone of life. The wisdom of the twenty-eighth chapter of Job, the secret, unfathomed and unfathomable wisdom, is only another name for the *mysterium tremendum*. And Goethe, who helped so mightily to open the portals of our modern world, had the same idea in mind when he wrote:

> Das Schaudern ist der Menschheit bester Teil
> Wie auch die Welt ihm das Gefühl verteu're;
> Ergriffen, fühlt er tief das Ungeheure.

I cannot translate these lines in any adequate way, but they mean that the capacity for awe is man's fairest endowment and, though the world makes the experience difficult for him, yet in a moment of rapture he may feel in the depths of his being *das Ungeheure*—and again this untranslatable German word may stand for the *mysterium tremendum*. And finally, there is a saying of the poet-philosopher Coleridge:

* Rudolf Otto in *The Idea of the Holy*.

"In wonder all philosophy began; in wonder it ends and admiration fills up the interspace. But the first wonder is the offspring of ignorance, the last is the parent of adoration. The first is the birth throe of knowledge, the last is its euthanasy and apotheosis"; which means, I take it, that the wonder with which we first look out on life is akin to curiosity and this prompts to the acquisition of knowledge, to science, but the wonder with which, in the end, we contemplate life and its mysteries is the wonder of awe which, with knowledge transfigured into spiritual insight, leads to adoration, to worship, and worship is the final and specific expression of religion.

THE NEED OF RELIGION

IN a recent *Oberlin Review* editorial there is the following significant comment upon an equally significant contribution: "It is probably true that the reason religion in the broadest sense . . . is not a serious consideration with most students is that there is no crying need for it on the campus," and the editorial writer suggests that this situation is simply a fact to be accepted. This is a serious situation, but it is even more acute than is here described. Not only on our campus, but in the currents of the world's thought that move around our quiet retreat there also seems to be little feeling of need for religion. On the one hand our material life is, for most of us of the middle classes, increasingly easy and sufficing, and on the other hand the great religious traditions of our Western civilization seem to be too clouded with doubt by the findings of science to furnish us with a support which we think we do not really need anyway. What I wish to do today is to protest, not so much against the situation itself, as against the complacency with which it is accepted.

It is the fashion at present to dismiss God with a supercilious smile and the fact of sin with a sneer. Professor Harry Barnes, in an address before the American Association for the Advancement of Science, has been one of many to deliver finalities on these subjects. Of course there is no God. Sin, however, is technically defined by the "Westminster Shorter Catechism" as "any want of conformity unto or transgression of the law of God." Hence if there is no God there is no sin. Q.E.D. The sense of sin (Mr. Barnes appears to admit the sense of it though not the fact of it) is merely "a psycho-physical attribute of adolescent sentimental development." Apparently, therefore, it won't bother you much after you have secured your A.B. degree. The Decalogue, he goes on to say, "is the product of a semi-barbarous people and should be overhauled by scientific and sociological experts," and "Christian solemnity should be exchanged for the joy of living." Just what the joy of living involves Mr. Barnes does not tell us precisely, though he seems to suggest that it implies a golden mean between Immanuel Kant and Fatty Arbuckle. Now what I object to most in Mr. Barnes and the gentlemen of whom he is a type, the Menckens, the Louis Brownes, and the rest, is their jauntiness. The longer I live the more I distrust smartness as a way of salvation. It is the men who have suffered who have most helped the world. I cannot find any indication that these men have suffered. They do not know the meaning of what they have lost, the richness and nobility of the Christian inheritance. They lump it all under Puritanism or Methodism and let it go at that. I doubt if any of them would understand that profoundly sad but beautiful line of Robert Browning in a poem which reluctantly suggests that the doubts of religion might become hardened into fact:

> All my days I'll go the softlier, sadlier,
> For that dream's sake.

The intellectual freedom which has been gained by this class of modernists and of which they are so very proud has been too cheaply bought to be of any real value. And being cheap, it is far more likely to shift its moral center of gravity from Immanuel Kant toward Fatty Arbuckle than to turn from Fatty toward Immanuel.

But there is one of these modernists, one of the most advanced of them all, who is of a different caliber, who faces with a mental integrity which cannot but be profoundly respected what modernism, as identified with the purely scientific and intellectualist movement, really means. He rejects religion intellectually, but he *realizes what he has lost.* There is, if I do not misread him, a yearning after what has departed, just as I believe in the hearts of every one of you, when in a casual moment you are honest with yourselves, there comes a wistfulness, a yearning for some sustaining force, you hardly know what, outside yourselves.

This supermodernist to whom I refer is Joseph Wood Krutch, the dramatic critic of *The Nation*. In a series of articles appearing in the *Atlantic Monthly* several years ago and later published in book form under the title *The Modern Temper*, he analyzed Modernism and told us just what we may expect from it. He shows that the same mode of argument which would dismiss God out of the universe would also eliminate every faith and ideal from life. The only real thing is nature, the nature with which the laboratory deals, the nature which can be weighed and measured, the nature which has quantity but not quality. For while nature, as he tells us, "is marvelously ingenious in devising means, she is barren of ends, and quality has to do with ends." Nature with its mysterious powers fills every nook and corner of this earth with life, but when the question is raised, Why? nature has no answer. All that is connected with purpose, with quality, is imposed upon nature by the imagination of men. There is nothing in nature to correspond to it. Hence as a purely mental product without any tangible basis in nature, all this realm of value, of ideal, is illusion. This is in striking contrast to the doctrine of maya or illusion in Indian theology. There the unideal is illusion; here the ideal is illusion. There is no justice, no mercy, no righteousness in nature. These are figments of the human mind, without reality. Krutch does not argue the elimination of God. To do that is no longer a necessity in our enlightened age. He does suggest the argument for the elimination of morals as implying any authoritative standards. The thing can be managed quite easily.

History shows that books which claim to be authoritative revelations of God's will are not really such. Anthropology and history, combined, show that there is no continuity in moral standards. What was regarded in one age as wrong in another age is held to be right. All morals are but social habits and habits change. Honor, patriotism, even respectability, are swept into the discard. As for the soul, it disappears altogether when subjected to the analysis of the laboratory, and will and consciousness themselves become a species of illusion.

But, as I have already said, Mr. Krutch is well aware of what he calls "the vast emptiness of life" which results from these eliminations. Their values he repeatedly admits. Only, when tested by the purely rationalist method, they are all equally unreal, equally illusion. In two remarkable articles, the first on "Love—or the Life and Death of a Value," the second on "The Tragic Fallacy," he shows with appalling clearness just what happens when we give ourselves over to the unchecked, unsupplemented power of rationalism.

Romantic love—it was scarcely known among primitive peoples. The Chinese still set more store by parental love than they do by marital love. Love as we know it has only gradually developed out of the biological demand of life. In the process it has surrounded itself with taboos, as the modernists are pleased to speak of them, veiled itself in mystery (romance) and taken on a whole series of associated, transcendental values. But in the imperious modernist demand for freedom all the mystery and romance of love, all its transcendental values are dissipated. Love becomes free, yes —and common!

And what is the result? "No inhibitions," Krutch tells us, "either within or without restrain [these advanced modernists], but they are asking themselves, 'What is it worth?'" Love, reduced to a purely physical basis, becomes to an Aldous Huxley, carrying out the principles of his grandfather to their logical conclusion, or to a Hemingway (I quote Krutch again) "at times only a sort of obscene joke."

Krutch admits that the illusion of love as a value has been one of the most helpful and beautiful of all our illusions, but with restraints abandoned and freedom gained by the aid of scientific analysis each of these modernists, he goes on to say, "has refused to surround [love] with mystical implications, and each, looking at it as a mere biological fact, has found it ridiculous and disgusting."

I turn to the prayer book and read in the order of the marriage service: "I, M. take thee, N., to be my wedded wife, to have and to hold from this day forward, for better or worse, for richer or poorer, in sickness and in health, to love and to cherish, till death us do part, according to God's holy ordinance, and thereto I plight thee my troth." That is love with mystical implications, undoubtedly. But are you ready, in the interest of a supposed liberty, to abandon the beauty of it, touched with sacredness, for an experience which will surely end in degradation? Krutch ends his article on love with these terrible words: "We have grown used to a Godless universe, but we are not yet accustomed to one which is loveless as well, and only when we have so become shall we realize what atheism really means."

In his article on "The Tragic Fallacy," by which he means the imputation to humanity of a nobility not inherent in it, Krutch is equally searching. He raises the question why no great tragedies are written today, like those of Sophocles or Shakespeare. His answer is, because we have lost the sense of the dignity of man. Great tragedy can only be written when the inherent nobility of man is presupposed. Great tragedy is only great when it leaves the reader with a certain sense of exultation in the realization that the human soul, in spite of all outward failure and suffering, has triumphed. It takes a man of heroic mould to be the hero of great tragedy. But man is no longer heroic. The "cosmic perspective" (Barnes) which we have gained through science, with its numberless galaxies of stars, millions of light-years distant, suggests that God, to return to Mr. Barnes's phraseology once more, "has little solicitude for our petty and ephemeral planet." But if so, what takes place upon this planet is still less significant. Human history becomes, in the words attributed to Balfour, "a rather disgraceful episode on one of the minor planets." Man himself sinks into insignificance and sooner or later we will all come to "lead trivial lives because we are trivial people"—to quote from that terrible play of Somerset Maugham, *The Circle*. Great tragedy cannot be written in such an atmosphere. And Krutch compares the magnificence of *Hamlet* out of Elizabethan England with what he regards as the greatest tragedy of modern times, Ibsen's *Ghosts*, in which the hero, who has inherited from his father an unmentionable disease that is sapping his reason, gets his mother to poison him, a perfectly futile outcome that leaves not exultation but only depression behind it. When man no longer believes in his own significance, the most pitiable and the most glorious, the most cruel and the most merciful, the most lovable and the most baffling of all the works of God will cease to be.

It is not my purpose to attempt any refutation of the modernist position. From the point of view of a purely scientific and intellectualist approach to the problems of life, it is a strong position. But a process of argument which leads, ultimately, to a complete devaluation of life and turns all human ideals into illusion must have a defect in it somewhere. The mind by the power of imagination creates all these glorious illusions, these castles in the air which Krutch again and again admits are necessary if life is to be endurable and organized society is to be preserved in any decency. The same mind by the power of rationalization destroys these castles and drives us out, homeless, into the desert and the dark. The mind generates faith and hope and love and the same mind gnaws at them until only shreds are left. We are cannibals who devour our own mental processes instead of our own flesh and blood. It is grotesque and horrible. Krutch, himself, at times seems to suggest that there must be some way out, that the intellectualist position in itself is not sufficient. It is Jowett, the great Master of Balliol, who tells us that "pure thought alone is ineffectual." Nature's urge for life is also a fact as Krutch admits and human life is also a fact. But without its faiths and its ideals human life would cease to be human.

I believe less and less that man can live a man's life by pure reasoning alone. Logic works precisely only when dealing with abstractions. It is always qualified by life. Man is a kind of monkey-wrench thrown into the perfect order of nature. Where he appears "the mystery of lawlessness" enters and logic ceases to be supreme. Man cannot solve his problems by adjusting himself simply to the order of nature. There is a transcendent element in him that refuses to be completely standardized to the level of an orderly animal existence. It is that transcendental element which craves religion, which craves value in life. In Oberlin, as in all colleges, the general approach to the various fields of knowledge is the intellectual approach. This is proper but it is one-sided. Jowett tells us again that "the secret of combining feeling and intellect seems to be lost in modern times." *It must be recovered.* You may not be aware of it, but you *do* need the balance of religion, especially on a college campus. For this reason our chapel was erected, in accordance with the beautiful dedicatory inscription in its vestibule, not only "that a son might honor the memory of his Father," but "that the youth of this Foundation of learning may daily meet to worship God."

ON THE REALITY OF GOD

LAST winter a young cousin of mine wrote me that her small daughter of five was beginning to ask questions about God and she did not know how to answer them. She herself had ceased to pray, since what she had formerly prayed for she felt to be mostly absurd. She found more help in John Haynes Holmes than she did in the churches of her neighborhood. "I have the feeling," she wrote, "that what I am looking for is to be found in ideal human conduct and character, not in the world of the spirit, and consequently I am in the greatest difficulty when Dorothy asks about God." I asked myself if I had anything I could say to her and I wrote her a letter which turned out to be a small essay, in which I tried to clarify my own thinking on this subject. I am venturing to read a copy of it at this chapel exercise, with some elisions and with the final paragraph added in the hope that it will at least contain some suggestions that may be of help to you:

"Your very frank, sincere and interesting letter has set me, I fear, an impossible task. I have had to change my views on many fundamental questions during my life, but even so it has been extremely difficult for one brought up as I have been to keep pace with the tremendous changes in thought and practice of recent years, especially since the War. I do not believe the younger generation can possibly realize in what a difficult position we who were born in the Mid-Victorian era are often placed, and how impossible it is for us to adjust ourselves to many of the present ways of thinking and acting, at least to adjust ourselves comfortably to them. Professor George F. Moore of Harvard, one of the few really great scholars we have produced in this country, once said to me that there was a greater difference between his father's generation and his own than there was between Aristotle's generation and his father's. The momentum of that change is even greater today. The new knowledge of the world in which we live has increased so enormously that it is impossible for any single individual to know it all or to realize its full significance.

"The impact of this vast accumulation of new knowledge is, at first sight, apparently very disintegrating in its effect upon older beliefs. A scientific study of the Bible for example, in which I have always been particularly interested, unquestionably requires very fundamental changes in our theories of the Bible, and this in turn seriously affects many of our religious beliefs. In the Reformation, Protestantism discarded the absolute authority of the Church and fell back on the sole authority of the Bible. But Protestantism, in its turn, is now discarding the absolute authority of the Bible. This means that our religion has ceased to be authoritarian in the sense in which this idea was once understood, practically down to our own day. We are now substituting the idea of the historical for the idea of the dogmatic. This means, in the case of the Bible, that it is now accepted by scholars as the classical expression of the Christian religion. In other words, if one wishes to know what the Christian religion in its essence really means, he must still go to the Bible, the Old Testament as well as the New, to find out. But that leaves the question whether this religion is true or not still open. We no longer believe it just because it is disclosed to us within the covers of the Bible.

"Now many Modernists, men like Mr. John Haynes Holmes, have taken a further step and practically cut themselves off from the religion of the Bible altogether, as well as from the Church, and look on both as impediments to true religion. In this I cannot agree with them. It seems to me that these men have been so carried away by the multitudes of new facts that they have lost their sense of the importance of the past experience of the race, especially of past Christian experience. Their perspective has become distorted and their conclusions unbalanced. I freely admit the great difficulty of keeping one's balance in these hectic days. But when such tremendous issues are at stake, caution rather than speed (the great obsession of our time and country) is the wiser policy. Certainly Mr. Holmes's statement, which you quote, that 'Christianity is an accidental and fortuitous phenomenon that has outlived its usefulness' is a very precipitate pronouncement to make upon a movement which has exerted so profound an influence upon the thought and life of mankind, and for so long a time, as Christianity has done. That which has struck its roots so deep into human life can be neither 'fortuitous' nor 'accidental.' Whether it has outlived its usefulness is yet to be proved.

"Now there is one notable characteristic of our new knowledge which should not be overlooked. It is almost exclusively a knowledge of the external world which secures to us an absolutely unheard-of control over nature. This control over nature has, in turn, externalized our lives, as I believe, to an alarming extent. Our inventions have ministered almost exclusively to our physical comfort or to our ability to destroy one another. So far as I can see, they have done nothing to improve our characters, to give us self-mastery. In fact, I believe there has never been a more neurotic age than the present one and never a more nervously high-strung and uncontrolled people than our own. I will not take time to prove that assertion though I think I could give plenty of evidence for it (our lawlessness, the extremely dangerous character of our mobs, our movies, our newspapers, our impatience with thinking, etc.). You can just put it down, if you wish, as a queer opinion of a senile cousin. It is my firm conviction that, as one often hears today, our material development has far outstripped our spiritual and character development in these past thirty years. A thoroughgoing materialistic (really mechanistic) philosophy has attacked our generation, especially in this country. It is expressed in one of the most characteristic trends of current philosophical thought, namely Behaviorism, which seeks to externalize our lives completely, and regards the human personality as a machine, without any self-consciousness or purpose or will—a thoroughgoing deterministic theory of life. The Behaviorists, indeed, use these terms but they mean by them something quite different from the meanings hitherto attributed to them.

"Another apparent result of all this new knowledge and new speculation is the breakdown of the idea of standards in life. A great many people just now feel entirely at sea about what used to be thought of as the fundamental moralities. It is at this point that the collapse of the authoritarian conception of the Bible of which I have spoken has contributed greatly to the acuteness of the crisis. In the universal challenge of all our former beliefs even the ethical ideals of the Bible have been challenged also.*

"And now, when you ask me about God—the greatest of all spiritual realities, if he *is* a reality—don't you see what a difficult question has been raised? In a world that is so thoroughly materialized and mechanized in its habits and its thinking as ours is, a world in which our lives have become so externalized, at a time when we almost never submit ourselves to any self-examination and deny that anything is real which is not capable of quantitative measurement, the realization of God, who cannot be measured quantitatively and hence belongs in a certain sense to the realm of value rather than to the world of science, has largely, for the time being, died out. For the time being! Forever? I doubt it. I am not prepared to believe that the human spirit will be willing or

* This denial of any valid ethical standards has finally resulted in the denial of any such standards in our international relationships and threatens a complete collapse of our civilization. It might be safer, in the long run, to recognize the biblical ethics as embodied in the much maligned Decalogue than to accept as a guide of life the present-day authoritarian state.

able to divest itself of all those values in life that give it its dignity and meaning. We *must* believe in a world of value if we are to retain our humanity. But a world of value is essentially a spiritual, not a material world. It is not subject, except to a limited degree, to scientific measurements. You can count heartbeats but you can't count love. You can count syllables and even measure rhythms but you cannot put a great line of poetry into a mathematical equation. Mathematics may underlie music, but there is something in the adagio of Beethoven's *Fifth Symphony* that eludes, and I believe will ever elude, quantitative, that is, scientific measurement.

"It seems to me that the difficulty about God for most of us lies in our inability to distinguish between quantitative and qualitative measurements, between the scientific world and the world of values and to believe in the reality of this latter world just as much as in the world of the senses. If we believe that thought is simply a more complicated form of motor reaction we will probably end by not believing in God. But if we believe that it is something more than that, even though motor reaction may be, in the present conditions of life, the mechanical means of thought, then in the end it will not be impossible to believe in God. If we can believe that our own personality is something more than the mathematical summation of all our muscular reactions, the way is open even to the possibility of our believing in God as a person. But if we believe that we ourselves are nothing more than machines, then, of course, it is not possible to believe in a personal God. From all this it is clear how difficult a belief in God is in an age that seeks to bring all things under the domination of quantitative rather than qualitative measurement, that is, to make the world of science the only real world at the expense of the world of values.

"It is at this point that the question arises: How are we to train ourselves to believe in God? More and more I believe that is the same sort of question as: How are we to train ourselves to appreciate beauty? We cannot learn God or beauty or teach them to others as we would learn or teach an arithmetic or Latin lesson. Belief and appreciation in this connection imply feeling as well as understanding. God and beauty are things to be felt even more than things to be understood. I had an interesting experience with a young lad some years ago when he was little. A friend of mine sent me a book of poetry for children which she had compiled and which she called *The Listening Child*. I did not at first realize the significance of that title. It was not the *Understanding* Child but the *Listening* Child, and the attempt was made to convey to the child the magic of words *before they were understood*. And so, in the world of values, we are to feel before we understand. If we ourselves believe in a world of values higher than the mere bread-and-butter material values of daily life, we are preparing the way for a belief in God. To my mind it is extremely important for us to cultivate in ourselves this sense for something of value, of supreme value, beyond ourselves, in human life. You write in your letter: 'I have the feeling that what I am looking for is to be found in ideal human conduct and character, not in the world of the spirit . . . I want my children to be taught about the life of Christ but I don't think the child can grasp much more.' I think that when this antithesis is drawn between 'the world of the spirit' and the world of ethical conduct ('ideal human character') a serious mistake is made into which so many of our modernist preachers and teachers have fallen. Jesus did not make this mistake. His ideal conduct and character were rooted in religion, that is, in his faith in and love of God as the supreme good, the supreme value. It is because the Christian religion has bound ethics and religion together as no other religion has ever done to an equal degree that it has taken such a powerful hold upon mankind. And this religious sense is found primarily in the sense for the transcendental, for that which is beyond and above ourselves and our quantitative measurements, for what Matthew Arnold calls 'the power not ourselves that makes for righteousness.' God will appear differently to different minds, but I believe that this sense of dependence is, as the great German theologian, Schleiermacher, points out, the very essence of religion and of belief in God.

"I realize that what I have been saying will probably seem very vague and unreal to you. I am groping these days as everyone else is. Nevertheless I am coming more and more firmly to believe in the validity of this distinction between the world of quantitative measurement (the scientific world) and the world of qualitative values (the spiritual world), to hold that the reality of this latter world is just as great as the reality of the scientific world, and that belief in God depends upon the firmness with which we grasp the fact of a world of values. But this means that we must run counter to some of the strongest currents of thought and action in our times and in our country."

Two weeks ago one of the most dramatic episodes in human history occurred. A scrawny, toothless, ugly little man, a prisoner, held in bonds by one of the mightiest empires the world has ever known, bent this empire and the clashing and tumultuous wills of a hundred million of his own fellow countrymen to do his bidding. How was this accomplished? By the use of fleets and armies, powder and dynamite? Not at all. It was an incommensurable spiritual force that did it. At the very time that our Western world seems inclined to make the great denial of the reality of anything that is not subject to quantitative measurement, Gandhi in the East— the great untouchable, untouched by the things of time and sense—makes in his life the great affirmation of the reality and power of the transcendental. When the full significance of this episode in a far-away Hindu prison is once recognized, perhaps it may help us to become aware of the reality of the world of values, the fact of the spiritual world; and in the process God himself, the final value or rather the entity behind this world of values, may draw nearer to us.

THE LAST SENIOR CHAPEL

I

Three Guideposts Along the Student's Way

FOR twenty-eight years I have stood at various times before this chapel audience and never yet have told you that I was "inspired by your bright young faces." If my silence on this animating subject should be continued, it might be construed as a personal slight. I should be sorry for that. So here goes: On this lovely June morning, as I look into your bright young faces, I am insp . . . Wait a minute. There seems to be interference. I can't get beyond that letter P. It is acting up in a queer way. It refuses to become just an ordinary middle letter of a long word and insists upon being the initial letter of a shorter one. But what is the word? There! The static is clearing up. It's coming over. I have it. It's spelled out by the announcer, P-I-T-Y— Pity! That can't be right. On this lovely June morning as I look into your bright young faces, pity—the word simply does not suit the context. But there it is, I can't get away from it. What is to be made of it? I fear a rather sad little thought.

When I think of the vast potentialities that are latent here and that one day *may* be developed, but also *may* be wasted, the feeling of pity does sometimes creep into the mind. The mere physical vitality of youth is a tremendous asset. And there are its natural courage, its idealism, even its inexperience which enable it to enter untried ways without misgivings. What could not such a body of young men and young women as this accomplish if it were concentrated with all its energy and enthusiasm upon some great purpose. We have today an astonishing example of what such concentration can do in the case of the Hitler Youth Movement, though, alas, in furtherance of a wrong ideal. You dimly feel this inherent power, yourselves, even though you may not be quite consciously aware of it. The proof of this is that you never imagine you can become, for example, like us of the Faculty, that "Rotarian group on the chapel platform," as the *Review* some years ago so felicitously described us. You can scarcely even imagine yourselves becoming like alumni ten years out. I remember the fine contempt I felt, when in college, for the decennial classes at their reunions. What a sad lot of ancients they were! Now this feeling is not altogether bumptious or without justification. It springs out of the conscious power in you to be something different, and that power is a real power. It is the ultimate asset which youth has and which is usually denied to age. And it is this fact which at times inspires (I cannot dodge that word after all) my hope when I look at you. But the fact that you *can* be something different is no proof that you *will* be something different, and here pity enters in. The danger is that many of you, by the time you reach middle life, will be exactly like the middle-aged people whom you now, to a certain extent, look down upon. I have seen almost ten complete college generations, at four years to a generation, pass by since I began to teach. Translated into terms of human generations, that makes some three hundred years—a sufficiently patriarchal age and experience to afford a basis for generalization. I can therefore prophesy, on the general law of averages (though my soul hateth laws of averages) that by the time you reach middle life the larger number of you will be quite as thoroughly conventionalized as we are (which ought, by the way, to be a link between us—we seeing in you what we once were, you seeing in us what you will become). You will then be indulging in the conventional pleasures which are rather vapid, enjoying the conventional successes, which will not turn out to be quite such soul-satisfying experiences as you anticipated, and a few, I fear, becoming conventional failures, wearily shuffling along at the tail end of the procession and waiting to make an unnoticed exit from a shabby life. The terrific power of the world to enforce conformity you are as yet quite unaware of, though if you would analyze the compulsion to conform even in your undergraduate days you might get an inkling of what is going to take place hereafter, when the larger world begins to exercise its steady, relentless pressure upon you.

Now I do not say that conformity, convention, is altogether a bad thing. In fact, it is quite important if the earth is to continue to be habitable. As you grow older you will find it to be almost necessary to pad yourselves out with a certain measure of protective conformity and convention in order to ease the bruises that come in the scrimmage of life, and also in order that others may be able to rub up against you without feeling that they have struck a barbed-wire fence. If each of you insists on always being edgy in the interest of self-expression, you are going to scratch and cut each other unmercifully before you are done. But on the other hand, the great danger is that the habit of mental and moral padding will so grow on you that in the end you will have completely disguised yourselves from yourselves, and beneath this disguise your real self will have shriveled up. And the tragedy is that when that happens you will not even be aware of it. The light that was in you will have flickered out into darkness.

May I be permitted to point out to you three ways by which you may avoid slipping into a merely commonplace and Babbittized life by the time you are fifty years old, even though you may have to endure some of the trimming and polishing off which the world thinks it necessary to treat you to in order to turn you into a neighbor who will not reduce the price of real estate where he happens to live. And these ways are not only open to you as college students, but they are the only ways in which you, as students, should walk. I mean, first, the cultivation of intellectual curiosity, second, the cultivation of sincerity, and third, the cultivation of the disciplined life. Intellectual curiosity will enable you to preserve an interested attitude toward life even after you have become more accustomed to its trodden ways than you are now. It will preserve the freshness of youth in the later years. It will prevent you from becoming that most deadly sort of person, a bored man or woman. Intellectual sincerity will prevent you from becoming conventionalized in the wrong way, or to the wrong degree. It will prevent you from ceasing to know yourself, which is after all your main duty in life. Finally, the cultivation of a disciplined life will prevent intellectual curiosity from degenerating into a curiosity of the merely pecking kind, like the pecking of chickens in a hen coop, and will add to sincerity the quality of humility, so necessary to keep sincerity from degenerating into egoism.

I wonder whether you realize just how much pleasure is to be found in intellectual curiosity, in being in love with a new idea. Romain Rolland says somewhere that "a new idea is a ship under way." Does that give you any conception of the joy of it? I remember the sensation I had the Saturday of the week I graduated from college, when I stood for the first time upon the deck of a swift liner bound for Europe. It was at the close of a terrifically hot day that we dropped down New York harbor. The evening was a clear, moonlit one in June. As we passed out into the open sea I stood at the bow of the steamer where I could breathe in the cool salt breeze and watch our prow cutting the gentle, silver rollers as we headed eastward to "the land of my dreams," the land of "cloud-capped towers and gorgeous palaces," of "castle walls where splendor falls," of "snowy summits old in story," that I had read about from the time I was a boy. This is no mere sentimentalism. The memory of that experience is too vivid and has lasted too long for that. A new idea is a ship under way. To what distant and beautiful countries may it carry you! To what further discoveries! Is your interest never aroused, your wonder never awakened, your desire to know more never quickened by the book you are studying? Does it never lead you to set out for yourself on a voyage of discovery? Have you no desire for intellectual travel unimpeded by trunks full of grades? Has your imagination never been caught by the "argosies of magic sails," winged ideas, sailing outward to "the horizon's utmost rim"? It is true there is another side to the picture. Not all ships that set out find a new continent, sometimes not even a harbor. The names of some of them are "sadly writ in water." Their epitaph is the tragic one—*spurlos versenkt* —sunk without a trace left behind. And so not all new ideas are seaworthy. Some are meant, not for far voyaging, but only for pleasure craft in sheltered inlets or quiet rivers. They have no stability, are easily unbalanced, quickly capsize. It is only the well-balanced new idea that can carry us safely into foreign parts and secure to us the joys of travel. Intellectual curiosity must be balanced by intellectual sincerity.

Now intellectual sincerity does not mean that you are to set yourselves in opposition to all the accumulated experience of mankind down to that momentous turning point in human history, the year in which you happened to be born. That is not intellectual sincerity. That is egoism. And intellectual sincerity not infrequently turns by the route of egoism into its very opposite, insincerity. Youth not infrequently appears to think that in order to be sincere it must deny everything that anybody else has ever held or thought of, that a thoroughgoing sceptical attitude toward life is the only one compatible with sincerity. But such an attitude may easily run into attitudinizing, may become only a pose; and a pose always has a measure of insincerity in it. Intellectual sincerity is not to be confounded with universal denial, any more than it is to be confused with universal affirmation. Sincerity is not so much exhibited in the conclusions you arrive at as in the way you arrive at them. Intellectual sincerity implies not only a willingness to face all the facts when they are once discovered but a readiness to take the trouble to find them all out, so far as it is possible to do so. And that is often a long and tedious process. I do not believe it can be followed through without a certain measure of humility and a rigorous self-discipline. Life is altogether too complex to be capable of easy doctrinaire solutions. It is fairly easy to arrive at a philosophy of life by ignoring whole series of facts which may not fit some given premise. But since induction has come to take the place of deductive logic in the discovery of truth, and we realize more and more that "one truth," as Browning says, "goes to the world's end," it seems a rather foolhardy undertaking to settle the universe on the basis of four years of miscellaneous study in college. The way toward truth is longer and more arduous than that. Happily, the great Victorian poet sets up three guideposts of the greatest value to help us along our difficult way:

> Self-reverence, self-knowledge, self-control,
> These three alone lead life to sovereign power.

Self-reverence is placed first by Tennyson, and not without reason. But self-reverence is not self-conceit. Conceit and reverence are incompatible. It does imply, however, that there is something in each one of us that is vastly precious, that must be preserved at all costs, that must be treated even with awe. After all that we gain from heredity and environment is peeled off from us, that something which is left appears to be only infinitesimal, it is true, but this minute residuum is the thing that distinguishes you from every other living creature. And it is the refusal to surrender your right to stand on this precious needle point of your own residual self that is the final guarantee that life will not shepherd you, none too gently, into the common herd.

Now the "I" in us being so very small, it takes a careful, microscopic examination, prolonged through life, to arrive at self-knowledge. But this careful and continued self-examination cannot be dispensed with. There have been times when men have fed too much upon their inward experiences, gnawed too much at their own heartstrings. That is not the danger today in our thoroughly extrovert world. In fact we have almost forgotten that there is anything inside us worth examining. The doors to the secret chambers of our hearts have been shut so long that cobwebs have collected over them and their bolts are rusty and hard to turn. Self-knowledge must be regained by men. One reason, perhaps the main reason, why civilization is floundering so hopelessly and in such bewilderment today is because men seem to have lost, temporarily at least, this knowledge of themselves. And more. The needle point of one's self can prick or it can stitch. It can be simply a nuisance in life, as in many forms of unregulated self-expression, or it can do constructive work. It all depends on how and to what end the point is sharpened.

Self-control must be added to self-reverence and self-knowledge if life is to be led on to sovereign power. And so I bid you to cultivate intellectual curiosity. Do not be simply casually curious, but rather persistently inquiring. By reading, by conversation, by observation of life, keep your minds alert and active. Be sincere. Be critical, but neither captious nor contemptuous; and with deep humility realize that the long way to truth carries us beyond the utmost horizon which we in our finiteness can imagine. Cultivate the disciplined life which is the only life that can endure the wear and tear of our existence, which alone can guarantee the continuance of our intellectual curiosity and the genuineness of our intellectual sincerity, for the undisciplined life will sooner or later become the disintegrated life, that precious residual self will disappear. "And what shall it profit a man if he gain the whole world and lose himself."

THE LAST SENIOR CHAPEL

II

The Dangers of Boredom, Bunk, and Getting By

SENIOR chapel always stirs me. I have watched you seniors gradually edging your way forward from the outskirts of civilization and the barbarian darkness of the back seats of the chapel till you are within reachable distance of the platform, where we of the Faculty sit, who, with some learning and a very great amount of labor, are engaged in the difficult task of polishing you off and getting you into fighting trim for your bout with the world. And now your weekly processional out of the chapel, ahead of all your teachers and fellow.students, sign and symbol of what is so shortly to take place in your lives, is almost over. We all stand as you go out, to do honor to adventurous youth advancing into the unknown.

I have a notion that when in afterlife you look back upon the four years you have spent together in Oberlin, these chapel scenes, in the recollection of many of you, will be among the pleasantest of your memories, even though the chapel talks may not be. To have sat side by side for four years under such trying circumstances as required chapel is considered to impose should knit you very firmly together for the rest of your lives. This by-product of the chapel service may prove to be after all no mean recompense for sufferings so heroically borne together.

There is one element in the picture of this senior chapel which I often think about. As the doors swing open to let you march out I sometimes catch a glimpse of the campus in its fresh green of spring, of the elms waving their branches gently overhead, and in the background a hint of the art building tinged with pink—a lovely scene. But is it a picture of the real outside world into which you are entering? Hardly. And then I begin to think of the contrast between the world I entered on my graduation and the world into which you are entering on yours. I do not think you can possibly realize the immensity of the change between then and now. You probably get tired of hearing our senile generation whose parents fought the Civil War chattering our astonishment at the present. But, really, it is the most tremendous experience of our lives—this contrast between the world of our youth and the world of our later years—and you must be patient with us as we try to reconcile ourselves to the new situation and to your apparent indifference to anything that took place before nineteen hundred.

When I went to New York for my postgraduate work at Union Theological Seminary, Fifth Avenue was still lighted with gas lamps. The Seminary was on Lenox Hill and almost every evening about five o'clock I used to walk over to the Avenue and watch the lamplighter at his work. The rows of the soft, twinkling lights, stretching away for blocks, made a lovely picture, especially on a frosty winter night. I liked it better than the garishness, almost the indecency, of the electric age with its piercing, all-illuminating searchlights. Even when I came to Oberlin fifteen years later I used to go part of the rounds with one of my students who had the job of lamplighter here. You remember Charles Lamb's saying: "Night and the candle light bring out the starry fancies." Though I had to get along, to be sure, with gas lamps instead of candlelight, I could still persuade myself that I sometimes had starry fancies. But the hard glitter of electric bulbs has a way of dimming even the stars.

What, in particular, set me to thinking of this great difference between the present and the past, between the world you are about to enter and the world your forebears entered, was a shock I received the other day in house cleaning. I was ordered by the powers that be, or rather the power that is, to clean out a certain old chest that stands in my room. It is a rude affair but capacious, and happens to be the container which a great-grandfather of mine used in lieu of a trunk when he went to Williams College about 1797 (he graduated in 1801). After an idle life of several generations this box has also been compelled to adjust itself to modern exigencies. I have been using it for some time past to store memoranda which have to do with current events, political and social, in which I have been especially interested since the beginning of the World War. Such a mess! I am not a very systematic sort of person and I seldom can find in that box what I am in search of. Yet I have gone so far as to write the contents on some of the envelopes in which the stuff is roughly distributed. Here are some random items: Literature on free speech. Reports of twelve leading lawyers on the illegal acts of the State Department. Manifesto of the German Intellectuals. Bryan on Darwinism at the Scopes trial (the closely reasoned argument of one of our great American biologists). Henry Ford on "history is bunk" (the illumination of another profound American scholar). Imperial Wizard Evans of the K.K.K. on immigration (the carefully digested convictions of a great political leader). Judge Gary on the Bible (the thoughts of a learned biblical scholar after the settlement of the steel strike). German atrocities (nursery tales to scare bad little children in peace and war). Tribute of General Pershing and others to General Sherman's doctrine and practice of *Schrecklichkeit* in war (at the unveiling of Sherman's bust in the Hall of Fame). Governor Smith's pardon of Larkin. Mussolini's assertion that he will trample on Parliamentarianism. Sacco-Vanzetti literature. Mooney literature. Centralia and Gastonia literature. Bulletins of the Civil Liberties Union. Bulletins of the Foreign Policy Association. The K.K.K. in Indiana (vintage of 1927). Colorado miners' strike (vintage of 1928). And then an envelope with this heading which made me feel really sorry for myself: "Rejected Patriotism or Thoughts on War and Peace, which I wrote out because I had to, though I found no publishers."

As I went through all this garbage of our civilization I began to wonder what my great-grandfather would have made of this veritable Pandora's box of social ills which had once served him as a trunk when he went to college one hundred and thirty years ago. He lived most of his life in an obscure little New England village amid only the elementary necessities of pioneer life and firmly believed in Satan, which settled a great many otherwise difficult metaphysical questions. What he would have made of the accumulations of his great-grandson in that old chest of his I cannot imagine.

I have spoken of that chest as being filled with the garbage of our civilization. Perhaps a less malodorous metaphor would be, filled with the unfinished business which my generation is passing on to yours. Its unsolved problems, the question of war or peace, the class struggle which we cannot blink while Russia is a part of Europe, the problem of ignorance, the problem of simple decency in our common life, the problem of our own heart life, into which we seldom probe in these days of the apotheosis of the extrovert, but the solution of which is fundamental to the solution of all the other matters—it is these things which in one form or another will face each one of you when you step out of this chapel for the last time and leave the relative quiet and security of this pleasant village. What seems most terrifying to one who grew up as I did in the Mid-Victorian era is the realization that you must meet these problems with all the former standards—religious, moral, social, artistic—in the melting pot. There is not an ancient sanctity which is not in these days openly attacked in newspapers, popular magazines or movies, on the thin mental pabulum of which so large a number of us live. The churches are largely ineffective in the general welter. Fundamentalism has lost contact with the present, is fatally anachronistic and is degenerating in many cases into ignorance and superstition. Modernism, on the other hand, has too often lost its anchorage in the past and is unconsciously drifting toward the sands and shallows of rationalism. You are perhaps unaware of all this. But not being Mid-Victorians you have never known what it is to feel either intellectually or spiritually secure. And so you have not yet keenly felt the real discomfort of your situation. But when *I* look out upon life I confess to a sense of bewilderment. The facts which science and history have dumped upon us are too manifold to be moulded into a new philosophy of life in a short space of time, and I warn you against any short cut to peace of mind. There is none. Meanwhile, what will be your attitude toward all this? That is a very practical and a very important question which *is* capable of solution and which every one of you will solve in one way or another.

Will you dodge the issue *by taking refuge in boredom?* That is certainly a practical solution. But I think there is more spiritual satisfaction to be found even in bewilderment than in boredom. I hate to think of any of you going out from college into the world already disillusioned and hard-boiled. I hate to think of any of you going out from college eager and curious, and returning to some reunion in the future hard-boiled. To grow callous to the sin, the suffering, the need of mankind, which is fighting so desperately hard to lead a life just a little more decent as time goes on, is to adopt an ungallant and a cruel attitude toward one's fellow men. The hard-boiled and the knightly, so far as I can see, have nothing in common. Will you dodge the issues *by taking refuge in bunk?* That, too, may be a practical solution of your life problem. But that is also worse than bewilderment. I can forgive a sweet young girl like Pippa for singing, as she passes along in the dawn of a bright May morning, "God's in his heaven; all's right with the world." I cannot forgive the ordinary boosters, who, with a smirk on their faces, chant the same thing, for all too often their God is not in the heaven at all, but, as St. Paul says, "their god is their belly," and all is *not* right with the world. Certainly all is not right with them. Too often they palm off their Messianic promises only for the sake of better business. You hate bunk in college. You know you do. Are you going to contribute to this rubbish heap when you get out into the world, or are you going to continue to hate it?

I believe there is just one fundamental grace in these days with which to encounter life. And that is sincerity. Let us study its connotations for a moment. Sometimes sincerity is confused with egotism and bad manners. It is assumed that in order to be one's self, to be sincere, one must break all the conventions. We forget that conventions are the shock absorbers provided for us by society to enable us to travel together through life without getting on one another's nerves too unbearably. Our compartment is pretty crowded and the journey rather long. We must be considerate of each other's feelings if we are to enjoy any of the scenery by the way. Some years ago the *Oberlin Review* fell into the hands of a young fellow of ultramodern propensities. He thought he saw a number of cobwebs obscuring the light of the college windows. He may have been right, for spiders *do* work at times in academic shades. But to get rid of the cobwebs he thought it necessary to smash the windows. A queer way of letting in light, but sincerity in his opinion called for nothing less. The broken panes of glass cut so many people about the campus that even the faculty worm felt it had to turn and take notice. The young man disclaimed any intention of hurting anyone and he was probably honest in his disclaimer. The trouble was that he was unable to distinguish between cleaning windows and hoodlumism, between criticism and vituperation. It was simply a case of bad manners. No, sincerity is not to be confounded with bad manners.

Sincerity is something more than what we mean by honesty as this word is commonly used, though it should include it. There is certainly a sufficiently loud call for honesty in our American life. The thing that worries me most, at times, about the future of our country, though a great many things worry me more or less, is just this growing indifference among us to common honesty. I remember, when I was in Syria, hearing of an English merchant by the name of Black who had spent most of his life in the Near East and who had conducted his business with such scrupulous honor and honesty that when the natives wished to take an absolutely binding oath they said, "I swear by the name of Black." That was a glorious achievement of Black. I commend it to you for your emulation.

Again, sincerity is something more than reliability, though in its higher forms it includes that also. And here we meet a third temptation to dodge the responsibilities of life which may be associated with the temptations to boredom and bunk. I refer to the temptation to just "get by." My old friend, President Hutchins of Berea College, was one day passing a gang of workmen making a sewer connection on a Cleveland street. He heard the boss call to one of the workmen, "Is it all right?" The workman answered, "No, it's not all right, but it'll do." I do not know how many coffins may have been carried out of the houses served by that faulty sewer connection, but the workmen who just got by had done their best to provide a deathtrap for the neighborhood. The foundations of the philosophy of getting by are often laid in college or in high school. This recitation or that term paper is a relatively unimportant matter and the exertion of doing one's best is at the moment too oppressive. The doctrine of getting by usually grows out of laziness, and laziness, when not too pronounced, is perhaps the most venial and lovable of all the vices. It is easygoing, comfortable, and often accompanied by a cheerful and pleasant disposition. But the habit of getting by, which may have started in laziness, soon takes on, if persisted in, a more sinister character. It becomes dishonesty, unreliability. The life lived on this principle becomes a shoddy life.

But sincerity, while it involves honesty and reliability, is a much deeper and subtler thing than these other virtues. They deal primarily with our relations to other people. Sincerity deals with our relationship to ourselves. It is first of all an inner grace, a temper of the mind and spirit. Are we honest with ourselves? The longer I live the more difficult I find it to be absolutely sincere. The temptation to juggle with one's own mind as one gets on in life is increasingly insidious. Our minds tend to harden as well as our bones. Our mental patterns (I believe that is one of the up-to-date phrases in psychology and education) become stereotyped. It becomes more and more difficult to change our minds, to modify former conclusions. Often the very conventions which are intended to make our social intercourse easier muffle us up in unreality. Above all, self-interest deadens our sensitiveness to facts as we get more and more enmeshed in the complicated necessities of making a living within this very badly assembled economic system of ours. In these circumstances we resort to all sorts of mental tricks in order to relieve our mental and moral distresses. In business we cultivate the legalistic mind which will permit us to circumvent the spirit of the law though we may not transgress the letter—this type of mind functions with tremendous efficiency on tax day. We fall back on deductive logic which has this great advantage, that, if we can only select a couple of premises which will serve our own interest, we can, by means of the syllogism, secure a great many additional perquisites. We learn to play with words, to quibble, and we soon find ourselves back again in the unreal world of boredom, or bunk or getting by. There is nothing more intellectually and spiritually disastrous than to get into this habit of juggling with your own minds. A world of bewilderment, if faced with sincerity, is preferable to a sham life, though a more comfortable one, in any of these other worlds. But need it be a world of continuing bewilderment? Intellectually, perhaps, yes. A new synthesis, a substitute for the unified conception of life which obtained perhaps in the great age of Greece, and certainly in the Middle Ages, is not likely to be formulated in my time or yours. Our knowledge is increasing too rapidly to permit of such a synthesis. But does this intellectual bewilderment necessarily mean spiritual frustration? Not if it is the result and accompaniment of sincerity, of the attempt to face life as it actually is. For sincerity, as we have seen, is an inward grace and therefore can be maintained against all external buffetings. Which means that we must hearken to the Word from the East:

> Then shall we understand the saying that is written:
> Peace I leave with you, my peace I give unto you:
> Not as the world giveth, give I unto you.
> Let not your heart be troubled,
> Neither let it be afraid.

THE LAST SENIOR CHAPEL
May 29, 1934
III
Reminiscences of a Senescent

THIS is the last regular senior chapel exercise of the year. It is the last one for you, and also for me. In a way we are going out together. This fact inspires in me a reminiscent mood. It is forty-six years since I left college in 1888. When you return to your forty-sixth reunion it will be in 1980—a time which probably looks to you as distant in the future as 1888 looks to you in the past. Indeed, the fall of 1884, the year I entered college, when the slogan "Rum, Romanism and Rebellion" sounded through the land in the James G. Blaine presidential campaign, seems even to me, in the dim perspective of the receding years, contemporary with the building of the pyramids. As a matter of fact, by 1980, if you reckon from the year of my birth, we will have more than bridged a century between us. In that remote future you will be as senescent as I am today, which means that you will be reminiscent, garrulous, and as boastful about your Class of 1934 as I propose to be about my class of 1888.

You are probably often thinking these days of the time when you arrived as freshmen in college. I am also thinking of the time I arrived at my college as a freshman, for I really was once a freshman (pedagogues have not always been *aged* pedagogues from their cribs, as is commonly supposed). I remember the first man of my class that I met. He was one of the Thomi (in those days we still cultivated the classics and took our Latin pronunciation from Oxford), as we designated the Thomas Brothers. He was lugging a study desk, so called, across the Campus. I think more cheese sand-wiches than books were subsequently devoured at it.

The second man I identified as a future classmate was sitting in the office of the main hotel of the town into which I had chanced to sidle in a humble, deprecating way as became a freshman. He wore a Norfolk jacket over a clerical vest and was reading through heavy bifocals Henry George's *Progress and Poverty* which had recently appeared. He looked sporty, clerical (hence his name, the Bish, short for Bishop) and intellectual, a combination to impose upon any freshman. A chance remark betrayed the fact that this impressive figure and I were to be classmates. Immediately I wished to be chummy. But he remained cold and distant. Naturally he was chosen as our first class president. We were all overawed by him until our first class meeting which, under his guiding hand, ended in a riot and the demotion of the Bishop from his high office.

Then there was the dear old Mast. He was one of the two tallest members of the class and correspondingly thin. Students did not have the uncanny faculty of organization in those far-off days that you display today, and the Mast and I were allowed to lock arms for the first class rush, a combination which did not make for efficient driving power. When the Mast graduated he inherited a good hardware business which he disliked, for he loved the things of the mind. He said he proposed to double it in ten years and then retire, which he did, and devoted himself to literature. He lived but a few years to enjoy this larger life. I visited him on his deathbed. There was not a trace of disappointment on his emaciated face. A beautiful, brave soul shone through the thin veil of flesh that tuberculosis had rendered so transparent.

There was Rusty. He always made the aggravating claim that he could beat me at tennis and generally made good his claim, which was still more aggravating. He was one of the earliest of the volunteers in the Student Volunteer Movement. But his eyes troubled him so he could not continue his theological studies. He went into business, made a competence for himself and his family, and then, remembering his boyhood vow, gave up his business and offered himself to the board of one of our greatest foreign missionary societies, to be used by them as they saw fit without salary, and has been serving that society ever since.

There was Bob, decorated by Theodore Roosevelt in person for special bravery at the battle of San Juan Hill. There was Chump, the inventor of our class. He, too, made a fortune and then retired to devote himself to literature and experimentation in a school of his own establishment for primary education. There was Allie who has spent his life largely in philanthropic work, and, as our loved class president, has held us together over all these many years.

Our class was a small one as compared with the hordes that now swarm over college campuses, but we have had our full share of men who have made the wheels go round. We landed one of our men on the Interstate Commerce Commission—our valedictorian (you who scoff at Phi Beta Kappa, please take notice). Another has succeeded, apparently, in tapping every known source of wealth in a great Eastern state, and another like him has been head of the traction system of one of the most important cities in the country. Their chief social service, however, is in furnishing the wherewithal to bring us economic parasites of the class—the pedagogues, preachers, et al.—back to the quinquennial reunions.

In addition to a large body of successful doctors, lawyers, teachers and preachers, we have also furnished a president for one of the foremost universities of our land. He and I belonged to the same club and ate together for four years a species of underdone griddlecake which went among us by the name of "malarial cakes." Four years after graduation we had sufficiently recovered from this diet to spend a summer idyll together in the Harz Mountains in Germany. Later on we returned to spend Christmas week with our kind host and hostess. One day of that memorable week the two of us walked by ourselves up into the mountains. The air snapped with frost. The tall and solemn pines were powdered with a fine snow. The sun went down behind the Brocken about 3 P.M. and a marvelous green light spread over the mountains and valleys. Now and then a deer would appear upon some high ridge, etched against the sky line. It was all overpowering. We broke forth into a duet, "In praise of Old Nassau," our Alma Mater song. It marked an era in the musical history of the land of Schubert and Brahms. "Dumbbells," I hear someone say. Maybe. But you see, we simply couldn't help it. The situation could only be done justice to in that way. It may sound strange to you reputedly sophisticated young ladies and gentlemen of the present age, but, honestly, the recollection of that episode with my classmate is priceless.

Our class entered college before the era of organization and standardization had fully set in. Organized cheering had begun, but laissez faire in the matter of individual yelling, in other words "let her go Gallagher," was still permitted. Our particular class, if a paradox may be permitted, was a kind of creative chaos. As in the days before the Judges judged in Israel, "every man did that which was right in his own eyes," and that was a lot. We were still an irresponsible and happy remnant left over from the era of nineteenth-century individualism. I have never been associated before or since with such a thoroughly uncoördinated number (you could not call them a "bunch") of human beings, except in one particular. We were all loyal to '88. And as the years have rolled around, now forty-six of them, that common tie has bound us all together and has added a charm to life that not one of us feels he could afford to lose. We have gone our several ways. Our interests in many cases have widely diverged. But the fact that we are all members of '88 binds us together in what, as we approach the sunset years, is coming to be almost a mystical union. For the union is now not only of the living with the living, as it was in the old days, but of the living with the dead. And that seems strange. For if there ever was a class with which the thought of death could be least associated, it was ours. But upwards of half our number have gone out beyond the "horizon's utmost rim" to that bourne from which no traveler, however vigorous and venturesome, ever returns. I have quoted before in this chapel the song we used to sing in College:

> Where, oh where, are the verdant Freshmen?
> Safe now in the Sophomore Class.
> Where, oh where, are the gay young Sophomores?
> Safe now in the Junior Class.
> Where, oh where, are the stately Juniors?
> Safe now in the Senior Class.
> Where, oh where, are the grave old Seniors?
> Safe now in the wide, wide world.

The interpretation we used to give to the idea of safety in that song was that at last we had skinned through the final examinations. But I now believe that interpretation to be a mistake. "Safe now in the wide, wide world"! What does that mean? Does it mean that we have all become *safe and sane?* I hope not. Such persons are no doubt needed in the world but they are usually awfully dull. Does safety mean that we have become *financially secure?* Some of us have succeeded along that line and some of us haven't. Those of you who have are, I think, exposed to one of the greatest dangers that can befall a young man or a young woman. They are too apt to become hard-boiled. I beseech of you, don't, all of your class, come back safe and sane in 1980. The reunion will lose a most pleasurable thrill if you do. Above all, don't any of you come back hard-boiled. By 1980 the Fascist Utopia may have arrived, the Utopia of the hard-boiled. But I warn you that, though you may journey hither in your own private airplanes from Kamchatka, Laguna or Mozambique (I don't know why I have located Oberlin Alumni "cells" in these regions unless it is to secure a Macaulay sonority), and though you may dine on undreamed-of viands which the McNally Doyle* of that distant era will spread before you, when the Aluminum Company shall have paid up all its back dividends, and the College is furnishing a free lunch, your reunion will none the less be flat, stale and unprofitable, if you return to it hard-boiled. The hard-boiled are apt to lose out of their lives the thing that lends to a reunion its greatest zest—the faculty of friendship.

I don't believe that our college faculties have yet learned to do a very adequate job in the way of educating you students who pour through our classrooms in such swelling tides. But there is one thing we do give you, to a degree scarcely attained in any other country, namely, the great opportunity in the Maytime of youth and in congenial surroundings to make life-long friendships. Perhaps that may mean as much as a technically more adequate education. Perhaps all these hundreds of millions of dollars of endowments that are put into your education could be spent to no better purpose—friendships help mightily to make the world truly safe. Without them the wide, wide world would be very wide indeed and very lonely.

May I add just another note, this time of warning. There have been some failures in my Class of '88. Not many, I am glad to say, but still a few. How do failures come about? Nobody deliberately sets out to be one. Nobody wilfully proposes to disgrace his class or make his classmates wish to avoid him when he turns up at a reunion. How does one contrive such a sad outcome for his life? There are two main ways of doing it. Sometimes we are overtaken by an unex-

* A celebrated Cleveland café.

pected, terrible temptation, or by a sudden gust of passion. We are *bombed* by life and are never able to gather our moral fragments together again. That happens very rarely. The more usual way to failure is the way of gradual, moral atrophy. Just as we often permit our imaginations to be slowly deadened, or worn down by the weathering effects of humdrum daily life, so we allow our moral faculties, our consciences, to become dulled by constant contact with the material world. We yield a bit here, a bit there, of our idealism. Compromises with our better selves become easier and easier. And then an unusually languorous and relaxing hour may come and one more compromise, a very little one, may be asked of us. We yield without really knowing we have done so. Some people die very easily, without a gasp or a struggle. It is all very quiet, very unobtrusive. Nevertheless it is *death*.

Safe in the wide, wide world! We are *never* safe. I have been out in it for forty-six years. I do not feel safe. It is so very wide, so very labyrinthine. One can so easily lose his way in it. But by holding fast to two golden threads he may win his way through without bringing shame upon his classmates. These golden threads are love and loyalty.

Someday you and I who go out from college life this year will attend our last reunion. The foreground will be strangely foreshortened. The horizon will be no longer distant. The wide, wide world will have shrunk till there is nothing but a brief, precarious foothold left, and time, too, that once seemed so unending, will have contracted to the final decisive moment that awaits each one of us. Then earth's labyrinths will seem constructed with a child's simplicity as we turn from them to face the solemn, baffling mystery of the life beyond. But perhaps these tenuous threads of love and loyalty, if firmly held, may lead us on encouragingly, invitingly, to explore in the amplitude of eternity that wider world which lies before us all.

PART II
THE GENIUS OF OBERLIN

THE OBERLIN CENTENARY

June, 1926

IT is one thing to see a place famous in history, another thing to feel it. There are two little Alsatian villages tucked away in a fold of the Vosges Mountains about two hours distant by railroad from Strassburg, which a casual tourist could "do" in a couple of hours and wonder why they were ever mentioned in Baedeker. And yet if their significance can once be felt, they will repay the trouble of a long journey. The valley is the Steintal or Ban de la Roche (almost every place has two names in this bilingual region) and the villages are Waldersbach and Fouday. It was here that Johann Friedrich Oberlin, as he was almost certainly baptized, or Jean Frederick Oberlin, as he later usually wrote his name, lived and labored.

The rather forbidding name of the valley, Stony Valley, suggests a desolate region, and its wildness has been dwelt upon by many writers, most of whom have probably never been there. As a matter of fact, the valley gets its name from the great castle, now a ruin, which stands on a lofty crag above it and which once belonged to the lords of Rathsamhausen. Contrary to expectation the valley proves to be pleasing to the eye, though the almost bare heights of the Vosges that rise just back of Waldersbach give to the scene a certain air of solitude and remoteness. The valley is only a little one, but its aspect is solemn rather than intimate. Its smile, for it can smile when the sun comes out, is somewhat grave. The two small hamlets, Fouday, the railway station at the mouth of the Steintal where it breaks into the larger valley of the Breusch, and Waldersbach, a mile or so farther up, are clean and neat, which cannot always be said of peasant villages in Europe, and have a general air of well-being and contentment that is somewhat unusual.

Of course, each village has its church. The one at Waldersbach is the less pretentious of the two, and its white plastered walls are less relieved by shade than is the case at Fouday where the burying ground with some fine trees adjoins the church. The church at Fouday has also made use of an ancient tower which adds to its architectural attractiveness. The tower belonged to an earlier church dating from pre-Reformation times, and in it there still swings a bell consecrated to the Virgin. I think Oberlin must have enjoyed that bell, for he called himself an "evangelical catholic," though he was pastor of a Lutheran church. Both churches have pulpits raised to the level of the galleries that run around three sides of the audience room, as is the case in many of our own colonial churches. In the gallery of the one at Waldersbach are great logs twenty-five or thirty feet long, but quite narrow, which serve for seats. There was no going to sleep on these *misericordia* when Johann Friedrich preached. And here in these two churches and three others which belonged to the same parish of Waldersbach, he preached for fifty-nine years. That was certainly a long enough time to justify his parishioners in taking an occasional nap. Instead, they grew wider and wider awake under the preaching of this remarkable man.

At Waldersbach is the parsonage just across the way from the church, a fine old house covered with vines and giving out on a roomy approach, half courtyard, half garden. Here Oberlin lived and received needy or admiring guests from all over Europe. By the church at Fouday he lies buried, and to his grave pilgrims continue to come from the ends of the earth as to a shrine. It was to this secluded valley and to these simple village churches that Mrs. Fullerton and I, with many others, repaired in June, 1926, to take part in the hundredth anniversary of Oberlin's death. Professor E. A. Miller and myself had been chosen to represent Oberlin College on this occasion. But Professor Miller was unfortunately prevented from attending by the strike in England. The only other Oberlin person present besides ourselves was Dr. Frederick O. Anderegg, of the Class of 1910, son of Professor Anderegg, the head of our mathematics department for many years.

It is impossible to go into all the details of the celebration. There were preliminary services held in Strassburg, Oberlin's native city, in which members of the theological faculty of the University of Strassburg and others participated, followed by a visit to the Alsatian Museum, in which two rooms were devoted to a most interesting collection of Oberliniana. This was on Thursday. On Friday there was an excursion out to Colmar, the city from which Oberlin's ancestors came to Strassburg. But the main part of the celebration took place on Sunday in the two churches of Fouday and Waldersbach. The morning service, which was the more formal one, was held at Fouday. After an excellent luncheon given to the visiting delegates, there was an open-air service in the afternoon at Waldersbach. A tea in Oberlin's parsonage completed the program.

I confess I was amazed at the size and quality of the audience which packed the church at Fouday quite literally to the ceiling. But it was not only the villagers who had trouped in from the surrounding countryside and helped to fill it; there were some of the leading representatives of French Protestantism, scholars and preachers from far-away Paris as well as from near-by Strassburg. There was a delegation from Switzerland which came to lay a wreath on Oberlin's grave (the relationship of Oberlin with Switzerland had always been intimate). There was the unofficial representative of the British and Foreign Bible Society in the person of Mr. Cowell, an English journalist, who has taken a great interest in Oberlin and incidentally in Oberlin

College. The official representative was unable to be present. There was General Reibell, to represent the French army, and the Prefect of the Rhine country, to represent the civil government. It was evident that France took this commemoration of Oberlin very seriously. I may add that there was great interest manifested in it also in both Germany and England, if one may judge by the newspaper notice which it received.

As the delegate of Oberlin College it was my privilege to pay as best I could the tribute of Oberlin in America and Oberlin in Shansi to the memory of Oberlin in the Ban de la Roche. The various speakers were unannounced except on the printed program. It is apparently not thought decorous in France to emphasize the personal note in a religious service. For the same reason the announcement of the College's donation of five thousand francs was reserved for the luncheon. When I climbed, in my turn, the flight of stairs that led up to the pulpit and stood in the place where Oberlin had stood so many times, and looked down into the faces of the descendants of those to whom he had preached and among whom he had labored so many years, it was one of the most memorable experiences of my life. It was then that I not only saw the outward environment of Oberlin but felt the far-reaching significance of what he had accomplished in this little valley more than a hundred years before. I realized what a man of piety, consecration and sincerity can accomplish in the most untoward circumstances, and that intellectual endowments of a higher order are not necessarily wasted when employed in the service of the lowly.

Young men and young women, if you have the good fortune to graduate from this college, you will bear the name of no ordinary person. Who was John Harvard? Who was Eli Yale? Who was Lord Geoffrey Amherst? Persons of no real consequence, whose fame depends on the chance attachment of their names to institutions which have succeeded.

But today two great nations, France and Germany, are quarreling over the question whether Oberlin was more French or more German, and each is unfortunately jealous of the other's claims. There is a rather flippant song in the Oberlin Songbook, the last verse of which, however, may be sung in all seriousness:

The rolling years have come and gone since the good old Johann died,
Yet still his name and fame live on through all this country wide,
And we, here, where his College stands with thousands more in alien lands
Now rise to bless the name and kin of Johann Friedrich Oberlin.

This College has an inheritance and a challenge in its name such as no other college in the country possesses. And why? What were some of the qualities and accomplishments of this humble Alsatian pastor which make the one-hundredth anniversary of his death a matter of international interest?

The Steintal was not always so prosperous looking as it is today. The Thirty Years' War had left it a waste, howling wilderness and almost depopulated. Later there followed new settlements of very heterogeneous character, composed of French, Germans, Swiss and even Italians. Poverty, ignorance and lawlessness prevailed. Churches and schools fell into decay. Strassburg divinity students considered it a punishment to be sent to Stony Valley and got out of the hole as soon as they could.

But when the call came to Oberlin in 1767 to go to this unenviable parish he went at once, and remained there for fifty-nine years. At that time he was a promising young man of twenty-seven. He belonged to an educated family. His father was a teacher in the Gymnasium at Strassburg. His mother was the daughter of a pastor and Canonicus at St. Aurelien and had received an excellent education in a French fitting-school at Nancy. One of his brothers was a noted Germanist and classical scholar of his day, editing texts of Ovid, Horace and Tacitus. Oberlin himself very early gave promise of great ability. At the age of fifteen he began to study theology. He took his bachelor's degree in Theology at eighteen, five years later his doctor's degree, and four years after that, in 1767, the year that he went to Waldersbach, he became *Magisterius* on the basis of a thesis: "Concerning the advantages and disadvantages of theological study." This academic discussion was to receive a very realistic illustration in the wilderness of Waldersbach.

Meanwhile he had been tutor in a wealthy French family where he had learned the graces and polish of French society. He was eminently fitted to become the popular pastor of some urban congregation, but, instead, he was to be called to lose his life in a remote, and at that time, wretched mountain village. But he that loses his life for my sake and the Gospel's, his Master had said, the same shall find it. He chose obscurity and found fame. Yet he must have felt the danger to his own intellectual growth in taking up his work in the Steintal, for from 1766–80, a period which includes the first thirteen years of his pastorate there, he kept a memorandum of books he had read, with comments upon them.

In these fourteen years, pressed most of the time by all sorts of "outside activities" (a plague upon them), he managed to read 538 works, an average of three per month. He would not permit his intellectual interests to be smothered by parish details, numerous and important though they were. For the Steintal needed everything—preservation from actual starvation because of crop failures (for several years previous to Oberlin's arrival on the scene, the people of the parish had been reduced to living principally on grass steeped in milk), training in agriculture, education, liberalizing contact with the outside world—everything to provide the opportunity of a decent mode of living.

One of the questionnaires which Oberlin sent out to his people begins with the inquiry: Do you regularly attend the worship of God with your families? and ends with: Have you proper receptacles for your manure and proper drains for your houses? He taught the people to make roads, build bridges, plant trees, etc., working with his own hands in these enterprises. They still point out on the otherwise bare heights of the Vosges around Waldersbach little groves which Oberlin planted to provide cool shady coverts for the wild game of the region during the hot summers, an act very characteristic of the man.

One of the most important things he did for the welfare of the valley was to establish a silk-ribbon industry in which he enlisted the support of an able and philanthropic Swiss manufacturer, Luc LeGrande. This industry has been continued down to the present and under the management of Luc LeGrande's successors, who have developed his work in his spirit, it has brought prosperity to the valley. In all these activities, which he combined with his studies and reading, Oberlin was a living object lesson of our College motto, "Learning and Labor," and a champion of what we now know as the social service ideal, which has always distinguished our institution.

The greatest attention was given to the education of the villagers, particularly to primary education. "Infant schools" were established and conducted on a plan that in many ways anticipated Froebel's kindergartens by upwards of fifty years. Oberlin's interest in education brought him into contact with Basedow, the great German educator of the eighteenth century. We find Oberlin and his wife contributing enthusiastically out of their slender means (for the first three years of his ministry his annual income was the equivalent of only $148 and part of this was in goods) to Basedow's rather ill-fated Institute, Philanthropin. When Professor Fiske visited the Ban de la Roche in 1912 he found a wreath laid on Oberlin's grave by a party of schoolteachers from Scotland, who wished to show their appreciation of one who had done so much in the cause of elementary education.

But Oberlin's interests were not to be confined to his own little valley, nor did he suffer his parishioners' interests to be centered on themselves. Oberlin's mind was essentially the adventurer's and explorer's. He does not seem to have traveled much, but his *mind* ranged to the ends of the earth. He displayed the greatest interest in missions, and only the outbreak of our own Revolution prevented him from going out as a missionary to the wilds of Pennsylvania. He was the first foreign correspondent of the British and Foreign Bible Society, and the peasants whom he found subsisting partly on grass were soon to send contributions to the support of this society, to the support of the missionary activities in Basel, and to the relief of the slaves in the West Indies. Oberlin, as usual, set the example in self-sacrifice. On one occasion he and his wife melted down all their silver plate except one spoon to send to Basel.

His regular custom was to give away three tenths of his income, one tenth for beautifying the services of the church, one tenth for general parish purposes, and one tenth for the poor. He went for a time without sugar or coffee as a protest against the slave labor which produced them. In these respects also we have inherited Oberlin's ideals. The problem with us is whether we will maintain them unimpaired.

But Oberlin was also intensely interested in the great political issues of the day. Racially he was born a German-speaking Alsatian. German was his mother tongue, and unquestionably the baptismal form of his name was German. His solemn dedication of himself to God at the age of twenty was written in German, and the beautiful prayer which he wrote for himself and his wife on the occasion of their marriage, asking the blessing of God upon it, was written in the same language. But nationally he was French, as all Alsace was at that time. The villages where he preached were largely French-speaking, and most of his sermons were therefore in French, and his letters and other documents are usually signed with the French form of his name. It is unquestionable that he was a loyal French citizen, and what is more, he was an ardent democrat and supporter of the French Revolution.

He saw in it the fulfilment of the prophecy of the little stone in Daniel, which was to destroy the kingdom of anti-Christ, that is of the aristocracy and the Clericals. The Declaration of the Rights of Man was in his view the beginning of the Kingdom of God. He was on intimate terms with at least one of the Revolution's most distinguished leaders, Grégoire, the Bishop of Blois and one-time president of the Convention. Grégoire once wrote to him, "I love you as much as I hate Kings." From his remark that "Kings are in the moral world what monsters are in the natural world," his appreciation of Oberlin may be measured. I fear many of our American tourists in Europe, of the kind who loudly praise Mussolini because they find travel in Italy more comfortable than in years gone by, and who are better acquainted with the toadying social columns of the continental editions of the English and American newspapers than they are with the Constitution of the United States, would have found in Jean Frederick, the revolutionary, rather a dangerous Bolshevist. He was dangerous even religiously. Though a Lutheran, he said his faith was not in Martin Luther but in Jesus Christ. He was willing to give the communion to Jew and Catholic as well as to Protestants in the church in whose tower swung the bell consecrated to the Virgin, and he actually dared to reject the doctrine of eternal damnation! A charge was laid against him on this score before the Board of Ecclesiastical Overseers in Strassburg.

As the years went by Oberlin's fame increased. The French Royal Society of Agriculture honored him with a medal for the work he had accomplished in making the Ban de la Roche blossom as the rose. The Revolutionary Convention sent him a letter of congratulation on his usefulness as a citizen, and later still, under Louis XVIII, he was decorated with the cross of the Legion of Honor.* The pastor of Waldersbach either corresponded with or received visits from many of the noted people of his day. The German poet, Lenz, one of the most talented, though one of the most dissipated, of the literati of the Storm and Stress period, visited the parsonage at Waldersbach in what seems to have been a fit of remorse and in a longing for peace. The novelist, Jung-Stilling, also went on a pilgrimage to "the righteous pastor of the Vosges," as he calls Oberlin. It is worth notice in this connection that Oberlin himself became the hero of one of the best-selling German novels, entitled *Oberlin, a Romance*. It appeared in 1910 and my copy belongs to the one hundred and forty-third edition.

One of Oberlin's most interesting guests was a Russian lady, the Baroness von Krüdener, wife of the Russian Ambassador at Venice and Berlin, a very eccentric, not to say neurotic, sort of person, but destined to play a curious part in one of the great dramas of the time. She had been converted from a worldly past to a belief in the speedy Second Coming of the Lord. In the strength of this belief she undertook the conversion of the Czar, Alexander II, who, after the fall of Napoleon, was the most powerful sovereign in Europe, and she exercised for a time a profound influence upon him. Out of the group which she gathered around herself and the Czar, and among whom were numbered such notables as Chateaubriand, Madame Récamier, and the Duchesse de Bourbon, emerged the mystical idea of a European civilization based upon the principles of Jesus Christ, an idea which took political form in the Holy Alliance, proto-

---

* It may not be known to you, though it should be, that a little over one hundred years later President King received the same great honor.

type of our League of Nations. The Baroness claims, probably correctly, to have suggested the idea of the Alliance to
the Czar, and that the draft of the strange proclamation in
which the Czar, the Emperor of Austria, and the King of
Prussia invited the nations of Europe to join the Alliance
and live as brethren in Christian Unity had been submitted
to her for approval before its publication.

This was in 1815. In 1812 and 1814 we find the Baroness
visiting Oberlin at Waldersbach. She was probably drawn to
him by the mystical side of his life, by his belief in the Second Coming and in occultism, a faith which he shared with
many of the leading men of his age in a reaction against the
rationalism which then prevailed and which sought to reduce
the complexities of life to the rules of logic. Just how far the
Baroness' ideas concerning the Holy Alliance may have been
influenced by Oberlin I am unable to say, but in any case it
is a well-authenticated fact that the Czar himself took a
great interest in the humble Alsatian pastor, for when the
Allies entered Alsace in 1813 the following general order
was issued: "In the name of his Imperial Majesty. All army
corps and all others who see these presents are commanded
to protect the house of Pastor Oberlin, at Waldersbach, and
to guarantee its inhabitants against any molestation or dam-
age of any kind."

Oberlin died at the age of eighty-six, loved by the humble
members of his parish, admired by the great ones of the
earth, and leaving a memory that was to affect in a remarkable way the life of this country through Oberlin College,
and the life of China through Oberlin in Shansi, the end of
which is not yet.

Let me close with a few brief documents which reveal in a
more intimate way the real nature of this remarkable man.

The first is a portrait of Oberlin by himself drawn when
he was eighty years old, for the translation of which I am
indebted to Professor Cowdery.

I am a strange composite of contradictory qualities. I am intelligent, nevertheless my ability is very limited. I am prudent, and more politic than the majority of my colleagues, yet I easily grow angry. I am firm, but I can also yield to others without difficulty. I am not only enterprising, but if need be courageous, and at the same moment in my heart of hearts I may be cowardly. I am very frank, but I love to please and because of this am not absolutely sincere. I have a vivid imagination but a weak memory. I am so sensitive that I cannot give expression at times to the feelings which oppress me and cause in me actual pain. Active and industrious, I nevertheless love indolence. I admire painting, music, poetry without having skill in any of these arts. Mechanics and natural history are my favorite studies. I have a passion for regularity. By instinct I am a soldier. I have always made an effort to be the first to run into danger and to stand firm against trouble. From my earliest childhood I have had an overwhelming aspiration for a higher life. Military order and discipline give me pleasure to the degree in which they compel the coward to show courage and the irregular man to be punctual. I have a tendency to be slightly sarcastic but without intentional malice.

The soldierly ideal just referred to is found also in a series of rules which Oberlin drew up for himself when a young man of twenty.

I will make every effort always to do the opposite of what the inclinations of the flesh might force me to do. Therefore, I will eat and drink but sparingly, never more than is necessary for the preservation of my health. As for those viands of which I am most fond, I will partake of them less than any others. I will seek to conquer anger. I will perform the duties of my state of life very exactly. I will begin [he is referring to his studies] on the stroke of the hour. I will be content with as little as possible in matters of wardrobe and furniture. Lay aside each day some portion of thine income for the poor, and manage these funds as a faithful steward.

This rather Spartan discipline was in the interest of spiritual efficiency, if I may be pardoned the phrase. It was not the expression of one who thought it wrong to take any joy in life. There is a charming portrait of Oberlin in his old age drawn by a Mrs. Cunningham, who visited him on behalf of the British and Foreign Bible Society. The picture is not of a soured man but of a very lovable one.

We set off for Mr. Oberlin's, and on the way we met this most venerable and striking man, the perfect picture of what an old minister should be. I never knew so well what the grace of courtesy was till I saw Mr. Oberlin. He treats the poorest people and even the children with an affectionate respect. He is, I think, well over 80, one of the handsomest old men I ever remember to have seen, still vigorous in mind and spirit, full of fervent charity. It is almost past belief what he has done and with very limited means. There is a spirit of good fellowship and kindness [about him] that is quite delightful.

Lastly I give a few extracts from Oberlin's solemn dedication of himself to God in 1760, when a lad of twenty.

In the name of the holy and blessed Trinity. Infinite, eternal, and blessed God, I yearn to set myself before Thee in deepest humility and lowliness of heart. I know well how unworthy such a worm is to appear before the holy majesty of heaven and Lord of all lords, especially on such an occasion as this, when I would enter into a formal covenant with Thee, O Holy God. I surrender myself to Thee in the most solemn manner. Hear, ye heavens, and earth incline thy ear. I today confess that the Lord is my God. Today I confess and testify that I am one of his children and belong to the people of his covenant. I consecrate to Thee all that I am and have, the powers of my soul, the members of my body, my time and temporal possessions. Help, Thou, O gracious Father, that all may be used to Thine honor alone and employed in obedience to thy commands. If I have accomplished Thy will here upon earth, call me hence when and how it pleaseth Thee. Grant me Thy grace that in the moment of my death and even at the gates of eternity I may think on my obligations and use my latest breath in Thy service, and Thou, O Lord, bethink Thee at that time also of this covenant. My God and God of my Fathers, who keepest covenant and showest mercy to the thousandth generation, I humbly do beseech that Thou wouldst, since Thou knowest how deceitful the heart of man is, that Thou wouldst grant me the grace to enter upon this covenant with all sincerity of soul and to confirm the solemn surrender made at my baptism. Let the name of the Lord be here eternally my witness, and now do I with my own hand freely and joyfully sign myself the Lord's.

JOHANN FRIEDRICH OBERLIN.

Strassburg, the first of January, 1760.

This formal self-dedication was no idle, rhetorical flourish, the daring expression of youth, unacquainted with the pitfalls of life. Ten years later, with a growing knowledge of its temptations, he read his vows over again and added the word *Bestätigt* (confirmed). And fifty-two years later still, the aged man, now eighty-two years old, took out once more the yellowing pages on which was recorded the passionate self-devotion of his youth, and under the date 1822 on the margin opposite the paragraph in which he vowed to be faithful unto death, added in French and German the prayer: Seigneur aye Pitié de moi, Herr ebarme dich meiner (Lord have mercy upon me).

Such was the man whose name we bear and such was the secret of his power.

IN THE HEROIC DAYS OF OUR YOUTH

Founders' Day Address, December, 1929*

Today? But what of yesterday? For oft,
On me when boy there came what then I called,
Who knew no books and no philosophies,
In my boy phrase, "The passion of the Past."

SO spoke the great Mid-Victorian thinker and dreamer. But his boy passion is not the ordinary passion of youth. Boys and girls, young men and younger women, incline to live in the present or future, seldom in the past. This is natural. They have not yet acquired a store of memories. How, then, can they know their value? They have not yet felt themselves to be an organic part of the society about them. They are still unaware of the numberless subtle links that bind them to the past. They little suspect that they are the product of countless hopes and fears, of resistances and acquiescences, of decisions and avoidances whose beginnings reach out into "the dark backward and abysm of time." What is true of individual young men and women is true of youthful countries. In this respect our own country contrasts strikingly with England. On the one hand, a nation with a homogeneous population, which has developed in an orderly fashion for many centuries, loving its past, guarding it at every

---

* In what follows no attempt has been made to discover any new facts. All those referred to are to be found in President Fairchild's *Oberlin, the Colony and College*, Dr. Leonard's *Story of Oberlin*, *The Oberlin Jubilee Volume*, edited by Dr. Ballantine, *The Oberlin-Wellington Rescue*, and Mr. W. C. Cochran's exhaustive study, *The Western Reserve and the Fugitive Slave Law* in Collections of the Western Reserve Historical Society, 1920. The address having been given within the bosom of the family, so to speak, I have permitted myself some informalities which might otherwise have seemed inappropriate. The address was delivered on Founders' Day, December 3, 1929, in the belief that once in so often the story of Oberlin's great past should be retold.

point with an almost religious devotion; on the other hand, a land of many uprooted peoples with mutually canceling and blurred traditions, with only a brief past to steady it, give it direction, provide the atmosphere of common sentiments and associations through which citizens can see and recognize each other at a glance. Under these circumstances it seems to me that it is most essential to any healthy growth in our nation that we should studiously conserve and remember every vestige of our all too limited history.

President Fairchild said fifty years ago that "a successful College is a growth." Oberlin is preëminently a growth. It did not spring into being at the touch of an Aladdin's lamp (or chandelier) of some millionaire as so many of our colleges and universities have done. It was not assembled all complete like an automobile so that one had nothing to do but to turn on the faculty gas and let her go. The thing that strikes me most painfully about many of our institutions of learning is that they seem to be aboveground. You can comprehend them at a glance—great factories for turning out Ph.D. degrees, admirably adapted to the purpose, efficient to the nth power, but as yet lacking that indefinable something which we call atmosphere. I like Oberlin because it is not made to order. It is not a manufactured product. It is indeed a growth. And sometimes when I get blue it comforts me to think that any honest day's work I may do actually becomes a part of this great college organism and will, in some mystic way, live on in its life long after I am dead and gone. Therefore I always welcome Founders' Day when tribute is paid to those who have already grafted their lives upon this wider and wider spreading academic tree which we call Oberlin, and I wish to thank President Wilkins and the Chapel Committee for the privilege extended to me of giving this memorial address.

As I read the story of the Founders I cannot truly say that

they were men who at first acquaintance arouse one's enthusiasm or even affection. Father Shipherd and Father Stewart, for example, were not men of great intellect, or profound learning, or very broad culture. There was something, at least so it seems to me, of the uncouthness and eccentricity of the pioneer days about them. This was of course inevitable. Mrs. Trollope, the mother of the great novelist, who spent several years in this country just about the time that Oberlin was founded, thought the "domestic manners" of our people as a whole rather forbidding when not amusing. We were all a bit backwoodsy in those days. Nor have we had any great and commanding figures, with one or two exceptions, on our faculty. In themselves and individually the members of the Oberlin faculty in those early days were distinguished for their character rather than for their academic attainments, though the latter are by no means to be underrated, and probably were equal and often superior to the abilities of teachers in other colleges at that time. But they were men of absolute integrity. Everything they did they did honestly. There was no sham about them and perhaps that is a more important factor in its influence upon impressionable youth than the possession of an M.A. or even (I hardly dare hint the blasphemous suggestion) a Ph.D. degree. But if we look at our forerunners collectively and not as individuals, I think a somewhat different estimate may be made of them. Collectively, our faculty has always been bigger than any of its members, and it is team play, not starring, that after all secures titles. But both individually and collectively the Oberlin faculty were great in another sense. They were great in that, almost from the start, they allied themselves with two of the greatest moral and political issues of modern times, the emancipation of woman and the emancipation of the negro. Freedom was a passion of these early leaders of Oberlin. By this noble passion they were themselves transformed, enlarged, ennobled beyond their natural attainments. I can touch only briefly on the first of these issues: Father Shipherd writes in a famous passage:

> The prominent objects of this seminary are the thorough qualification of Christian teachers both for the pulpit and the schools, and the elevation of the female* character by bringing within reach of the misjudged and neglected sex all the instructive privileges which have hitherto unreasonably distinguished the leading sex from theirs.

This sentiment of our Founders was, however, by no means exceptional. Interest in the better education of women was growing at that time throughout the country. What made Oberlin unique was its theory of coeducation and its admission of women to the college courses. In 1837 four young women were admitted to the college course, three of them graduating in 1841, the first of their sex to receive the degree in Arts in this country. It must have been pretty hard sledding for these adventurous young women for at that time they were required to work three hours daily at some form of manual labor at three cents an hour and until 1839 New Testament Greek was compulsory. But even so, the logic of coeducation was not fully worked out till after a considerable interval, for it was not until 1859 that the young ladies at graduation were permitted to read their own essays from the Commencement platform, the professor of rhetoric having up to that time performed this duty for them. Nor was it till 1870 that a woman was permitted to teach on the faculty, and not until 1890 was a woman actually appointed to a professorship. But in spite of this very cautious development Oberlin was always in the vanguard in the education of women and what was regarded at first as

---

* "Female," by the way, is the regular term in this earliest Oberlin literature applied to the "misjudged and neglected sex." It seems to have been regarded as the most elegant way of referring to them. I have noticed that Cooper, in *The Last of the Mohicans*, uses the same term when he wishes to be most formal and proper.

a radical departure from the appropriate conventions, namely coeducation, is now a matter of course, especially in our great state universities, and has spread to other countries. When I was at Tübingen three years ago, I had to rub my eyes as I saw the inroads the once "misjudged and neglected sex" were making upon the University life. In the good old days at Berlin, in the early golden nineties, not a petticoat was to be seen within the sacred precincts of the University, and the students still sang

> Studenten Herz was macht dich trüb?
> Dass Ich so fern bin meiner Lieb.
>
> O student Heart, what makes thee smart?
> Ah! my Love and I are far apart.

That song can be sung no longer, it does not fit the facts. So far as I can see, the only refuge for us men from female competition, now that even Turkey and Afghanistan have adopted Oberlin ideals for women, is the plateau of central Arabia where under the benign rule of Ibn Saoud and the Wahabis, the slogan of Mohammedanism—I am for men—still resounds full-throated over the desert wastes.

But it was along the second line, the emancipation of the negro, that the genius of Oberlin expressed itself, not more fully, perhaps, but certainly more dramatically, in those early days. The story of how this came about is an interesting one.

Oberlin was founded in 1833 when the great tide of antislavery sentiment was beginning to rise. Two years earlier (1831) Garrison's *Liberator* was first published. In the same year that the colonists gathered at Oberlin the American Anti-slavery Society was formed. Arthur Tappan, a wealthy New York merchant (the walk that cuts through the campus and leads beneath the Martyr's Arch is named in his honor), was its first president, and a certain Theodore Weld was a delegate at its first convention. In the fall of 1834, Oberlin

having somehow managed to weather its first year, Mr. Shipherd set out for New York in order to find a president for
the institution and some badly needed additional endowment. He started east by going southwest to Columbus. As
if this were not a sufficiently circuitous route, when he
reached Columbus Mr. Shipherd, moved apparently by some
inner prompting of the spirit, decided to reach New York by
going southwest by south, via Cincinnati. His pocket compass seems to have suffered on this trip very violent per-
turbations. After several days' journey in a two-wheeled
mail cart he reached Cincinnati and got into communication
with members of the Lane Theological Seminary.

The Seminary was just then in an uproar. (What I have
to say at this point has a special personal interest for me as I
taught at Lane for eleven years before coming to Oberlin).
A large number of mature men were in attendance, among
them Weld. As a group, they were described by a contemporary as "a noble class of young men, uncommonly strong, a
little uncivilized, entirely radical, terribly in earnest." Weld,
burning with antislavery zeal, was their leader. He insti-
tuted a series of discussions on slavery. Eighteen nights they
debated. The result was the adoption of what were at the
time extreme Abolition views. In a statement published by
the students, summing up some of the results of their debates, they said: "Free discussion with corresponding effort
[they were not mere talkers] is a duty and of course a corresponding right. . . . We prayed much, heard facts,
weighed arguments, kept our temper and after the most patient pondering we decided that slavery was a sin and as such
ought to be immediately renounced."

But Cincinnati was a border state. Very strong Southern
sentiment prevailed there. The faculty, though not altogether approving the action of the students (faculties never
do), had not attempted to stop the debates; but the trustees
became alarmed at the criticism provoked by the agitation of

Weld and his followers, and during the absence of the professors on their summer vacation (among them Lyman Beecher and Professor Stowe, father of Harriet Beecher Stowe) they passed the following resolutions:

1) To abolish societies formed in the seminary relating to slavery; 2) to make it unlawful for students to have public communication with each other at table or elsewhere without leave of the faculty (a resolution of rather monastic rigor for a Presbyterian institution); 3) and to give the executive committee of the Trustees power to dismiss any student when they shall think it necessary to do so.

At the same time they dismissed Professor Morgan who sympathized with the students. The action plunged the institution into the wildest turmoil. Mr. Mahan, a member of the Board, resigned in protest. Some eighty students refused to be muzzled. They actually revolted and established themselves in a suburb of Cincinnati where a house was put at their disposal by a sympathizing citizen, James Ludlow, and organized a theological seminary on their own account. Arthur Tappan heard of the revolt, sent on $1,000 to help the rebels and urged his pastor, Mr. Finney, to go to their assistance.

At this juncture Mr. Shipherd, led by that errant compass of his, arrived on the scene. He immediately extended an all-inclusive invitation to Professor Morgan, Mr. Mahan and all "the rebels" to come to Oberlin, offered the presidency to Mahan and the chair of Theology to Weld. Weld said he was unfitted for such work and suggested Mr. Finney for the chair. (It is curious that I never heard a word of this story while at Lane.) So Mr. Shipherd resumed his journey to New York, now accompanied by President-to-be Mahan, to see if they could secure Mr. Finney.

At first the great metropolitan preacher did not seem to be much attracted by our swamp, as the campus then was, but, urged on by his parishioner, Mr. Tappan, who promised to give all of his enormous income of $100,000 a year, except

what was required for the personal needs of his family, to
support the institution, he agreed to come on two conditions:
1) that the trustees should never interfere with the internal
administration of the College (a lesson learned from the
Lane mess and an educational principle which has been one
of the most characteristic features of our Oberlin life ever
since), and 2) that Oberlin should admit colored students
on the same terms with the whites.

Mr. Shipherd wrote to the Board of Trustees December
15, 1834: "I desire you at the first meeting of the Trustees
to pass the following resolution, to wit: Resolved that students be received into this institution irrespective of color."
This letter precipitated a crisis. Such a proposition had never
been heard of. What would its effect be? Would not the College be overrun by colored students? Should not the fact
that there were so many young women here give pause to
such a radical step? The young women themselves at first
objected. Many of them had come from refined, New England homes. Should they be compelled to study with slaves?
Some of them threatened, if the action were passed, to return
home even if they had "to wade Lake Erie" in order to get
there.

The trustees hesitated. Mr. Shipherd wrote a second letter: "Whatever the expediency or prejudice of some may
say," he urges, "does not duty require this? . . . Why
should beloved Oberlin wait to do justice till others have
done it? Why hesitate to lead in the cause of humanity and
God?" He gave twenty points in favor of the proposition,
most of them on the highest plane of morals and religion.
He also informed them that the coming of President Mahan,
Professor Morgan, and Mr. Finney, the endowment of eight
professorships, and $10,000 for running expenses depended
upon their action. Still they hesitated. It was decided to hold
their next meeting January 1, 1835, in Elyria where they
could be free of the excitement in Oberlin which was now at

fever heat. The colonists sent in a petition requesting that "your honorable body will meet at Oberlin in order that your deliberations may be heard and known on the great and important questions in contemplation." They demanded "open covenants openly arrived at."

On February 9, 1835, the trustees met again, this time in the home of Father Shipherd. Father Keep, president of the Board, presided. Mr. Shipherd himself was still absent; only Mrs. Shipherd was at home. She could not resist the temptation to listen at the door of the room where they met, which was ajar. Father Keep came out and told her the decision was doubtful. She immediately ran out, got other ladies together, and began to pray and never stopped till the decision was made. The vote in the Board stood four to four. Father Keep was obliged to cast the deciding ballot. He cast it in favor of admitting the negro. The destiny of Oberlin was sealed in good, orthodox fashion by a five to four decision. Mahan, Morgan and Finney agreed to come.

Mahan arrived about the first of May, 1835, and shortly afterward the Lane students, some thirty of them, began to appear. The last Lane rebel landed in Oberlin some seventy years later in 1904. By a strange coincidence my own arrival coincided with his. With the help of these men the forerunner of Council Hall was erected, 144 feet long, 24 feet wide, and one story high, built, we are told, of beech logs and battened on the outside with slabs with the bark on. It stood about where the Soldiers' monument now stands, on the edge of the forest. This glorified shack was called Cincinnati Hall, Slab Hall for short (they were as irreverent then as they are now toward the home of us theologues). But it was the coming of these mature and very earnest men whose numbers were augmented by revolters from Hudson (the forerunner of Western Reserve), and the establishment of the Seminary, with Mr. Finney, a man of unique power and commanding personality, to guide its progress that secured the future of Oberlin. The Oberlin Institute now became a college in the true sense of the word.

There was great excitement when the College again opened. How many colored students would there be? Everybody was on the tiptoe of expectation. At last one lone colored boy entered the village. A small son of one of the trustees was the first to catch sight of him. He rushed home shouting: "They're coming, father, they're coming." Shortly afterward, in the fall term of 1835, Weld delivered before College and community twenty lectures on slavery. The result was decisive. From that time Oberlin was committed with all its soul to the cause of Abolition. Thus from the start Oberlin was something more than a college. At the dedication of Council Hall in 1874 Dr. Peabody of Harvard said of us: "The establishment of Oberlin marks an era. It was the first seminary of learning expressly designed to be a focus of moral, social, and political propaganda."

But here was a combination—coeducation of the sexes and the presence of colored students—which ran counter to the prevailing sentiments and the strongest prejudices of the time. From the point of view of that day Oberlin was radical, ultraradical. And it had to pay the penalty for this in social ostracism. When it extended asylum to the rebels from Lane and Hudson, this did not endear it to those institutions. The beginnings of our rather intense rivalry with Western Reserve in football probably go back to our more fundamental differences in early days. Our most noted personality, Mr. Finney, taught a theology which was obnoxious to the controlling minds in the Presbyterian and Congregational churches with which Oberlin was most nearly associated. And in those days theological differences were far more divisive among educated people than they are today. Oberlin began to be looked upon as a settlement of cranks and fanatics. It was an outcast, politically, socially, ecclesiastically. The American Board would not accept its students for missionary service, and pulpits were denied to them. A certain Dr. Lyon, pastor of the most important Presbyterian church in Erie, Pa., said on one occasion: "I have not had a conversion in my church for three years but I have kept Oberlinism out." (Today Oberlin welcomes Erie boys and girls in ever-increasing numbers.) Another clergyman proudly said: "I would go fifty miles and back to shut the doors of one of our churches against an Oberlin man."

Poverty added to the perplexities of the situation. Mr. Tappan, who had made such generous promises to support the institution, failed in the great financial panic of 1837. Oberlin was stranded. Did it capitulate? Did it abandon its principles with its change of fortunes? Far from it. In the school of adversity these principles became its great and sustaining passion. Let us echo back the words with which Mrs. Lucy Stone began her address at Oberlin's fiftieth anniversary: "Oberlin is proud of its founders, of their poverty, of their faith, of their perseverance."

I shall pass over some twenty-five years of honest work in Oberlin and of growing tension in the nation over the slavery question and let the curtain rise on the next great scene. In the interval the soil was being prepared for the sowing of the blood of a million men. The great struggle was rapidly approaching. In 1850 Clay's compromise, defended by Daniel Webster, was passed. It admitted California as a free state, but this gain was purchased by the adoption of the notorious Fugitive Slave Law. The North was shocked by it. Its feelings found expression in Whittier's memorable poem, "Ichabod," in which he arraigned Daniel Webster for his recreancy to the cause of Liberty. You remember how it begins:

> So fallen! so lost! the light withdrawn which once he wore!
> The glory from his gray hairs gone forevermore. . . .
> All else is gone; from those great eyes the soul has fled:
> When faith is lost, when honor dies, the man is dead!

Even after eighty years to read the provisions of this terrible law makes one's blood boil. In 1857 the Dred Scott decision was handed down by the Supreme Court. In it the ground was taken that the negro was property exactly like any other property and Chief Justice Taney announced the terrible doctrine that "the negro had no rights which a white man was bound to respect." Though Taney was referring to the preconstitutional period of our national life when he uttered this doctrine, it was equally applicable and was understood to apply to the present also, as being involved in the theory of the negro as property.*

Oberlin refused to accept such ideas. It believed with Thomas Jefferson that "the Almighty has no attributes that can take sides with those who deny the rights of the negro." It had been one of the main stations on the Underground Railway. Fugitive slaves were cared for here while they waited for sailing boats at various points on the lake shore between Cleveland and Sandusky to transport them to Canada. In other words Oberlin was carrying on, in the language of today, bootleg operations. Slave catchers often appeared in the village. In September, 1858, one of these villains, for they were a brutal lot, came to town in search of some runaway slaves. He did not find the man he was after, but there was a colored boy here, John Price, newly arrived from the South, and him the slave catcher decoyed out of town and took to Wellington in the hope of getting him to Columbus and thence to Kentucky. The news of the kidnapping spread like wildfire. A crowd of fifty or sixty people went to Wellington where its numbers were greatly augmented and without any real violence rescued Price, took him back to Oberlin and hid him for twenty-four hours in the attic of President

* It is only fair to say that one of the most brilliant of the younger Oberlin alumni, Professor Irwin Griswold, claims that injustice has been done to Taney's position by opponents of the Fugitive Slave Law. Into the merits of the case I am not at present able to enter.

Fairchild's house, much against Mr. Fairchild's will. It was a case, as he himself admitted, "of flagrant resistance to the Fugitive Slave Law." Was the authority of the Federal Government to be thus impudently flouted? Was it too supine or too cowardly to enforce its laws? On December 7 some thirty-seven citizens, twenty-one from Oberlin, were arrested and indicted, among them Mr. Fitch, who had been superintendent of the Sunday school in Oberlin for sixteen years, Henry Peck, Professor of Moral Philosophy, and Ralph Plumb, the banker of the town. None of these three had anything to do with the rescue, but the District Attorney afterward stated that "the Oberlinites are the ones the Government wishes to punish; we shall convict all the Oberlinites." The *Ohio State Journal* commented: "It would seem, then, that it is not so much a violation of the Fugitive Slave Law which is to be punished by the United States as the anti-slavery sentiment. . . . It is *Oberlin* which must be put down. *It is freedom of thought which must be crushed out.*"

Owing to the good character, however, of the defendants, they were at first released on their own recognizance until the trial should come off. They returned to Oberlin January 11, 1859, and held the famous "Felons' Feast," as it was called, a great banquet in the hotel in which town and college participated. The following toasts were made among others: "The inalienable rights of man, loyalty to God and loyalty to human government *when it is loyalty to God*," to which Professor Peck responded, saying: "They will be traitors if they obey the laws which break the laws of heaven"; and another toast by Mr. Plumb to "The Antisedition Law of 1798 and the Fugitive Slave Law of 1850." These toasts have a strange other-worldly sound in these days when thirty-four states have adopted antisedition laws, most of them since 1917, and on the table of Congress there now lies sleeping a law ready, when the next war is declared, to wake, to spring, to raven like some fierce tiger snarling over the blood and bones of its prey. This is no idle rhetoric. I have an intense fear of these laws. The fact that they have been passed by our legislatures so easily and with so little opposition from the people is a symptom of our growing Fascism. They are not scraps of paper, but they threaten to make our Bill of Rights a scrap of paper. I am glad that Oberlin protested in early days against the first of these dangerous laws.

After the usual law's delays the trial opened on April 5, 1859, before a packed jury. Every one of them was a Democrat though Cleveland was overwhelmingly Republican, and one of the members was actually a deputy United States marshal. Into the details of the trial it is impossible to go, but several points in the argument for the defense were, to say the least, unusual. One was the appeal to the higher law, the law of Christ, which was also supported, it was claimed, by the Constitution. Another was the justification of the use of technicalities. Mr. Riddle, counsel for the defense, begins by expressly announcing himself as a votary of the higher law:

Right and its everlasting opposite, wrong, existed anterior to the feeble enactments of men and will survive their appeal. . . . He who has no higher regard for the right than that which is enforced by the penal code of the country, whose moral sense does not rise above the coerced observance of the criminal statutes, is neither a good citizen nor an honest man. . . . Are we at the point that no man can be a good citizen or patriot unless he believes not only in the Union, the Star Spangled Banner, the American Eagle, and Bunker Hill as we all now here do, but our faith must reach every act of Congress and every ruling of the Federal Court?

The Fugitive Slave Law, he goes on to argue, is a thoroughly bad law, contradicting the moral sense of mankind. It may be an act, but in no true sense a law, a distinction later drawn by Mr. Nock in an article in *Harper's* (December, 1929) on "Officialism and Lawlessness"; and then

Riddle makes the following very interesting point: Men can obey a bad law in either of two ways, first by observing it, and secondly by deliberately and voluntarily subjecting themselves to the penalties it imposes if they disobey it. Men who do this are not lawless but law-abiding. Yet the law in question being as bad as it is, it is perfectly legitimate to utilize every technicality available to secure acquittal, a method which Mr. Riddle admits would be pure chicanery if it were employed in the interest of injustice. But in behalf of the Oberlinites it is legitimate, for, he says: "Spite of early prejudice, misrepresentation, and a ribald intolerance, the claims of Oberlin are finally recognized and acknowledged. From her class-rooms and recitations have gone forth strong, pure, earnest-souled men and women through all the ways of life. . . ."

Judge Belden for the prosecution retorts: "Your Higher Law, as interpreted by the saints at Oberlin, is just that law which makes every man's conscience and private opinion his guide. Such doctrine would make chaos. . . . Don't talk Higher Law as God's law; it is devil's law and it would make Hell upon earth. Higher law people run into the predicament of infidelity and free love. If St. Peck and St. Plumb go off on this higher law," Judge Belden advises them to go "where some good man preaches the Bible and not politics. Render to Caesar the things that are Caesar's."

Judge Bliss, also for the prosecution, contributed the following gems:

The students who attend that Oberlin College are taught sedition and treason in connection with science and literature and they graduate from that institution to go forth to preach opposition and treason. . . . Yes that [rescue party] had turned out well, for that old buzzards' nest of Oberlin, where the negroes are regarded as dear children—that nest had been broken into and one of the brood had escaped. . . . That was an army that old General Satan himself might have selected from the chief spirits of Hell.

Evidently opinions about Oberlin in those days differed rather sharply!

Bushnell, the first man tried, was convicted. The next to be tried was Langston, a colored man. The presiding judge ruled that the same jury which tried the first case should try the second. This so outraged the defense that all the indicted men refused parole and went to jail and there they stayed for eighty-five days. The speech of Langston before receiving sentence was the most thrilling part of the entire trial. One brief passage will give some notion of its intensity.

There is not a spot in this wide country, not even by the altars of God—no, nor in the old Philadelphia Hall, where any colored man may dare to ask a mercy of a white man. Let me stand in that Hall and tell a United States marshal that my father was a revolutionary soldier . . . and fought through the whole war and that he always told me he fought for my freedom as much as for his own, and he would sneer at me and clutch me with his bloody fingers and say he had a right to make me a slave. And when I appeal to Congress they say he has a right to make me a slave . . . and when I appeal to your honor, your honor says he has a right to make me a slave . . . for [and here he quotes Chief Justice Taney's fatal words] black men have no rights which white men are bound to respect.

Can you not feel in these words the soul agony of those tremendous days?

But the trial had its amusing aspects. According to the Cleveland papers the jail, on the first Saturday of the incarceration of the Oberlinites, appeared "more like a fashionable place of resort than a prison; hundreds of ladies and gentlemen of the highest standing called on the Oberlin prisoners." The next day, Sunday, Professor Peck preached to a crowd of six or seven hundred who jammed the jail yard and crowded the roofs of the surrounding buildings. He protested that his disobedience to Caesar was not divisive. A spirit which is obviously generous and benevolent never divides. Selfishness divides society; the good will which Christ exhibits unites it. On May 24 a great mass meeting was held on the Public Square at Cleveland. Between ten and twelve thousand were present to protest the Fugitive Slave Law and the injustice of the trial. Six carloads came into Cleveland from Elyria, thirteen from Oberlin. On July 2 four hundred Sunday school children came up from Oberlin to visit their superintendent, Mr. Fitch, in jail—not the usual place for Sunday school picnics.

The trial finally ended in a fiasco. Lorain County brought suit against the slave catchers for kidnapping and pressed it so vigorously that the Government finally compromised and let the prisoners go free on July 5. The *Plain Dealer* has this comment to make at the close of the case:

So the Government has been beaten at last with law, justice, and facts on its side, and Oberlin, with its rebellious higher law creed, is triumphant. . . . This is Mormonism with Professor Peck acting the part of Brigham Young, and it will have to be put down, as Mormonism has been put down, with the strong arm of military power.

But in spite of this blast, a hundred guns were fired in Cleveland at the prisoners' release.

On July 11 a great celebration was held in Oberlin in the "immense" church (to quote from a contemporary account), whose "spacious galleries presented a beautiful spectacle, being almost filled with the ladies of the College and neighborhood." Bands from Cleveland, Wellington, and Elyria led the procession to the church, where there were speeches and singing by the choir. In describing the scene in the church the reporter for the *Plain Dealer* makes amends for previous slurs.

But the dessert of the feast was the choir led by C. H. Churchill, esq. Talk of Sontag and her supporters, or Piccolomini or Jenny Lind or Strakosch—we have heard all with stoic composure, but yesterday we surrendered at discretion on hearing the first piece by the choir. We pondered long how we could get the piece repeated, for we were sure they could sing nothing else that way. At length, solitary and alone in the midst of the choir, a beautiful lady arose and struck the glorious Marseilles . . . and when she approached the chorus (To Arms, to arms) the whole galaxy of stars arose and sang together.

It was my intention to point a few morals which this tale suggests for our own time. What is Oberlin's attitude to be toward the race question in the coming years? To the problems of liberty in all their various phases? To such an increasingly significant social phenomenon as the conscientious objector? But the discussion of these and other questions requires far more time than is left to my disposal. There is opportunity for only one closing word.

Father Keep, in welcoming back the "Felons," said to them: "In your imprisonment you have nobly represented a great principle, the divine Law supreme everywhere, human law subordinate. Your testimony will leave a permanent record in history." Will it? That depends upon us and those who come after us. Will Oberlin in its prosperity be as true in the future to its great moral mission as it was in its penury? We were born free. Will we stay free? When the "unimaginable touch of time" shall have dissolved our outward forms into dust, will those who follow us be able to catch from us the same inspiration for service in the kingdom of truth and righteousness that we can catch from the Fathers?

OBERLIN, COLLEGE OR CAUSE?

Given before the Social Science Club of Oberlin College
*January 18, 1926**

PERHAPS it would be more fitting for one who has been born out of the curricular travail of Oberlin, fair Mother, and baptized with her A.B. degree to speak upon this particular theme than for an alien to do so. Yet, alien though I was, originally, I am an adopted son of this institution and have at last attained my majority. I have been a part of Oberlin for twenty-one years. I sit on the front row in chapel and am steadily moving toward the emeritus chair next the pulpit, from which I will one day be thrust by the automatic action of time.

But perhaps I have a deeper claim than mere length of service to speak upon this theme. I came here from Lane Seminary in Cincinnati. I came, not because I wished to come, but because I had to. I was forced out of Lane when that Seminary changed from its New School and more liberal theological tradition, and when, at the same time, my own views had become clarified, after a long struggle, along modernist lines. But even then I left Lane with reluctance, as I was greatly attached to it for family reasons. When I arrived here, I learned for the first time of the "Lane rebels," that group of theological students whose interest in the antislavery movement aroused such opposition in Cincinnati that they finally migrated in a body to Oberlin and became a very important factor in its early history. Significantly enough, I never heard of this historical episode while at Lane. I could not avoid associating in thought my own little hegira with

---

* The following address has been left very largely in its original form with only here and there references to changed conditions in 1938, inserted for purposes of comparison.

theirs from the same institution. We were all seeking greater freedom and at Oberlin we found it. Oberlin has given me my chance. It has given me my professional opportunity, which had largely been denied me until I came here, and, along with it, it gave me my home. I should indeed be ungrateful if I did not have a genuine affection for this institution which has done so much for me. And perhaps this affection entitles me to speak upon the theme of this article. I believe we are to face, in the next five or six years, what promises to be the most serious crisis in our history since Father Keep cast the decisive vote which admitted the negro to the privileges of Oberlin. If I raise a warning finger now, believe me, it is out of no desire to pass any captious criticism upon present tendencies but out of an honest wish to further, if possible, the best interests of this institution which has done so much to further mine.

I

THERE can be no question that originally Oberlin was a cause as well as a college. Mr. Shipherd's first idea was to found a colony whose aim would be "to glorify God and to do good to men," and by means of which the Church should be "restored to Gospel simplicity and devotion." This is a cause. Mr. Stewart was primarily interested in a college. The two ideas were combined and Oberlin Colony and College were the result. But the cause was at least as dominant as the college in the minds of the Founders. "Prominent objects of the Oberlin Institute," we have already seen, were "the thorough qualification of Christian teachers both for the pulpit and the schools, and the elevation of female character . . ." The rather vaguely defined desire of Mr. Shipherd to have a colony generally useful to the Kingdom of God now combines with the idea of the college and assumes at one point a more specific meaning. The College becomes interested in the higher education of the "neglected sex."

While this cause has been one of Oberlin's chief glories and titles to distinction, it has become so merged into the life of Oberlin as a college and into the educational life of the country as a whole that it no longer calls for any special remark. Cause and college at this point have become organically one.

It was not till the arrival of President Mahan, Professor Morgan and Mr. Finney in 1835 that the great cause, as distinct from more collegiate and academic aims, which has secured for Oberlin its national and international fame, became sharply defined—the cause of liberty. Under the conditions that then existed this passion for liberty expressed itself in the decision to admit colored students on an equality with the white students. The coming of these three powerful personalities who were to exert such a determinative influence upon all our subsequent development was made contingent upon this decision. Through it Oberlin became identified with the greatest political and moral cause in the first century of our national life, the antislavery movement. While the Board of Trustees at first hesitated to admit the negro, and while the resolution which was to decide the issue is almost comically ambiguous, nevertheless the decision, once made, consolidated the institution. The faculty presented a united front on the subject of slavery and the main support of the institution came from politically liberal-minded men both in this country and in England. I may point out, in view of what is to be said later, that under the historical conditions that then obtained this struggle for the freedom of the negro was a struggle primarily for *political* liberty.

I would also point out two other factors in its early history which are of great importance if we would understand the peculiar genius of Oberlin. These have more to do with it as a college than as a cause. The first is its interest in art, originally in the form of music. This interest was manifested practically from the beginning. But even here the idea of cause is not wanting. The first two teachers of music were called "professors of *sacred* music." Music was primarily cultivated in the interest of religion.

The other factor is of immense importance. This was the principle of faculty control in all things which have to do with the academic side of the college life, all questions not only of curriculum but of general educational policy, of selection or removal of teachers, etc. For this principle we have to thank Mr. Finney and the object lesson of Lane Seminary.* This principle eventually led to the organization of the faculty into two bodies, the General Faculty, which includes all teachers on more than half-time appointment, and the General Council, which includes all full professors, associates and assistants on more than half-time appointment. It will be noticed that by definition members of the General Council are at the same time members of the General Faculty. Both divisions also include a number of deans, librarians and so forth who are elected by the divisions. By faculty in what follows is meant the faculty as thus organized and it is upon this body that the final settlement of all academic questions has devolved. The trustees do not settle them. The administration in its own right does not settle

* The magna carta of Oberlin is found in Mr. Finney's letter accepting his appointment as Professor of Theology in the Oberlin Institute, dated June 30, 1835, a copy of which has been kindly furnished to me by Professor Fletcher. In it Mr. Finney lays down certain conditions of his acceptance among which the third and last condition is the most important, namely, "that the Trustees give the internal control of the school into the hands of the Faculty and leave it to their discretion to admit or reject those who, in their judgment, shall be proper subjects for admission or rejection irrespective of color. If your Board consent to these conditions, as I understand that they are willing to do, you may, if you please, record my acceptance of the appointment. Your brother in the Gospel of Jesus Christ, C. G. Finney."

The fact that the general principle of faculty control was applied by Mr. Finney only to the question of admitting colored students is not to be regarded as a restriction of the underlying principle of "internal control." It is rather an instance of the most extreme application of the principle that could be imagined in those early days of Oberlin's development.

them. The president adopts no policies without the approval of the faculty. He is chairman of the faculty and as such is *primus*, but he is only *primus inter pares*. If I understand our organization correctly the president is the executive but the faculty, with the president at its head, is both the legislative and judicial body in our system of government. In this respect Oberlin has probably been and continues to be the most democratically organized of all our colleges and universities.

The result of the development of Oberlin during the first fifty years was a synthesis of extraordinary interest, a synthesis of the religious and ethical (the moving passions of Mr. Shipherd and Mr. Stewart) with the intellectual and artistic, for the purpose of advancing human freedom. College and cause during all these years were indissolubly bound together. Oberlin does not believe that any of these purposes should dominate the others. It believes that they should merge together into a full and rounded life. If I interpret its spirit aright, Oberlin would have its religion and its ethics emancipated by the intellectual and artistic sides of its life from the falseness of superstition on the one hand and from the ugliness and disproportion of fanaticism on the other.

Again it would have its intellectual life freed by its religious and ethical interests from a purely academic and aristocratic intellectualism on the one hand and a self-indulgent or nonmoral emotionalism on the other. And it is because Oberlin has not been merely a college in the ordinary acceptance of the word, but has developed as a great educational, social, religious and artistic experiment that it has hitherto felt itself entitled to take an active part in that struggle for a completer life both in the individual and in society which is represented by the word "democracy." College and cause have been inextricably interwoven. No happier illustration of this fact can be found than the legend inscribed upon the façade of our Art Building, "The cause of Art is the cause of the People!"*

II

FROM the close of the Civil War to the beginning of the Great War the development of Oberlin lacked the dramatic character which characterized its heroic era. I am not familiar with the history of the institution in the earlier part of this second period. All I can do is to argue back from the tendencies which I have been able to observe since 1904 and which may fairly be regarded as accelerations of tendencies which had been more slowly and more silently maturing in the preceding decades. Though generalizations upon this period as a whole are somewhat risky, I would suggest the following as its prominent characteristics.

The outstanding fact is the development of Oberlin as a college at the expense, to a certain extent, of Oberlin as a cause. This was natural, perhaps inevitable. After the tremendous struggle of the Civil War, the idealism of the nation was for the time being exhausted. No new great issue had as yet arisen or at least none had made itself felt with the insistence with which the antislavery movement had impressed itself upon the life of the nation. The political freedom of the negro was now won, or seemed to the majority of people to be won. The cause for which Oberlin had so definitely and bravely stood had apparently triumphed. There seemed to be nothing else to do along that particular line. What was to take its place? It was very natural, under the circumstances, that the College should devote itself during this period to its development mainly along educational lines. This development culminated shortly after I came here in a two years' discussion by the faculty of our educational policy and the revision of the curriculum along the lines

* A quotation from William Morris, selected by Professor Wager.

within which we are still operating (1926). When the job was done, I doubt if there was a faculty in the country more alert to the problems of education or better informed than ours. We have been going on the momentum of that effort for many days.*

Yet the idea of Oberlin as a cause was by no means altogether lost. The old religious and ethical fervor continued to manifest itself in various ways. The passion for liberty which was concentrated upon the freedom of the slave now became diffused into the ideal of social service which has so strongly marked Oberlin's history. This ideal was of course present from the beginning. It is expressed in the name of the College. And Oberlin has succeeded in instilling into large numbers of its alumni this ideal for which John Frederick Oberlin stood.

In this connection, Oberlin very naturally attached itself to the Y.M.C.A. and Y.W.C.A. movements, which reflect this ideal so typically. Yet I feel obliged to say that in the very close association with these organizations there has been an element of weakness as well as of strength. They have unquestionably done an immense amount of good. They have done their part in recalling the Church to functions which it had too long neglected, and they have been able to enlist the youth of our country in religious and social endeavor when the Church had failed to do it. Nevertheless, there is one serious weakness in them as movements. Their intellectual content is meager. For that reason their work has been palliative and supplementary rather than original and constructive, and therefore I cannot foresee any very permanent influence which they are likely to exert either upon society or the Church. I think that the large influence which

---

* The more recent revisions are like the earlier ones in their emphasis upon the academic side rather than upon the reforming interests. But that was to be expected.

these organizations have exerted upon the life of our students has not been without its dangers. They have stimulated good will rather than the intelligent expression of it. They have too often been taken, quite unconsciously, as substitutes for more fundamental attempts to correct the abuses of our present civilization.* However, in the latter part of this period our fine Shansi work has been developed— one of the first and one of the best enterprises of this kind to be inaugurated by any American college. And the strong interest Oberlin has always shown in the cause of temperance, particularly in the work of the Anti-Saloon League, may also be cited.

But more important than any of these expressions of the original spirit, and what I would suggest to be Oberlin's outstanding contribution in this period, is the work of President King and Dr. Bosworth. These two men have been able to accomplish for Oberlin what has been accomplished for no other institution in the country to the same degree. They have managed to effect a change of religious base without serious losses to the religious life of the institution. They have placed the religious life of Oberlin squarely upon a modernist basis and yet preserved the earlier religious interest and missionary zeal which characterized the old evangelicalism. Under their leadership Oberlin has sought to coördinate religious experience with the findings of the laboratory. From my point of view this is an extraordinary

---

* The continuing decline of the Y.M.C.A.'s influence upon our college life in these more recent years would seem to justify the doubts expressed above. Just how far the religious interest of Oberlin has maintained itself during the last decade it is difficult to say—especially for those of us who are older and inclined to identify religion with certain forms of religion to which we have been accustomed, but which are now rather conspicuous by their absence. We are inclined to make generalizations which might be too pessimistic. Yet there is one question that may, I think, be properly raised. When selecting new members of the faculty is there anything like the same interest taken in ascertaining the religious attitudes of the candidates as in making sure of their academic standing?

achievement, all the more so because it was done with so little controversy. Our students are taught the modern interpretation of religion as a matter of course, and the absence of all theological polemic, of the rabies theologorum, is one of the happiest and most helpful features of Oberlin's spiritual life.

Politically Oberlin's development has been almost stationary. It was very natural for the College to attach itself after the Civil War to the party which had fought the war and freed the slave, and so Oberlin has gone regularly Republican. The two exceptions were the Bull Moose campaign and the second campaign of Mr. Wilson. The first of these reflected the interest of Oberlin in social service but did not speak so clearly for its political sagacity. The more lasting effects of Mr. Theodore Roosevelt's intriguing personality have been in my judgment hurtful rather than helpful in the life of the nation. But this of course is a purely individual opinion. The second apostasy from stalwart Republicanism was occasioned by the World War. I raise the question in all seriousness whether our predilection for the Republican party, natural though it was, has not been a real injury to us. Because the party was originally identified with the great cause of freedom we took it for granted that it would always be so identified. Therefore we have been slow to realize that the Republican party of the last twenty years and the Republican party that fought the Civil War are entirely different entities, standing for very different ideals. Political habits are hard to break, political idealizations hard to destroy. I am strongly inclined to think the Old Guard form of Republicanism has stood in the way of the development of Oberlin as a cause. It has blinded us to the moral meaning of the economic tendencies which no party has come to represent.*

* In the two campaigns of Franklin Roosevelt, there has been a marked increase in the Democratic vote, a hopeful sign of independence.

III

THE Great War threatens to be a turning point in Oberlin's history as it has been in the history of the world. We could not expect to remain untouched by such a cosmic catastrophe. It is not my purpose to recall the details and incidents of those fierce days which it is better to forget, though I would like to record my judgment that we came through the ordeal far more satisfactorily than most other institutions did. But it is necessary for my argument to point out that for the first time the unity of the faculty was seriously threatened in the face of one of the most tremendous political and moral crises in history. This is not to be wondered at. The struggle was so vast, it had so many different aspects, that sharp differences of opinion as to its true significance were bound to arise. The large majority of us seemed to interpret the war, as later the Versailles Treaty officially interpreted it, as an unprovoked attack of a single arrogant and criminal nation upon the most precious heritages of our civilization, an attack to be resisted with all the courage and self-sacrifice we could command. There was a smaller group who were at first suspicious of what seemed to them to be an oversimplification of the case, and who gradually came to see in the war the symptom of a deadly disease which had attacked our entire civilization and not one particular nation.

To discuss the rights and wrongs of these theories is not germane to my purpose. But what *is* of fundamental importance is to note *that the division which arose among us as to the interpretation of the origin and significance of the war prevented us from adopting a united front with respect to the problems of reconstruction.* These problems have largely gathered about the Treaty of Versailles and the Covenant of the League of Nations. Some of us saw in the conditions of the Treaty a severe, but a justly severe, penalty laid upon Germany for its crimes, and in the League an expression of the highest idealism in international affairs to which the world had as yet attained. If the Treaty had anywhere over-stepped the limits of justice the League could be relied upon to correct its errors. The League would reform the Treaty. Others of us saw in the Treaty one of the most treacherous and malignant documents in history, and in the League either an instrument to enforce its terms, or at least an expression of idealism compromised by the Treaty. The Treaty would corrupt the League. Thus, in the most obvious postwar political issue which has confronted the United States, the decision upon which was fraught with momentous consequences for the future of our country, the voice of the College was uncertain. Either side, pro-Leaguer or anti-Leaguer, would have felt aggrieved if the other side had attempted to commit the College to any official action upon this subject.

But I do not think this result of our divisions in the war is the most important one, so far as the question whether Oberlin is to continue to be a cause as well as a college is concerned. There is another line of cleavage, somewhat wavering to be sure, yet far more fundamental in its effect upon our future.

I can best lead up to an analysis of this cleavage by asking a question. How did it come about that those who were (for the most part quite wrongly) called pro-German during the war were dubbed (with equal inaccuracy) parlor-bolsheviks after the war? I suggest that the minority who saw in the war a symptom of the disease of our Western civilization as a whole rather than of the criminality of one particular nation *were driven by their position to interest themselves more directly and more deeply* in the nature of this universal disease than were those who adopted what I have called a simplified theory of the war. The former think they find the answer in the present competitive structure of our society with its resulting imperialism, militarism, and accentuation of race hatreds in international relationships, and class wars within the various nations.

Incidental to but closely allied with these great issues is the issue of free speech. For those who seek to change the present structure of society by political means rather than by force and violence, the freedom of speech which is guaranteed by our Constitution but which is being steadily restricted by our antisedition laws is of vital concern. Now it is these great issues, partly economic, partly political, but in their deepest essence moral, with which the world is today confronted, with which our own country is very menacingly confronted. These are the issues which, in this country, have taken the place of the old antislavery problems. The antislavery issue was fought out in the interest of political democracy, of political freedom. Oberlin's stand on this question was clean-cut and consistent, in spite of the opprobrium and ridicule that was for a long time heaped upon us by the majority in Church and State. But Oberlin's view, courageously adopted when it was still an unpopular view, finally prevailed and the College, in identifying itself with this great cause, won its title to fame. The issues of the present day mentioned above may be summed up in the phrase, "industrial democracy." Upon this question we have taken no correspondingly clean-cut position. Upon the great politico-moral problem of our national life in the first half of the nineteenth century Oberlin's voice rang clear and true; upon the much greater and more difficult problems which confront our nation in common with all other nations in the first half of the twentieth century, our testimony is hesitant and confused. A year ago the question was raised in the Social Science Club: "What great cause has Oberlin stood for in recent years?" The only reply was, "the Anti-Saloon League!"

I do not mean to deny that Oberlin has done some fine things both during the war and since which show that the old passion for liberty still has vitality. The faculty permitted the publication of the *Rational Patriot* at a time when Oberlin, as well as the country at large, was in a very tense mood, and the great majority of us had no sympathy whatever for its views. In the one loyalty case which occurred during the war, the faculty insisted upon its traditional right to adjudicate the case against the strongest sort of pressure from some of the Trustees to take a certain action, and it conducted the case with a fairness and impartiality which I think could hardly have been duplicated at that time in any other college in the country, and this, too, in spite of the fact that feelings in Oberlin, also, were very deeply involved.

When the war was over and the Student Liberal Club started on its brief, but hectic career, a freedom of action was allowed to it that was almost unprecedented in colleges or universities at that time, and at least once, officially, through the mouth of the president, the College spoke out in behalf of amnesty for political prisoners when it was still very unpopular to do so. The faculty twice refused an appeal from one of the greatest railways of the country to permit students to help break the great outlaw strike of 1922. All these things are very much to the good and should warm the heart of every alumnus who has any appreciation of what Oberlin stood for in its earlier heroic days.

Yet on the other side there is evidence that while we obeyed the law of our tradition in the cases cited above, we did it without much enthusiasm. With us "it was dogged as does it." As evidence of the justice of this criticism I cite four facts, (*a*) the death of the Liberal Club, (*b*) our general indifference to the free-speech issue in this country, (*c*) the general management of the endowment campaign, and (*d*) our present attitude on the color question. I expect sharp dissent from what I shall say on each of these heads.

a) It is a very singular fact, when one stops to think of it, that a Liberal Club should have died in Oberlin, of all places in the world. One would naturally have supposed that on a campus dedicated to the cause of freedom such a club would have enjoyed perpetual youth. I know what will be at once said, that those who dominated the club were a lot of cranks, unbalanced, extreme, undisciplined, etc., and that some of them were for various reasons unpopular with the student body as a whole. Undoubtedly the club made mistakes, undoubtedly the question of personalities entered into its fortunes. But I do not believe these incidental features of its life were responsible for its early death, and certainly not for the fact that it has never been revived.

The young people who were most interested in the club were young people of unusual ability. That may not have been recognized at the time by the faculty. Youthful revolters always seem terribly callow and silly to the academically minded, especially when they are espousing unpopular causes. Immoderate they may have been; when was youth, possessed of ideals, ever known to be what middle age calls moderate?

But if one has followed the careers of these young men and young women since graduation, I am sure he will be convinced that a very able group has come out of the old Liberal Club, a group that is likely to confer real distinction upon us in the future. No, I do not believe it was because of any mistakes that may have been made that the Liberal Club died in Oberlin. I believe the real reason was that the club found itself, curiously enough, in an environment which was on the whole unsympathetic, though it was honestly seeking to interpret the old ideals of Oberlin in modern terms. The faculty was true to the Oberlin tradition in permitting the club to exist while passions were still hot; but the faculty as a whole never encouraged the club, and I think the general feeling was that it was a nuisance.

In my view, the death of the Liberal Club in Oberlin College is a significant fact as to which way the wind has been blowing since the war. It has been blowing quite strongly away from Oberlin *as a cause*. In the fifties and sixties of the last century the club's fortunes would have been different. In those days of its youth Oberlin itself was a Liberal Club and it also seemed immoderate and offensive to those who were suspicious of its ideals.

b) The tradition of the College would naturally lead us to expect that it would take an advanced stand upon the question of free speech, and, as we have seen, it did speak out once in favor of amnesty for political prisoners. But again, the war feelings and the tendency to identify all economic heresy with Bolshevism have blinded our eyes, in a measure, to the seriousness of the situation in our country. I would expect a resolution in the faculty to endorse the work of the American Civil Liberties Union to be voted down. Yet this is the only organization in the country actively engaged in protecting freedom of speech, of the press, and the right of assemblage. If it were urged that Oberlin as a college has nothing to do with such an organization, I would concede the point, but I would urge in reply that as *a cause*, identified with the struggle for liberty, it has.

c) The third example I would cite is the method of our campaign for endowment. Was there any *special* attempt to enlist the interest of the liberals in the country in Oberlin as a liberal college both politically and socially, in Oberlin as a cause as well as a college? In the early days when funds were sought those were approached who were interested in Oberlin as a cause as well as a college. This was notably true in the case of the delegation which was sent to England at the time when we were so miserably poor. If we are really not simply a college, but a distinctively *liberal* college, why should we not make our special appeal to those in the country who would be especially interested in such a college? The Seminary is frankly modernist. It would not expect to be supported by fundamentalist money. Why should the

College, if it is as frankly modernist in its political and social outlook as the Seminary is in its theological outlook, expect support from those who would not naturally sympathize with such an outlook?

A college which is simply a college may make a legitimate appeal to everyone, conservative, liberal or radical, who is interested in education, but a college which is at the same time a cause must be content to rely upon a more limited but a more devoted group for support.

d) My last example is our present attitude toward the colored problem. I raise the question whether our testimony on this problem has not become rather conventionalized and lukewarm. I also raise the question whether this is just the time to become conventionalized and lukewarm on this particular subject. Racial antagonism is more menacing today in this country than at any time since the Civil War. The Southern attitude toward the negro is penetrating more and more into the North. A sectional point of view threatens to become a national one. There are those among our alumni and even among us here in Oberlin who would like to have the College rid of this problem. But would Oberlin's abandonment of any attempt to solve it further its solution? Would not our abandonment of it in order to avoid embarrassments add very greatly to the complications?

If the problem of the relationship of the white and colored races cannot be worked out in a just and satisfactory way in Oberlin, a place dedicated almost at its birth to the cause of emancipation, it cannot be worked out in the nation at large. In that case this problem can only mean a growing terror and an increasing pain to the nation at large which will be incalculable. The agony of the Civil War will be slight in comparison.

In all these instances I see evidence of a shift, largely unconscious, from the idea of Oberlin as a cause. This shift was natural, perhaps almost inevitable under the circumstances.

Again I would recall the terrific complications of the situation in which we found ourselves during the World War, and in which we find ourselves today. Most of us are teachers primarily interested in our own particular fields of investigation. To master any of these is usually a lifework in itself. On the other hand mastering the economic and political questions with which we are confronted also takes a lifetime of study. Who is sufficient for all these things? It is no wonder that Oberlin hesitates to take sides. But the unfortunate thing about the situation is that all these questions are ultimately great moral questions and have to do finally with a new heaven and a new earth, and the fact remains that we are still in unstable equilibrium.

What part are we to play in the new world? With what movements will we ultimately align ourselves? With those tendencies, now very manifest, which culminate in a rich and repressive America, an America both socially and politically reactionary, or with those movements which are voicing the new longings, the new religious and ethical insights and convictions that are inevitably preparing the way for the realization of a new world? We are, I fear, unconsciously drifting away from the idea of Oberlin as a cause and, as we tend to disengage ourselves as a college from these new movements, there is nothing left for us to do but develop ourselves solely as a college. In other words, the tendency to shift from cause to college manifested in our middle period has been greatly accelerated by the events of recent years.

But this is not all. There has been an internal development which tends very strongly to further hasten this process. During this time we have been hesitating, our internal policy has also been changing to a marked degree. What may be called the departmental idea in our college organization has been developing rapidly. This finds its most obvious expression in the rapidly changing complexion of the faculty. Over 50 per cent of the members of the General Faculty in 1926 were graduates of other colleges. Out of the fifty-eight new appointments (officers, teaching faculty and administration assistants) in 1937–38 only sixteen are Oberlin alumni. But this by no means tells the whole story. A large majority of the heads of departments are not Oberlin men. The most striking example of this tendency is found in the Theological Seminary. Of the seven active members of our faculty only Dr. Bosworth was, in 1926, an Oberlin man. He graduated from the Seminary though not from the College.*

Now the reasons for this are obvious. As the College develops as a college rather than a cause, the departmental idea more and more prevails. The increasingly complicated organization of college life also almost necessitates such a change. But the result is that the various departments will desire, above everything else, to secure professionally qualified men. The first question apt to be asked is whether a teacher is technically fitted for his departmental work rather than whether he is in entire sympathy with Oberlin's traditional attitudes or with Oberlin as a cause.

Now this means two things. It means that at a time when the College is undecided on the great politico-moral issues of the hour, the dominating influences in the faculty are ceasing to be Oberlin influences. It should be said, however, by way of qualification, that the older members of the faculty who are not Oberlin graduates have been here long enough to have the Oberlin stamp to a very considerable degree, and thus far we have, on the whole, been very fortunate in securing teachers technically competent and at the same time sympathetic toward our traditions.

In the second place, the departmental idea may become a serious menace to our peculiar organization of the faculty,

* In 1937–38 Dr. Robert Brown (1901) is the only Oberlin alumnus on the Theological Faculty.

which we have seen to be the most distinctive academic contribution we have made to the educational system of the country.

I can illustrate by two instances how the departmental idea which leads to the selection of men primarily for professional and technical reasons and hence to the frequent selection of men outside the Oberlin constituency, unconsciously influences the functions of the faculty. The other day the head of a department who is not an Oberlin man said to me in effect, "I have been looking over the reports of the departments in the President's Annual Report. I do not like gumming up the machinery by making suggestions outside my own department." And an assistant professor, again not an Oberlin man, said to me, "What is the use of speaking in faculty meeting anyway; the responsibility for policy rests finally upon the president and he must in the end decide these questions; we younger men do not feel that it is our place to butt in." Probably it would not be their place to butt in in most colleges, but it *is* their place in Oberlin. As members of the faculty it is not only their right but their duty to do so.

But if the unrestricted departmental idea is to prevail here, this may mean departmental rivalries. Blocs will be introduced into Oberlin life. The only way in which the resulting impasse can be overcome is by a dictatorship. The president will have to be the dictator if we are to get along at all. And then we will say farewell to the faculty as it has existed in Oberlin and to our thoroughly democratic form of government. To some this will be a glad release from the irksomeness of committee work. All such work can now be turned over to the administration. But the time and strength spent in faculty committees is the price we pay for our liberties. Perhaps the departmental idea is inevitable in view of the very rapid development of the College and the correspondingly increasing complexity of its organization. But it will almost certainly result in a still further shift of the emphasis from Oberlin as a cause to Oberlin as a college.

From my point of view our democratic organization is a needed protest against the growing power of the executive in our college and university organizations throughout the country, a power which is immediately connected with the more commercial aspects of our educational systems.

And this leads to my last warning. Oberlin is now confronted with the opportunity and also with the menace inherent in great riches. How hardly shall they that have riches enter into the kingdom of God! I do not believe this warning holds good only for the individual. Groups and organizations are also exposed to the temptations of money. How are we going to spend all this money? Are we going to develop ourselves along university lines? Are we going to build up technical schools? In either case we will almost inevitably cease to be identified with any cause. The purely intellectual, academic and professional interest will definitely predominate, if not over the artistic side of our life, at least over the religious and ethical side, as it has done in so many of our institutions of higher learning which were originally founded largely to further the interests of the Church.

What is likely to happen, unless we are constantly on our guard, is this: With all these millions Oberlin will become a more and more attractive place to live in—not bad in itself. It will appeal to wealthy Clevelanders with a certain measure of intellectual interests as a very desirable residential suburb—again, not a thing to be deplored in itself. But what we will be very strongly tempted to do in these congenial surroundings is to sink into them with luxurious acquiescence and make ourselves over into a second-hand Eastern college. It will be second-hand because we do not share the traditions of our Eastern academic cousins. Our background is different. In other words we may become a parvenu, not to the manor born. I do not believe the fear of this possibility is an idle fear. I believe the danger is a very real one. How can we best nerve ourselves to meet this temptation? I suggest in the following ways:

1) We can lay an increasing emphasis as the years go by upon the social sciences, and we can make sure that the teachers who man these departments shall always be forward-looking men. Such an emphasis is in entire harmony with our traditions as a cause.

2) We can develop, more than we have done, an interest in internationalism. (An interesting memorandum on this head has been prepared by Mr. Don Brodie for the Alumni Committee on "How May the College Test Its Product?") This would be an organic and very necessary development of our historic interest in missions. As a matter of fact present international behavior is undercutting the entire missionary structure. The so-called backward nations whom the West for a hundred years has been exploiting are turning against the religion of the West as well as against its political and economic domination. Missionary propaganda along the usual lines cannot be carried on much longer unless the international situation is materially changed. Oberlin need not give up its interest in missions, but if this interest is to retain any vitality, it must be enlarged so as to take in the whole field of international relationships. Lectureships should be established by means of which our students would have the opportunity to hear a constant succession of representative men and women from all over the world. I believe I am correct in saying that not one representative of the English labor movement, one of the most vital political and social movements in the world today, has as yet (1926) addressed the College. Oberlin students should be trained to tingle with interest in the great movements which are occurring to-

day all over the world through becoming acquainted with the many vivid personalities who represent these movements.*

3) *Above all, Oberlin should renew its testimony to the great cause to which it was dedicated in early days, and this not so much for the sake of the negro as to save its own soul.* President Fairchild once said that the presence of the negro in our student body was as important to the white students as it was to the colored students themselves. I am not advocating turning Oberlin into a colored school. I am not urging that the proportion of colored students to the whites should necessarily be much if any larger than it is today. I am not even advocating any material change in the relationship of the whites to the blacks. On the whole, the situation, when examined year in, year out, is probably as good as one could expect under present conditions.

What I do advocate is that Oberlin should not only be interested in the individual colored students who may come to its doors, but should seek to interest its white students in the tremendous problem entailed in the juxtaposition of these two very distinct races within the same nation. We should certainly give more degrees than we do to colored men and women of distinction. We should have colored men of broad vision, and there are many such, speak to our students more often in chapel on the peculiar problems of their people. Perhaps we should introduce some colored teachers into our faculty. We should keep our students acquainted with the advancement of colored people in literature, art, music, economics. In other words we should *deliberately* seek to interest our students in the great group movements of the colored people which are taking place in our country. Colored people should be made to feel that we are really interested

* Nineteen hundred thirty-eight shows decided gains over 1926. The Students' Peace Society and Public Affairs Society are fine examples of the growing thoughtfulness and balance in our student life.

in them and really seeking to support them in their desperate struggles against heavy odds. If this were done, we might get the very pick of the race here in Oberlin, who would become in course of time the natural leaders of their people. I believe it is only along some such lines as these that our ancient testimony could be efficaciously renewed under modern conditions, and there is just as much need for witness bearing along this line today as there was in the fifties and sixties.

4) Lastly, we must hold fast, in spite of every temptation to transform it, to our peculiar faculty organization, as the agency by which all problems are aired and all policies determined. If we are to continue to be interested in the cause of human freedom, we ourselves must be free.

By following these lines, Oberlin would not become a university or a technical school. It would not add simply one more unit to the increasingly standardized educational system of America. It would remain a college. But also it would remain a cause.

IN MEMORIAM

Dr. Bosworth

THE first day of July, 1927, was a beautiful midsummer day. The opulence of nature was manifest on every side. The obvious boundlessness of its resources for the present and the future seemed to suggest a sort of gay carelessness of the past. Yet there is one thing the creative power of nature cannot do. It cannot duplicate its own work, at least its patterns in personality, and on July 1, when Dr. Bosworth died, there passed out of our Oberlin life a spiritual essence which is irrecoverable. Of the sixty-six years of his life five were spent here as student and forty as teacher. For twenty-one years of these forty he was Dean of the Graduate School of Theology, and in the difficult war year of 1918–19 he was acting president during the absence of Dr. King. This life of service was varied only by occasional trips abroad, to Europe, to the Near East, to Japan, for study and rest. Judged by externals it was an uneventful life, without startling or dramatic episodes. Passed unobtrusively in a home that breathed repose, under the shadow of one of the most graceful and at the same time majestic trees in Oberlin, with a lovely flower garden behind it upon which the door of his living room gave invitingly, what was there in this life to appeal to adventurous youth? What was there in it to account for the shock to this community when it was whispered from friend to friend on the street corner or in the shop, "Dr. Bosworth is dead"? What was there in it to explain the profound sense of personal loss with which the news of his death was received by thousands of Oberlin's sons and daughters throughout the world. We do not read *Hamlet* or the Book of Job for the action of the story. We read them for their revelation of the possibilities of the human soul. And we are interested in the life of this dear friend of ours, our colleague, our teacher, not because of any exciting external incidents that attended it, but because of its inner meaning. And what is its meaning?

No highly endowed personality will make precisely the same appeal to everyone. Its varied capacities will make a different impression upon different minds. I cannot pretend to draw the complete portrait of Dr. Bosworth as this was gradually revealed in countless subtle ways to those who knew him in Oberlin for nearly half a century. I can only speak of some of those traits which made a profound impression upon myself and which, I venture to believe, have enriched the life of Oberlin College immeasurably, and will, it is to be hoped, continue to inspire us through the generations which are to come.

I shall never forget the first time I met and heard the man who was to become so close and valued a friend. It was upwards of thirty years ago. The occasion was a conference of theological students in Cincinnati. At that time I was passing through a severe mental struggle. I was feeling more and more forced to revise the religious views in which I had been brought up and which I still cherished for the love and reverence I felt for my father. Dr. Bosworth spoke on intellectual sincerity, with all the earnestness and quiet power with which we are familiar. His message came like a refreshing breath from the Great Lakes in the sultry theological atmosphere of southern Ohio in which I was then living. It gave a new confidence, a new feeling of security, a new inspiration to live one's life honestly. This experience of mine has been undoubtedly repeated in countless instances among students of Oberlin.

This quality of intellectual sincerity was one of the organic elements in Dr. Bosworth's character. It was the quality which kept him a fresh and inspiring teacher up to his last teaching hour, for it is only the intellectually honest mind that grows, and it is only the constantly growing mind that can retain the student's interest. His mind was always open to new facts. His lecture notes were never "in the sere and yellow leaf." He kept himself abreast of the best work in his field. The New Testament section in the library for which Dr. Bosworth was responsible is probably one of the most carefully selected sections in it. The last book orders which he handed in show how particular he was to choose the solid works which really contribute to knowledge. One feature of his open mind was his catholicity in reading, and he was undoubtedly one of the most widely read men in our faculty, though here, again, he did not waste his time on ephemeral literature but sought out the books that abide. He was often troubled with sleeplessness and in the wakeful hours of early morning he did much of his general reading. He especially enjoyed Plutarch's *Lives* which he read again and again. Rhodes's many-volumed *History of the United States* and Pepys' *Diary* alike interested him. Once I surprised him during an attack of grip deep in Gibbon's *Decline and Fall of the Roman Empire*. These varied books of history and biography, of which he was so fond, contributed to that tolerant view of life which he always instinctively entertained but which grew more and more mellow with the years.

And this leads me to speak of another characteristic of Dr. Bosworth which was a most valuable qualification of his intellectual honesty. It is the temptation of many minds, especially of youthful ones, to express intellectual sincerity in iconoclasm. They are not content with discarding an old idea; they must insult it, smash it, blow it up. This was not Dr. Bosworth's method. The cautiousness of his Scotch ancestry taught him a better way. He was not only tolerant of new ideas, he was also tolerant of old ones. He respected the historical; he revered the sanctity of old associations. This blend of cautiousness with an open-minded sincerity is a rare and much-to-be-cherished gift among teachers. It enabled Dr. Bosworth steadily to advance in his own thinking without antagonizing those who were still wedded to older views, or unsettling inexperienced minds. Nothing, I think, has characterized our religious life in Oberlin more than the absence of theological controversy. And to no one, not even to Dr. King himself, are we more indebted for this healthful and happy situation than to Dr. Bosworth. In the classroom or in personal conversation this rare combination of open-mindedness and caution was conspicuously exhibited. By his close, insistent questionings he stirred the laggards to think honestly, and by his own cautiousness he was able to clip the wings of the flighty. He had that best gift of the teacher, the ability at once to stir curiosity and to check undisciplined speculation. He never condoned mental inertia in a student, and on the other hand he never took that poisonous pleasure in which teachers sometimes indulge of leaving a student "up in the air." He did not abandon old positions because of the lure of novelty, but only when he thought honesty compelled him to do so, and then he took the step without haste or assertiveness. He did not seek to impose his own way of thinking upon his students, but neither did he think it was pedagogically sound to abandon immature minds to blind gropings in a new and unknown world. He always sought to show a way out, though the student was left to follow it or not as he chose. I do not believe Oberlin can be too thankful to have had, as one of its two chief guides in religious matters for so long a time, a man who thus combined so harmoniously intellectual sincerity and cautiousness. Dr. Bosworth and Dr. King together enabled generations of Oberlin students to effect an intellectual change of base without the loss of a genuine religious experience, truly a great work.

I have just spoken of Dr. Bosworth's lack of assertiveness. Temperamentally, he was a very shy man, or so he seemed to me. He always modestly kept himself and his opinions in the background so far as he was able. And yet there was no member of the faculty whose opinions were more sought after and more highly valued by colleagues and students than Dr. Bosworth's. He had a curious way of aiding those who came to him for advice. How often have I threaded the mazes of Council Hall to that prophet's chamber in the sunny, southwest corner, burdened with a sense of the impending collapse of civilization, due to the obstinacy of some colleague, or the folly of some General Faculty action, or some ill-considered editorial in the *Review*. And what would he say or do? Sometimes nothing at all. He would just sit and look at me from behind his desk with a kindly, quizzical smile and let me sputter until it began somehow to dawn on me that my colleague might not have been as obstinate as I was, that there was some ray of intelligence left in the faculty, that the *Review* editorials often provided innocent entertainment in our academic life, and that civilization was still intact. I often came out of his office wondering just how he did it. Without a word of controversy or rebuttal, sometimes by only an indirect suggestion, or by the tone of the voice in which it was conveyed, he could make you feel the absurdity of your own position.

Possibly this result was also due in part to the fact that Dr. Bosworth could look on life with a gentle humor. This saved him from taking too deadly serious a view of relatively unimportant matters. His perspectives were always normal and wholesome. Like his Master he enjoyed beautiful things, sunshine and laughter. The last lectures he gave were delivered in Athens—a fitting place to end the teaching activities of a life such as his. In these lectures he raised the question: What is man? He defined him by the affirmations man is able to make about himself. One of these is, "I can understand a joke and laugh." With an almost naïve realism he describes heaven as a place where "there will be much hearty laughter," and even speaks with the mystical bold-

ness of an Eckhardt of "the laughter of the life of God."
Another of these affirmations is, "I can feel beauty, the
beauty of the sunset flowing in radiant colors across the
Salamis waters into my soul, as I stand on the Parthenon
steps." I am sure that sentence is autobiographical and most
revealing. So far as I know, Dr. Bosworth was not endowed
with the gift of expressing himself in poetry, but he had the
poetic feeling and the poetic imagination; and one can almost see his eye kindle as he stands on the Parthenon steps
and drinks in the beauty of the scene. I shall never forget
how he told me just before he sailed on his last journey to
Greece of a little episode in his first journey thither with that
sweet lady, his wife, then a young bride. They were walking
one evening in the moonlight at Olympia when the old care-
taker of the great Hermes of Praxiteles espied them and
invited them in to see his treasure half revealed and half concealed in the shadowed moonlight within the museum. Somehow, with a subtle touch all his own, Dr. Bosworth con-
trived to make me see and feel through the fragile medium
of this slight reminiscence something of the tender romance
of life and of the pure beauty in the world which he himself
had seen and felt. This refined feeling for beauty which he
possessed expressed itself for us in Oberlin nowhere more
fully than in his prayers at chapel. The aesthetic quality of
these prayers answered perfectly to a definition I once came
across of the Greek style, "an unobtrusive propriety of dic-
tion." The style of these prayers was a part of the man.

But Dr. Bosworth's prayers were not a continuation of his
addresses to the students, as college chapel prayers are apt to
be. They were, in the truest sense, prayers, a communing of
the soul with its God. And here we touch upon something
profounder, more impressive in Dr. Bosworth's character
than anything to which I have yet alluded. There was a
poise about this man that expressed itself even physically in
the firm, unhurried step with which he crossed the campus to

and from his daily lectures, a peace of spirit which sprang, one at once felt, from sources that lay deep within him. Yet this serenity of soul which seemed to us to be so much a part of him was not altogether native to him. I understand that he was naturally of a quick temper. Nor were his patience, his tolerance, his gentleness, his peace the easy acquisitions of a character without initiative or force. They were the hard-won fruits of a life that had been schooled by much suffering and anxiety. He told me once, alluding to a certain tragic episode in his life, that he had felt at that time what seemed to him to be the very ultimate of pain. Yet few who met him and who looked upon his kindly, unfurrowed face realized that he had been acquainted with grief. He did not wear his sorrows on his sleeve, and the majority of us probably forgot that he ever had any, so silent was he about them. His self-control, his poise, his serenity were not the marks of a passive nature. They betokened in his case a strong one.

The great words of Isaiah at once come to mind in thinking of Dr. Bosworth: "In returning and rest shall ye be saved, in quietness and confidence your strength shall be." The secret of this "soul-rest," to use his own phrase, was religion, religion of a profound and intimate character. I have always felt, and the conviction has been reënforced as I have read, recently, his last lectures on "The Christian Religion and Human Progress," that Dr. Bosworth was essentially a mystic. His feeling of the "vast life of God"—to use again a favorite expression of his—surging up in him, or of himself as living in this vast, vital stream, was a mystical feeling. His yearning for the "civilization of the friendly men," when "everyone shall have a fair chance at all good things," for a civilization of "invincible good will" was a mystical yearning. It was not definitely connected with any reform programs, with the concrete realities of the present. This hope was rather a reflection of the radiance of another world. These ideals are mystical ideals, like the great ideals of St. John's Gospel, love, life, truth. Indeed, there was a quality of mind and character about Dr. Bosworth that naturally recalls the disciple whom Jesus loved. It is in this profound, mystical experience of God that Dr. Bosworth's real greatness and power lay. I have often felt in conversation with him that here was one who had actually experienced what to many seems only a mirage, who was actually living in the unseen world which seems so remote and insubstantial to our day and generation. But is not this the real reason, after all, why one so modest and retiring has exercised such an extraordinary influence upon our college and community for more than a generation? And is not this influence a challenge to the scepticism and materialism of our day? Does it not force upon us the question whether the Prophet's saying is not ultimately true: "Not by might, nor by power but my spirit, saith the Lord"? Cannot this hard, self-assertive and blatant world, living in externals, neurotic, and with less and less of inner power to steady it, take to heart the lesson of such a life, that only the things unseen are eternal? Should it not give pause to those of us who may fatuously trust in the high-power methods of modern industrialism to spread the kingdom of the spirit, when we remember that the influence of this shy, unobtrusive, and simple man, who has walked among us so quietly for forty years, has reached out to the very ends of the earth? Of him, as of his Master, it may be said:

> He did not cry aloud, nor lift up his voice,
> Nor cause it to be heard in the street.

And yet of him it may also be said as of the silent, unhurrying stars:

> His line is gone out through all the earth,
> And his words to the end of the world.

IN MEMORIAM

Dr. Currier

PROFESSOR Albert Henry Currier was a worthy representative of the New England strain which, from the beginning, has enriched Oberlin life. He was born at Skowhegan, Maine, on the fifteenth day of November, 1837. He died on November 11, 1927. If he had lived four more days he would have attained the age of ninety years.

He was educated in the best New England tradition, graduating from Bowdoin College in 1857 and from Andover in its great days in 1862, and receiving the M.A. from Bowdoin in 1866. The first nineteen years of his professional life were spent in the pastorate, three years in the rural parish of Ashland, Massachusetts, and sixteen years in the industrial center of Lynn.

This varied experience in country and city pastorates admirably fitted him for the work to which he was called at Oberlin in 1881, when he was invited to accept the Holbrook Professorship of Sacred Rhetoric and Pastoral Theology in our Seminary. He came to us with a mind disciplined by as fine an education as those days afforded, cultivated by wide reading, and enriched by the experiences of a faithful and successful pastor. His attainments he placed, without reserve, at the disposal of his students and colleagues for twenty-six years. He was deeply attached to this institution and his loyalty was unswerving.

In those days the financial difficulties of Oberlin were very great, and Professor Currier was unremitting in his endeavors to supplement the meager income of the Seminary by enlisting the interest of influential friends whom he had made in his pastorates. But he did not seek to increase the pitifully small salaries which were given then; he was primarily interested in providing scholarships for students, and in this respect the financial service which he rendered, as Dr. Bosworth said at the time of his retirement, "was greater than anyone but himself realized." That phrase, "but himself," is significant. How many students have gone through the Seminary and accomplished a fine work in the kingdom of God because of the aid secured through the self-denying and *unadvertised* work of Dr. Currier none "but himself" will ever know.

During all this time he was actively engaged in preaching and in this way endeared the name of Oberlin, through the winning presentation of his message, to a multitude outside our immediate environment. His Alma Mater recognized his services by giving him the degree of D.D. in 1884, and Oberlin itself reëmphasized them by conferring the same degree in 1922. On his retirement in 1907 he continued to live in Oberlin for twelve years, devoting himself to literary work, though the later years of his life were passed in the home of his daughter, Mrs. Healy, in Cold-Spring-on-Hudson. I think Oberlin has been singularly fortunate in the kind of lives our emeritus teachers have lived among us. When their official teaching and example ceased, that has not meant a cessation of their usefulness; but in countless ways they have continued to enrich our lives.

Most of the important books of Professor Currier were published after he became an emeritus. His work on the *Present Day Problem of Crime* appeared in 1912, and in the same year his volume on *Nine Great Preachers* was published. These were followed in 1915 by *Biographical and Literary Studies*, and in 1923, at the age of eighty-six, when literary initiative has failed most men who live to such an age, he published a little work on *Robert Leighton*. These books show a wide range of reading, especially in Christian biography and the best homiletical literature of England and America, and on every page betray a refined and cultivated mind. He loved to associate in his reading with the great and good of the past, with such characters as Augustine and Knox, as Fuller and George Herbert. They, next to the Scriptures, were his spiritual refreshment.

Professor Currier belonged to a generation, the one which was coming to its prime during the Civil War, whose finest flower, I venture to suggest, was a culture distinctly religious and still more distinctly biblical. That generation was steeped in the Bible. The allusions which it at once understood were Scriptural. Its phraseology and literary style were largely formed by the King James version (witness Ruskin, Tennyson, Kipling, or almost any Mid-Victorian writer). Its very humor often had a biblical flavor. It was a culture marked by much moral idealism (the profound interest in slavery indicated that), but at the same time it was qualified by a certain otherworldliness. It was a generation which expressed its deeper religious life in the prayer meeting and the family altar. Who can estimate the effect which the daily family prayers, not only in the homes of the clergy but of many of the laity as well, had upon the life of that generation? To begin or end the day with prayer gave a certain sanctity and dignity to life which served to steady it and enlarge its meaning.

It has been my great privilege to know a number of older people who were steeped in the religious atmosphere which I have tried to describe, and they always seemed to me to have a certain indefinable something about them that was very precious, but which is tragically missing out of the life even of most religious people today. I do not refer to their morals or religion as such. I refer, rather, to what I have called their culture, taken in its broadest sense, a culture religiously nourished on the Scriptures. It produced a beauty of character, a tone, a temper, a certain spiritual and otherworldly quality, a subtle essence which has largely evaporated in our day and left our lives drier, harder and more brittle in consequence.

My two former colleagues, Dr. Currier and Dr. Wright (and I am sure Dr. Currier would be glad to have the name of his dear friend associated with his own in this connection), have always stood out in my mind as admirable examples of this religious culture of the preceding generation. Their lives, in one respect at least, were like the life which Dr. Currier so beautifully describes in his essay "On the Value of the Imagination." He says that life is sometimes like a sea shell, whose exterior is rough, corrugated, weather-stained; but the inner concave of which is tinted with the colors of the sunset and appears like the image of the sky. Its beauty is the beauty of the interior life which shines out upon the world. The homes of Dr. Currier and Dr. Wright together radiated this gentle, earnest, kindly Christian culture, purifying and uplifting to all, and they were many who came in contact with it. A community in which such homes have existed is to be accounted highly favored.

To Dr. Wright we were called upon to say goodby some years ago, and Dr. Currier has been one of the few remaining links that have bound us to the generation that preceded us. Today, with affection and reverence, we say goodby to him also. With gratitude we remember his life. "Thou hast come to thy grave in a full age; like as a shock of grain cometh in in its season." Ninety years of refined, gentle, and holy living is a legacy which our generation can least of all afford to be unmindful of.

PART III
A SABBATICAL IN WARTIME

WARTIME SNAPSHOTS IN SYRIA

I

A Sunny Landscape

June 29, 1914

THE *Assuan* put into Smyrna for the day. We have seen our first camel *in situ*, so to speak. He was kneeling in the shadowy courtyard of a khan. We also had time to make a pilgrimage to Polycarp's tomb. As we set sail for Beirut in the afternoon the harbor was full of picturesque life. Italian, French, Austrian and Russian warships were lying at anchor, and among them our own little *Scorpion*. They have come here, we understand, on a curious mission. They have brought the diplomats whose solemn duty it is to whitewash the recent Turkish massacres of Greeks and so relieve the growing tension between the two nations which, it is feared, might lead to awkward complications in the Balkans and endanger the peace of Europe. As we passed, the Italian cruiser hoisted its anchor to follow us. Its flag was at half-mast. Somebody said the news had just come of the assassination of the Archduke Ferdinand of Austria. What tempest in a teapot will this stir up, I wonder? We threaded our way through the mine fields by which the Turks had protected the harbor of Smyrna from the Greeks into the open sea just at sunset. It was a world of calm and radiant water.

> Silken Mediterranean waves
> From isle to fabled isle
> Flowed softly north to Sunium.

The Italian cruiser is following us with its flag at half-mast.

July 2

We were awake and out on deck at 5 a.m. Early rising for a sabbatical. What a view! The Mediterranean dancing to some "soft Lydian measure" behind us, and the Lebanons rolling up to the sky like a Hallelujah Chorus in front of us. Little white villages ripple down the terraces of the lower slopes wherever the eye turns. We wondered which of them was Abeih, where we are to spend our summer. Six months ago we looked it up on a Baedeker map—a little dot about an eighth of an inch from the dot named Beirut—conveniently near, we thought. It's difficult to visualize dots and contour lines. Away up there beyond the olive groves, evidently a long carriage ride, lies Abeih.

July 3

We left Beirut in the morning, planning to reach Abeih in time for dinner. We made a mistake. The Syrian sun must always be reckoned with. I supposed I was proof against ordinary hot suns. But the Syrian sun is not like our suns. It is not always a hotter sun, but its specific gravity is different. The heat has weight. You can feel it pressing down upon your neck like a great burden. It does not seem to blister like our impetuous and vehement suns. It crushes. It does another thing. It bleaches the color out of the landscape. It is best to start for Abeih in the afternoons, as we found out afterward. Then, as one mounts the long, white road, French built of course, with easy gradients and luxurious curves, one can feel the cool breath of Jebel Sannin and Jebel Keneiseh falling upon one from their perpetual snows, and enjoy in physical comfort the transfiguration of the world that takes place at sunset. It is in the evening lights that one should drive up through the olive groves and by the terraces of vine and fig and mulberry, past Ain Anub and its bubbling fountain, and Shimlan clinging to the top of the ridge, and the little *kah-*

weh at Kubureshmun, from which can be seen in the distance, across the great gorge of the Damur, the main range of the Lebanons, then round the great bend which circles the Wady Arid, full to the brim with fruits and flowers—to Abeih.

The little village struggles up steep terraces almost to the top of the ridge some two thousand feet above the Mediterranean. The largest olive grove in Syria covers the slopes below it, looking like soft gray moss in the distance. Then comes a rust-red sand dune, then a faint, creamy line of foam, and then the sea.

We had engaged rooms at the old mission house, now turned into a small pension. As we stepped from our carriage at the foot of a steep path that led between high stone walls, we were met by a fine looking, broad-shouldered Scotchman, with iron gray hair and blue eyes, our host, Mr. Macfarlane. He led us up the path and through a gateway into the garden terrace, shaded by fine plane and cypress trees. The garden looks down upon Beirut fifteen miles away and out to sea through the pillars of Hercules and beyond, to the Statue of Liberty! After dinner we were taken to our rooms in the adjacent castle. It's a real one, no doubt about that, now partly in ruins, with broken arches in the courtyard framing bits of blue sky, lightless dungeons under our bedrooms, bloody history clinging to its walls as thick as ivy. I find that it was begun by the famous Druse family of the T'nuchs in 1315 and successively occupied by the Ma'an and the Shihabs, the three most famous feudal families of "The Mountain," as they call the Lebanon, and now in turn by the F—s of Ohio. Our room is as large as a chapel. The ceiling is some twenty feet high and beautifully groined. The clothes closet is let into the wall, which at this particular point is nine feet thick. Very little furniture in the room except a cool wind that blows through it delightfully—better than an electric fan. There is a glimpse through the south window of a little hermitage occupied by a lone Maronite monk. In the moonlight this evening he walked upon the roof of his hermitage and then stood with folded hands looking down upon the olive groves and the sea far below. As we entered our castle for the first time this afternoon, it seemed as if we had stepped into an old romance.

July 7

THIS day we visited the lower threshing floor. The crops are being gathered and stacked in great heaps about the floors. It seems to be a time for family picnics. Everybody turns out with smiles. Parents and children take turns riding on the threshing sledge in order to press it down more effectively into the grain. The urchins tumble about in the new-threshed straw, our own among them in the internationalism of play. We find the threshing floors usually located in some open place on a hillside where the wind blows freely, and hence they seem to be naturally associated with spaciousness and wide horizons. The ox which is *not* muzzled when he treadeth out the corn, the baby asleep in its sister's arms and circling round on the threshing sledge in the pleasant sunshine, the wind blowing freshly and making the heat quite tolerable, distant glimpses of the sea below and of terraced hills above—these are the pictures which I know I shall see in time to come when I shut my eyes and dream of Syria. Who would wish to exchange such heaven-sent toil for the fierce whir and grind of a flour mill? May Mr. McCormick and his mowers and his reapers and all the deceitful, labor-saving devices upon which we pride ourselves, but which invariably increase the nervous strain of life, never succeed in banishing the threshing floor from Syria. If we could only use more muscles and less nerves we would all be healthier and wiser and nobody would wish to be wealthier but the fools who are like the chaff which the wind bloweth away.

July 8

WE walked over to Ain Kesur this morning and got a drink from its famous fountain, the best water in the neighborhood, soft and cool. A lamb drank first, then I, then an ass. It is pleasant to feel one's kinship with the rest of God's creatures, a kind of St. Francis sensation. It prevents provincialism, also. We are apt to go round and round in our own little circle of two-legged friends and forget the centipedes and quadrupeds. This is narrowing. For instance, we are becoming quite tolerant of that marvelous world of the bacilli. Travel in the East broadens one's sympathies, at least when one has been properly inoculated and vaccinated. We no longer feel a race antipathy to a germ. We are becoming accustomed to live with him, eat with him, sleep with him. Anyone who takes a snobbish view of germs will be uncomfortable in the East. Here, every bacillus has as good a right as I have to life, liberty and the pursuit of happiness.

Every village has its Ain or fountain by which the sheep and goats lie down and to which the Druse women in their white veils and with their red water jars on their shoulders come several times a day for water. Farther south, we are told, the jar is carried on the head. In Palestine, alas, the five-gallon Standard Oil can is rapidly supplanting the jar of Rachel and Rebekah. The words of the Preacher will have to be revised. Soon the pitcher will no longer be broken at the fountain, but the Standard Oil can will rust there. As for myself, I prefer a potsherd to a rusty tin.

July 30

A HARD day's trip yesterday. I left Zidon early in the morning to drive to Tyre and back, a ten hours' journey. A young boy from the Presbyterian Mission School accompanied me to interpret. His name was Elias. It is the month of Ramadan, the great fast month of the Mohammedan year. Between sunrise and sunset no good Moslem is supposed to swallow a

morsel of food or a drop of water. When the fast falls, as in
this year, in midsummer, the suffering is intense. My driver
often filled his mouth with water in the sweltering hours of
the long day, but not one drop did he swallow. The horses
were better off. They plunged up to their bellies into the
cool, deep flow of the Litany, and as we left the main road
some two miles north of Tyre and drove along the hard seashore, formed by the silt of the sand against Alexander's
causeway, they trotted briskly through the fringes of the surf
and entered Tyre in fine fettle. Not so the rest of us. The
noon hours had accomplished what the drive had begun. We
were wilted. Elias and I attempted to walk about the town
in the burning heat and see the wreckage of the ancient har-
bors. The two sights that alone appealed to me on this day
of fever were the naked boys who waded back and forth between a little schooner and the shore unloading watermelons,
and the fallen columns of the ancient palaces of which we
caught opalescent glimpses beneath the turquoise water.
Their lines had fallen in pleasant places. There were other
columns not so fortunate, particularly the giant monoliths
that burned in the hot sand where once stood the Venetian
church of St. Mark's, the reputed burial place of Frederick
Barbarossa. As we stood for a moment by the largest of these
columns, the staccato cry of a woman mourning for a son
just dead cut through the blazing air like a sharp knife.
Everything seemed dry and hard and poignant except the
wading boys and the columns washed by the sea.

We got back as soon as we could to a little locanda that
hung over the seashore. It had not been swept since the days
of Jezebel and Dido. But a few trees shaded it, and through
the window by which we sat came the salt breath of the sea.
Elias sent out for a melon. As we opened it, our landlord,
who squatted beside us, looked longingly at its luscious interior. We invited him to eat with us. He shook his head
despairingly. It was Ramadan. But as he saw the fruit

rapidly disappearing, the lust of the eye proved too strong for him. After peering around to see if anybody was about, he stealthily drew the dingy draperies across the window, settled back in a shadowed corner and feasted with guilty satisfaction.

We left Tyre in the smother of the midafternoon and the next three hours were a blank. At sunset we rested at a little wayside locanda. It was filthy, of course. Chickens were picking about on the dirt floor, goats and dogs were running in and out. The maid who had just come in with a basket of freshly baked bread let the loaves fall into the rubbish. It did not trouble her. All she had to do was to pick them up and dust them off. Neither did it trouble me, for all I had to do was to sit in my carriage under a lattice awning of vine and fig leaves and bathe myself in color and the sea air while the horses were unhitched and rubbed down for the remainder of the journey. And then in the cool of the evening, with the day and its heats behind us we started on. A full moon was rising behind the great ridges that jam their rocky flanks, as hard as iron, into the sea. Now, in this magic light, they are transformed. They are giant galleys launching into the surf with the foam tossing about their plunging prows, ready to sail away for Carthage or Iberia. The smell of the sea spreads over the grassy meadows that lie between the headlands. Far above, on the right, there are one or two faint lights. It is Sarafand where once the Syro-Phoenician woman challenged the Lord himself. By the low wall of a khan fifty or sixty camels are swaying and moaning in the misty light. My driver begins to sing. It is one of those curious chants which the camel drivers love, full of half tones and unexpected cadences, the music of nature, of the wind in the stone pine tree, of the flowing brook or falling moonlight. "What is he singing, Elias?" I ask. "Oh, it is not much of a song, Effendi, only a few words." "But what are they, Elias?" "He is singing, Effendi, 'Oh, My Night!'"

WAR-TIME SNAPSHOTS IN SYRIA

II

Storm Clouds

August 2, Sunday

I AM still resting from the Phoenician trip, tired out. Allan Montgomery came down to the castle late this afternoon to tell us that a European war has just broken out. It's absurd.

August 3

THE rumors of war are being confirmed. We are all in a great state of excitement. Allan's tale seems to be true after all.

August 4

OUR British friends, Sheppard and Gilbart Smith, went down to Beirut today to see what news they could pick up. All Europe seems to be on fire. The suddenness of it is paralyzing. Mr. Macfarlane and his brother, Dougal, assure us that there is no danger in "The Mountain." Its liberties, it seems, are guaranteed by the Powers, and Turkish control over it is merely nominal.

August 6

I HEARD today the first authentic news from Dr. Hoskins of the Presbyterian Mission. He is in close touch with the Russian Consul. The Consul had received a wireless dispatch from London that had been picked up by two French steamers. It said: "England will interfere by sea and land." After dinner, a party of us walked along the brim of the Wady Arid in the moonlight and sat under two old olive trees.

August 17

A WIRELESS message has just been received by the French Consul from a French boat stating that the German Emperor and forty thousand men have been captured. Nejib Hadad rushed into the dining room this evening breathless with the news. The English are jubilant. The ladies, in particular, are for sending the Kaiser to St. Helena.

August 25

THE *London Times* of August 7 arrived last night. We are falling upon it like famished wolves. I had my turn at it this afternoon. Toward sunset I took my usual walk to Kubureshmun (the grave of Eshmun; it must be some ancient sacred site). A goatherd was playing on his pipe and singing to his flock as I passed by. The amber colors on the yellow sandstone this side of Ain Kesur are marvelous in the evening light. As I returned, a crowd of forty or fifty men were listening to one of their number translate the war telegrams from the *Egyptian Gazette*. At the news of German reverses they cheered lustily.

Sept. 5

I WALKED down one of the stony paths below the town to the village of Androphile (beautiful old Greek name) to take a picture of some wonderful clusters of grapes. I can now believe the stories of the spies. These Syrian grapes do not have to be bruised into wine in order to make glad the heart of man. Their flavor is as delicate and joyous as a song of Schubert. A man in a fig tree that overhung the path climbed down as I passed by and offered me all the fresh figs I could eat for nothing—gentle people these Druses and Maronites seem to be, always good natured and kindly to us wherever we go.

Alarming reports have come in this evening from the interior, especially from Damascus. The British Consul has

asked all the English subjects in the Lebanon to select run-
ners whom he can send to warn them in case of emergency.
The Macfarlanes are confident, however, that we will not
be touched. The Lebanons are free. Turkey would not dare
to molest the guaranteed rights of the Lebanese.

Sept. 9

MR. MACFARLANE, Professor Montgomery and I went down
to Beirut this morning to see what could be done about
finances. The results were discouraging. The Deutsche-Palä-
stina Bank would not pay a cent on my account with them
till October 3. The Ottoman Bank refused to give me any
money at all except on condition that I would "leave this
damned country at once," as the director of the bank gra-
ciously phrased it. Bankers are all fidgety and our Consul is
non-committal. At the end of the Beirut car line, just beyond the shadowy line which marks the boundary between
the Lebanon and the Turkish vilayet of Beirut, we found a
couple of hundred carriages and horses. They belonged to
the Lebanese. If they had ventured to cross the line they
would have been commandeered by the Turkish authorities.
We cannot drive any more into Beirut. As we rode home in
the evening and reached Shimlan in the gloaming, Venus
was so brilliant that she left a path in the calm sea below
like a moon path. But I feel ruffled. I have only nine pounds
in my pocket and am some six or seven thousand miles from
home.

Sept. 10

SAW the first American papers today since the war began.
We had just made up our minds, in spite of slender finances,
to risk a trip to Damascus when word came that the Turks
had announced they would soon annul the Capitulations. In
that case we will be without any protection by our consuls if
we get into trouble, and will be under the jurisdiction of the
Turkish courts.

Sept. 11

THE plot thickens. We heard guns down in Beirut yesterday. It turns out to be a Turkish celebration of a telegraphed report of the German occupation of Paris! Will that lead Turkey into the war? In that case what will happen to us?

Sept. 13

THIS is the eve of the festival of the Invention of the Cross. We climbed the hill back of our village to the little Moslem shrine from which we could see all the sea slopes of the Lebanon from Jebeil on the north to Zidon on the south. Everywhere, in the valleys and on the hillsides, bonfires were blazing and lights twinkling. The stars seemed to have fallen out of the sky upon "The Mountain." Where the villages were, there the constellations were caught. It is pleasant to think that all Syria is luminous as a Christmas tree tonight and has been so on this particular festival night through all the centuries since St. Helena first flashed the news, by beacon light from the Holy Sepulcher to Constantinople, along the headlands of the Syrian coast, that the true cross had been discovered.

Sept. 22

TODAY I have been studying up the massacres in 1845 and 1860 which happened here and in which our castle figured. It is curious to find ourselves in a psychologically similar situation. The old accounts tell of how the missionaries here in Abeih longed to see a United States man-of-war, and when she finally did appear what a burden was lifted from their minds. So we, today, are wondering when our cruiser, the *North Carolina*, which is rumored to have left New York long ago for the Levant, will appear. People feel that if a strong man-of-war is in the harbor of Beirut it will tend to quiet the growing excitement.

Sept. 27

WE had again planned to risk our trip to Damascus, starting tomorrow, but the news has just arrived that on Wednesday, positively, the Capitulations will be denounced. In that case nobody knows what will happen. The Macfarlanes still feel confident that the Turks will not disturb the privileges of the Lebanon, but they keep on asking me why our cruiser does not come. Who am I to summon Leviathan from the vasty deep?

Oct. 3

THE Damascus trip is all off. The excitement in Beirut is approaching panic. All sorts of rumors are afloat—that Egypt has been taken over by the English, that Enver Bey has been deposed, that England has given a twenty-four-hour ultimatum to Turkey, that each Turkish soldier has a sack which he is to fill with sand in order to dam up the Suez Canal on a proposed expedition against Egypt. The Moslems are fleeing in great numbers from Beirut (some thirty thousand of them I afterward learned, mostly women) as it is reported that on midnight next Friday the English will bombard the town (why at midnight?). The trains to the interior on the Damascus railway are all jammed. Only the dear old Scotch lady, Miss Dobbie, of the British Syrian Mission, and ourselves are left in Abeih. In the midst of the hubbub, Miss Dobbie, the Macfarlanes and ourselves read *The Innocents Abroad* aloud every evening. Nothing else seems to relieve so effectively the tension of our nerves.

Oct. 4

THROUGH Dougal Macfarlane's spyglass we watched four Turkish gunboats maneuvering in the harbor of Beirut this morning. And then, glory hallelujah, we saw our own *North Carolina* steaming grandly in from Port Said. She looked like a queen, of the Amazon type to be sure. The very sight

of her gives new confidence. Fresh reports have also arrived
from Beirut that a proclamation has just been published to
the effect that no trouble exists between Turkey and England, and that the troublemaker, Enver Bey, has been either
shot or deposed. We have finally decided in this lull to take
tomorrow's steamer for Jerusalem and have sent off our
trunks by mule to Beirut. After they had gone, we were told
there was no carriage to take ourselves and no seats left in
the Bosta. Later on in the day we heard that we might be
able to get a carriage by 10 a.m. tomorrow. So we start for
Jerusalem tomorrow, but how we are to get there we do not
know. *We* seem to be the New Innocents Abroad.

Oct. 6

HERE we are in Damascus (!) instead of in Jerusalem. Most
unexpectedly. We did manage to get down to Beirut yesterday, only to find that the steamer for Jaffa had left and the
next sailing would not be for a week. I made a final assault
upon the banks and the Consulate and squeezed out the
promise of some sixty pounds to be paid within the next few
days. With this joyful assurance and with the *North Carolina* lying in the harbor we resolved to go to Baalbek. The
North Carolina might fire a protecting barrage that far!
Damascus seemed out of the question. Not only was it
crowded with soldiers and refugees and reported to be in a
very excitable state, but cholera was also rumored to have
broken out there and the quarantine might be imposed. In
that case anyone caught in Damascus might be compelled to
stay there indefinitely. So this morning we boarded the train
for Baalbek. As good luck would have it, we met a fine old
gentleman in our compartment, with his two daughters. He
turned out to be Canon Hannauer, a noted missionary of the
London Jews' Society and a famous archaeologist into the
bargain. For years he had been stationed at Jerusalem, but
had recently been transferred to Damascus whither he was

now going. He had lived in the East long enough to be un-
troubled by rumor and seemed utterly unconcerned about
the situation in Damascus. He and his daughters proved to
be so entertaining and inspired us with such confidence, at
least for the moment, that at Ryak, the junction for Baalbek, we decided to stay on the train to Damascus. So here we
are in the large Hôtel d'Orient with only three or four men
besides ourselves to share its roominess. The tourist trade
dried up long ago. The soldiers are here, thousands of them,
and the refugees are here. We saw the women in their long
black veils wandering disconsolately up and down the platform of the Beramkeh station. So far, rumors are confirmed.
But the cholera, we are thankful to say, has not yet broken
out. We separated from the Hannauers at the railway station and the New Innocents are alone in Damascus. The
fountain is playing in the courtyard of the hotel and our
small boy is learning for the first time the wonders of refrac-
tion as he sees his little cane apparently bend when under
the water in the fountain's basin. He does not realize that his
father is a bit bent, also, under the accumulated doubtful
joys of a sabbatical year in wartime.

Oct. 7

DAMASCUS is a blur, a wild phantasmagoria. Crowds in the
streets, crowds in the *kahwehs* smoking, soldiers drilling on
the parade grounds for the possible parade through the desert to Egypt, ruins of bazaars, recently burned, scattered
around, which nobody seems to care to clean up, dust flying
through the air after the long rainless summer, filth and
foulness everywhere. Only two clean, sweet things in the
city, the cool airy interior of the great Omaiyade Mosque
and the clear waters of the Barada rushing through the city
in a thousand channels. We arrived at the mosque just after
prayers were over. Groups of men remain to read. They listen to a leader expound the Koran. Their faces are intent.

The Koran is a passion with them. Near-by is the shrine in which lies the head of John the Baptist. Women are sprinkling themselves with water before it. If we could only stay in the mosque, away from the noisomeness of the adjacent bazaars! We chance to emerge into one of the vilest of them. We pass a little booth not more than four feet square, with tawdry trimmings flapping in the reeking air. Inside sits a giant black toad of a woman, a witch that lives and battens in that cage. A little farther on I see a huge bloated worm come crawling toward me rapidly. I turn my boy's face away so that he cannot see this vermiform beggar following fiercely after us on his belly in order to extort baksheesh.

We find ourselves standing in a narrow alley and staring up at a great crossbeam over a gate in the wall of the mosque which we have just left. We are told that there is a Greek inscription on the beam which reads, "Thy kingdom, O Christ, is an everlasting kingdom, and thy dominion endureth to all generations." When the Christian Church of St. John was transformed, centuries ago, into the Omaiyade Mosque, this inscription was unnoticed and has remained undeleted to this day. We are informed that we can climb a ladder and examine it for ten mejidis ($8.00). I concluded to take it on faith. Certainly its contents must be taken on faith. There are no tangible evidences of its truth about us at this moment. Standing in this horrible gutter of an alley, with humanity rotting about us, almost overcome by sickening stenches, and taxed ten mejidis to verify the statement that His dominion is an everlasting dominion! No thank you. We make our escape out of the welter and board a trolley (a trolley in such a place seems almost incredible). We ride out of the city to Es-salehiyeh. It is a famous point from which to view Damascus. We climb a hill and turn around to look. The sun is setting and below us lies the city out of which we have just come. It is no longer a festering sore. Sunk in luxuriant foliage, its graceful minarets flaming softly in the sunset glow, enveloped, as if with flowing silk, in the rose and violet and amber colors of the desert, Damascus is a vision of loveliness incomparable in the world. Beauty is real as well as ugliness. Perhaps, after all, faith *will* survive the filth and wretchedness and indecencies of the world.

Oct. 11

On Board the Porto di Rodi

Good-by to Beirut, to Syria, to "goodly Lebanon"! We left St. George's Bay at five o'clock this evening for Jaffa. The past two days have been harassing in the extreme. The bankers went back on their promises to me made last Saturday that they would cash my letter of credit. It began to look as if we would have to winter as well as summer in Syria. But at last our Consul came to the rescue. The *North Carolina* had brought gold. I had seen a great safe being roped up the stairway of the Consulate with many curses and cries to Allah. I knew why it was so heavy. But could I lighten it? That was the question. Then I reflected that it was American gold, therefore it was *my* gold. My taxes were in that safe, at least symbolically, and after Damascus I trusted more in symbolism. The bread cast upon the great river that flows through Congress and out through the pork barrel as through a mighty spigot hole should now return to me after many days. I rang the bell of the Consulate with resolution, and stated my case with an assurance that concealed fear. The Consul went to the safe and returned with a box that weighed heavily. He counted out on the table one hundred and fifty napoleons. I had never seen so much gold before, and it was *mine!* My pockets bulged with the coin. I bought a money-belt and resigned myself with immense content to the certainty of drowning in case of a wreck. In spite of the ballast, my heart was lighter than it had been for several months. We had at last a chance, even in these troubled times, to visit Jerusalem and win the right to carry the pilgrim's palm.

As we sailed out of the harbor we looked up at "The Mountain" where we had spent so many weeks of mingled anxiety and happiness. There were the little cascades of villages still rippling down their terraces, and now we could distinguish Abeih, *our* Abeih. We knew Dougal Macfarlane would be watching our departure through his spyglass and Miss Dobbie would be walking up and down the garden terrace with little Thistle at her heels. The evening air would be stirring in the great plane and cypress trees and the Wady Arid at this hour would be brimming with color. What would become of them all, these friends of ours, and all the friendly villagers, Maronite and Druse, with whom we had become acquainted through the medium of smile and gesture during the past three months? Would the privileges of the Lebanon continue to be respected? Was the confidence of the Macfarlanes well founded? In the magic light, Abeih, high up on "The Mountain," seemed to be secure in a beautiful world of dream. Alas! The seeming security was as insubstantial as a dream. The flag at half-mast on the Italian cruiser in the Gulf of Smyrna had come to be not simply a conventional token of respect for a dead duke, but a symbol of a world bereaved. The terror out of the West was creeping daily nearer that fair land. Within a few weeks Turkey was to enter the war. The Lebanon was to be invaded. A battalion of cavalry was to be stationed in our peaceful little village and our kind friends who had trusted in the guarantees of civilization were soon to be transported as prisoners to Damascus and finally to Urfa, while the famished villagers were to be reduced to living on roots. The shadow of coming events brooded over our spirits. The unearthly beauty of the scene seemed to contain within itself a prophecy of dissolution. It was too perfect to endure. The eye was full of it but the heart was sad.

JERUSALEM AND THE WORLD WAR

IN what precedes I have tried to sketch our day-by-day experiences in Syria as the storm of war drew nearer and nearer. For nearly four months we had been marooned for lack of money in Abeih, a lovely little village high up in the Lebanon Mountains. Finally our cruiser, the *North Carolina*, arrived bearing gold with which to replenish our exchequer and strike for home. But should we avail ourselves of this opportunity? Of course, that would have been the sensible thing to do. Friends at home had been urging our return. Friends in Syria, especially our English friends, warned us that war between Turkey and England was inevitable and in that event nobody could tell what might happen. As a matter of fact, the English White Paper on the relationship between Turkey and England afterward disclosed how many telegrams were winging their way like birds of evil omen between London and Constantinople just at that time, telling of the seriousness of the situation, and within a few weeks some of the friends who had so kindly warned us were themselves to be prisoners in Damascus. But Jerusalem was as yet unvisited. Could we bring ourselves to forego catching at least one glimpse of the Holy City? We resolved to make the attempt. Our plan was to go to Jerusalem and pay a flying visit to the sacred sites, even if we were compelled to leave the day after our arrival. We would at least have won the right to carry the pilgrim's palm.

On a beautiful evening just at sunset we boarded a small Italian steamer, saying farewell to glorious St. George's Bay and goodly Lebanon. The wind blew fair and soft, and as we dropped anchor off Jaffa next morning and were rowed ashore over the lazy undulations of the sea in the warm

October air, the prospect seemed altogether reassuring. The Holy Land looked indeed like the Canaan of psalm and hymn, a land of serenity and peace, fit emblem of the Rest that remaineth. It seemed as if it were still dreaming of its milk-and-honey past or of the heavenly future, and as if the fierce present concerned it not at all. Our journey up to Jerusalem from Jaffa was sufficiently commonplace. As we crossed the famous coastal plain I suppose we should have been thinking of Philistine, Saracen and Crusader. As a matter of fact we spent the most of the time in conversation with the only other traveler in our compartment, an agreeable young man who was representing the Standard Oil Company. He was one of the few Americans still remaining in Jerusalem. Save for the missionary, the Standard Oil explorer seems to be the first to arrive in the far-off or dangerous corners of the earth and the last to leave. The company had been prospecting to the south of the Dead Sea and had started to build a road from Hebron to the reputed sites of Sodom and Gomorrah in order to tap the second causes of their overthrow. It was making good progress when the war broke out. The Turks afterward extended this road, I believe, as an important link in the line of communications for their Egyptian expedition and the English no doubt also used it when they paid their return call.

As we approached the Holy City our hearts beat faster and we pressed our cheeks against the window panes to catch a first glimpse of its walls and towers. But if we had been compelled to restrict our sojourn in Jerusalem to the day or two which we had originally allowed ourselves, our first impressions would have been disappointing. To love Jerusalem one must live there and must probe deep below its surface. Not till the soles of one's feet have become sufficiently sensitive to be able to distinguish between a twenty-foot layer of debris and a forty-foot layer simply by walking over them, will one begin to prefer Jerusalem above his chief joy.

The first appearance of the city, as we rode from the station in the fading light of the late afternoon, was distinctly uninviting. It looked dusty and haggard after the summer heat. The upper part of the valley of Hinnom, which lies to the right as one enters the city, was slummy and unkempt. I should never have been tempted to worship Moloch there! The gaping Birket-es-Sultan on the opposite side of the road, with some slimy green water collected at its lower edge, was equally unattractive, while just above it the barrack-like structures of the Montefiori Jewish colony inject their ugliness into a scene already sufficiently painful to an expectant imagination, and the bulky German Church of the Dormitio that sits like a huge paperweight on the traditional hill of Zion does nothing to relieve it. This church, by the way, is out of all proportion to its environment and assaults the attention of everyone who approaches the city from the railway station. The interior is beautiful, chaste and serene, and the service, conducted by the Benedictines, is one of the most devout to be found in the city, but the exterior is aggressive and irritating. Wherever one goes about Jerusalem this great pile strikes the eye with the brutality of a mailed fist.

The only really beautiful object which we passed, from the Jaffa Gate at the south of the city to what was to be our pleasant home in the American Colony half a mile beyond the Damascus Gate at the north of the city, was the tower of St. George's Cathedral. But even this bit of architecture, which is fine in itself, is not, aesthetically, altogether satisfying. Rising, as it does, out of a grove of olive trees, this thoroughly English tower seemed to be an exotic in its Oriental environment. I often meditated upon those two churches in the weeks that followed—the German church at the south of the city and the English cathedral at the north of it. They are the two architectural features which are most conspicuous from practically every vantage ground. Even seen from the Mount of Olives these modern upstarts thrust themselves upon the unwilling attention, symbolic of the present struggle for Jerusalem, *but both outside the walls!* Is there not a spiritual hint in that latter fact? Can Jerusalem be Occidentalized, Teutonized or Anglicized? George Adam Smith in a happy moment calls attention to the fact that the geological dip of the city is toward the East. Zechariah, it is true, anticipates some strange transformations in the topography of Jerusalem hereafter, but he does not appear to contemplate such a change in the geology of its site as to compel the city to bow in worship toward the West instead of toward the East.

On our arrival all that we had heard of the dangers and difficulties of a visit to Jerusalem in those troubled times seemed to be wide of the mark. Instead of a day's flying visit we settled down to a prolonged stay, and for the first two weeks of it we went about the city and its immediate environs in a leisurely, comfortable way.

The city was, of course, even then under martial law, but this signified only an increased security. Jerusalem is not a turbulent city even in ordinary times when police regulations are not so stringent.* Few crimes of violence occur there and such as do usually arise among the jealous Christian sects or quarrelsome Jewish parties, rarely between Moslems and Christians. But the strict military discipline effectually checked any violence whatsoever. Indeed it should be said in justice to the Turkish authorities that both before and after Turkey declared war the order in Jerusalem throughout the fall and early winter of 1914 was admirable. This was due in large measure to the good sense and moderation of the military commander, Zeki Bey.

After war was declared police regulations were of course somewhat more rigid than before. No one was supposed to leave town without a permit; no one was to be out after

* This observation does not apply to the situation in 1938.

eight o'clock at night; no one was to speak ill of his neighbor's religion. This last regulation would have proved to us that we were in an Oriental capital even if our sense of smell had failed us. But none of these regulations hampered us to any extent. We did not become sufficiently intimate with anyone in the gossipy capital to feel aggrieved by a prohibition to curse his father's religion or his grandfather's beard. As there were no picture shows in the city we could stay at home after dark by our little drum stove quite contentedly. So far as leaving town was concerned, we had no difficulty in obtaining permits from the authorities to visit the surrounding districts. But this proved to be a mere form. Only on the Nablous road did we find a guard to question our right of egress, and by going a few hundred feet east or west of him across the upper hollows of the Valley of Jehoshaphat, he could be circumvented without difficulty. The one locality which we were forbidden to visit after war was declared was Hebron. As Hebron was at that time the main southern base for the Egyptian expedition, this restriction was not to be wondered at. To the north the unsettled conditions of the times and the restlessness and suspicion of the population made travel practically out of the question.

Thus, for the ten weeks of our stay, we were compelled, whether we would or not, to concentrate our attention upon the strange city. But we were not left without our reward. Jerusalem revealed itself to us as it had revealed itself to no one, perhaps, for generations. Our good friends, the Montgomerys (Professor Montgomery was the Director of the American School for Oriental Research that year, and I was the student body!), and ourselves were the only persons in the city who by any possibility could be classified as tourists, a situation scarcely duplicated since the days of the Bordeaux Pilgrim (333 A.D.).

Now, the tourist unavoidably carries with him an atmosphere that communicates itself in a subtly damaging way to all the scenes he visits. He is automatically a vandal. He cannot help himself. The most beautiful and sacred objects inevitably take on a bored and blasé air after they have been described in Baedeker and stared at by sight-seers decade after decade. It is as if, under cover of indifference, the choicer things in nature, art and history wish to hide away their heart secrets from the sacrilege of the idly curious. I can well imagine that Jerusalem defends itself in this way during the tourist season, and it is doubtful if the average traveler ever catches anything but the faintest suggestion of the real city of Zion.

I shall never forget the quiet rambles we took about the city in those autumn days. Not even beggars molested us. The fake beggars who came crawling and limping in from the surrounding villages to demand baksheesh during the tourist season did not think it worth their while that year to stir from the shelter of their homes. The few beggars we saw were genuine ones whose pedigrees reached back to blind Bartimeus. On a Friday we would follow the weekly Franciscan procession, as it entered the Church of the Holy Sepulcher out of the Via Dolorosa, and wound its way with lighted tapers through the dark ambulatory and down into the blacker chapel of St. Helena, its murmuring chant resounding through the Church and finally breaking into a stately hymn, as the monks ascended the steps to Calvary. On a Saturday we might find ourselves in the synagogue of the Karite Jews—the oldest synagogue in all probability in Jerusalem. Only five families of this heretical Jewish sect were still left in the city. Their synagogue was a diminutive one, partly underground, and out of repair. On the day we visited it the rain was leaking through the roof. But it was spotlessly clean and redolent of devotion, in striking contrast to the stinking vault of a Sephardim synagogue in the same neighborhood. We sat for two hours while the rain pattered on the roof and listened to the cantillation of the Sabbath lections. There were only four men present and three women in a balcony above. The official reader was too blind to read the service and the other three men read in turn. At the end of the service they shook each other's hands and wished each other "peace," then wrapped their beautifully illuminated Bible away in a silk handkerchief with loving care. Outside the city wall on the slopes of the valley of Hinnom is the dreary cemetery of the Karites, with its rude and nameless stones, where no doubt these last representatives of the sect will one day be buried.

Our favorite walk was down the Kidron Valley. Halfway down we would turn into Gethsemane and sit under the shade of the old olive trees in the balmy air and look up at the great eastern wall of the city and the Golden Gate, while kindly Fra Giulio picked us posies from his lovingly tended garden.

I have said that the first aspect of Jerusalem is rather un-inviting. It is not a city of artistic charm. In this respect it is in sharp contrast with almost any Italian city one may visit. When one has named the glorious Crusading Church of St. Anne's, the charming little Convent of the Lentils (St. Nicodemus), tucked away in a back alley of Bezetha and not even mentioned in Baedeker, and the Mosque of Omar, he has named the three really beautiful architectural objects in Jerusalem. Most of the churches seem to be caves or dungeons. Religion is largely troglodyte there. The pictures that decorate the walls of the churches and monasteries are usually atrocious and there is practically no statuary. The general impression which the city makes is rather grim and austere, and the vast rubbish heap of Ophel which marks the site of the ancient City of David, with its ash-gray slopes of potsherds, decorated with old tin cans and cabbage patches, is positively ugly.

But there is one feature of the city which is always enchanting—the walls. Our favorite view of them was from the Garden of Gethsemane. Sometimes they would be the mellowest golden-brown when the sun rested on them. Under a passing cloud they would change to soft greens and mottled grays. One evening we were walking up the Kidron at sunset. The shadows had already gathered in the lonely gulch and the tomb of Absalom looked like a gigantic ghost as we passed it. But the sun had thrown a last jet of fire across the city above us and struck the wall of the Viri Galilaei that rims the brow of Olivet on the opposite side of the valley. The wall stood out above the darkness below like a softly flaming coronet of gold. Isaiah must have had some such scene in mind when he likened Samaria on its hilltop to a crown (Isaiah 28.1).

Sometimes we prolonged our stroll over the Mount of Olives to Bethany. The inhabitants of Et Tur on the top of the mountain, who have a rather evil reputation, never troubled us at all. We never tired of watching from the summit the vast, majestic reaches of the wilderness of Judea or the changing colors of the mountains of Moab and the Dead Sea. There is a saddle on the eastern slope of Olivet just beyond the Franciscan site of Bethpage and a few minutes before you arrive at Bethany. It is a very quiet place with marvelous views toward the Frank Mountain on the southeast and toward the Jordan Valley and the upper end of the Dead Sea on the northeast. A little olive grove is there and I have sometimes wondered if the original Garden of Gethsemane was not in that neighborhood, remote, unmolested, with a sense of vastness pervading the landscape—no fitter place for prayer and meditation can be found around Jerusalem.

In these many walks about the city and its environs the utter quietness of it all impressed us constantly. As I think back upon those days it seems as if a strange and solemn hush had fallen upon the city and the hills around it. A subdued and mournful expectancy seemed to tremble in the air.

O<small>N</small> October 31 we saw on our morning walk an ominous sight. The Italian flag was flying over the Russian Consulate. On our return home we learned that war had been declared between Russia and Turkey, that the Spanish Consul had taken the French interests in charge, and that our own Consul, Dr. Glazebrook, had been requested to look after the British interests. We seemed to be in for it at last, actually trapped in a war zone. That afternoon we walked again through the city. The day was Saturday, the Jewish Sabbath, and happened to be at the same time the Mohammedan feast of Abiram. All shops were closed and the streets empty. The stillness of Jerusalem had deepened until it had become uncanny, and it seemed as if the sorrowful forebodings of the past few weeks were about to be realized. That ancient capital knew what war and bloodshed meant. In its heart were the recollections of countless agonies, in its ears the cries of the widowed and the fatherless of unumbered generations. Its garments were stained with the blood of butchered multitudes. Were all these awful experiences to be again repeated? Alas! the four years to come only too well justified those early fears.

But for a time things went on, at least for us, about as they had done before. We resumed our explorations of the sacred sites, faked and genuine, and the spell of the past reasserted itself even in the midst of the commotions of the present. We were subjected to only two annoyances of any consequence. The first was the failure to hear anything definite from the outside world or for that matter from the world immediately about us. Until war was declared we had at least the French and Reuter telegrams with which to balance the German, though the former could not even then be posted on the streets without the danger of being torn down. But after the war began all the Allied sources of information failed us. We were limited to the German and Austrian dispatches. These were meager in the extreme and seldom ad-

mitted any reverses. Even though one was morally certain
that there was another side to the story, the effect of constant
iteration and reiteration of the same news over a period of
several weeks was depressing. The only offset to this discouraging telegraphic influence was an occasional rumor started
by some unknown person who had talked with some other
unknown person when the latter had landed at an unknown
date from an unnamed Italian steamer. Rumors with such
pedigrees did not inspire much confidence though they could
be used to cancel the wild claims of the Turkish telegrams
which now began to be posted up. We were thrown back for
fuller information upon our papers from home. These arrived
from a month to six weeks after their publication. While our
friends were reading extras morning, noon and night, we
were being schooled in the useful Oriental lesson of patience
and scorn of speed. So far as Jerusalem news was concerned
all we could learn was by word of mouth. The only papers
in circulation were in Hebrew and Arabic and they were of
course heavily censored.

It is really surprising, when I think back upon it, how
very little we managed to find out of what was going on immediately about us. Fortunately, and rather remarkably, too,
our home papers were admitted without much censoring.
Our private letters were opened, of course. But I doubt if
they were read. This was lucky, for our friends indulged in
all sorts of tirades against the "unspeakable Turk" which
the unspeakable Turk usually allowed to pass with the most
exemplary lack of resentment. In some cases, however, he *did*
seem to scent some cryptic danger to his fatherland. A letter
came to a Swedish friend of ours in which the innocent ex-
hortation, "love to the baby," was smudged over by the censor's thumb. The French Consul wished to send a telegram
home to his wife, and to assure her that he was safe and at
ease he mentioned the fact that he was playing bridge. The
reference to "bridge" sounded suspicious. Was military in-

formation being given to the enemy? Was there a plot to blow up a bridge? The Consul had to appeal to the commandant before he could send his telegram through. When leaving the country I had upwards of three hundred slides and a considerable amount of manuscript which I wished to take out with me. I was cheerfully assured by friends that these would give me much trouble, that if the manuscript was found I would probably be put in prison till it was read through. To save trouble at Jaffa I had them all passed and sealed by the censor at Jerusalem. The only thing objected to was a note on a scrap of paper by my wife stating that one morning she had seen twenty peasant women with bales of *tebn* on their heads being driven into town by soldiers. Our kindhearted censor did not like the idea that gallant Turkish soldiers were *driving* peasant women. I glossed over the memorandum with the qualification that what the soldiers were really doing was simply *guiding* the women to their proper destination. When I finally reached Jaffa the officials there ignored the Jerusalem censor's seals but on the payment of baksheesh allowed the slides to pass as being "a help to the country." They paid no attention to my manuscripts, but in the search of my person on the dock before embarkation they kept a copy of my will!

The other annoyance to which we, or rather our friends, were subjected for a time arose from the censor's regulations respecting the composition of our own letters. English was debarred. They must be written in Turkish, Arabic, French or German. As German was the only one of these languages we could handle we elected to send home our Christmas greetings in this speech and they fairly reeked with our *"fröhliche Weihnachten"* and *"herzlichste Grüsse."* Happily the restriction upon English was lifted after a couple of weeks.

MEANWHILE the effects of the changed situation began to manifest themselves in ways decidedly distressing for others.

Requisitions for the army from every possible source of supplies became more frequent and tyrannical. After the first of August when the general mobilization of the Turkish troops was ordered, the condition of the fellaheen had gone from bad to worse. The government had no means to support an army and so turned it loose to live off the country. A man in the cavalry service told a friend of ours that his pay was a ruba (a shilling) a month. While we were in Egypt an Australian trooper received six shillings a day. Even in the early days of the summer the newly levied soldiers had to provide their own outfit and rations for five days. But a man could still buy himself off from conscription by the payment of forty napoleons—only he ran the risk of being drafted again after the payment. After the war actually began requisitions and conscriptions enlarged their maws and gulped down what was left of the peasantry and their livelihood. In Bethany we saw one day a proclamation to the effect that if anyone attempted to avoid the conscription he would be shot with a rifle and a canon and sabered in addition. We chanced to meet there the present innkeeper of the Good Samaritan Inn, a distant glimpse of which can be obtained from Bethany. He had come in to town to answer the draft and escape a bloody end. We asked him what he thought of it all. He laid the blame on Germany but seemed quite willing to go to war. We asked him what the women and children would do in the meantime. "Work and die," this successor to the kindly host of old answered laconically.

One day we heard that our poor old egg-man at the Colony had come to grief. He and his donkey had been requisitioned to go to Beersheba. He went to the officers to find out more particulars and had a tooth knocked out for his impudence. Poor old fellow! We used to watch him counting out his eggs, singing their numbers to himself in a kind of chant and always omitting to speak the number seven lest it should bring bad luck. His circumspect enumeration had not saved him or his tooth.

On another day we were visited by a party of Bedouin from the Bene Sachr tribe. The son of the sheikh who was with them, a lad of only fourteen, was one of the handsomest boys I have ever set eyes on. He was a walking arsenal; guns, cartridges and daggers were festooned about him.* They had brought in five hundred camels which had been requisitioned from their tribe. The party was full of war, said they were not afraid of any cannon (which they had probably never seen), could muster 30,000 guns and horses, and claimed they were equal in prowess to any four other nations. These Arab tribes under the King of the Hejaz later favored the cause of the Entente. The long camel trains, bringing ammunition and provisions for the Egyptian expedition, were among the commonest sights we saw those autumn weeks. They came trailing over the slopes of Scopus from the north in a never-ending stream. Taxes, of course, in Turkey are always cruelly heavy. Even before the war, many olive trees which had taken years and years to grow were cut down because of the heavy tax upon them. With the war the tax levies became intolerable. One day we saw a large number of signs being taken down from the various shops about the Jaffa Gate. The signs were taxed and as tourist trade had all dried up, it no longer paid to keep these heavily taxed advertisements.

The Jewish inhabitants of Jerusalem were obliged again to endure the sufferings which the Jewish people of Jerusalem have always had to endure throughout the countless ages of its history. Jerusalem is a great pauper asylum even in times of peace. Of its population of 70,000, at the outbreak of the war, nearly two thirds were Jews and the great majority of them were more or less dependent upon charity. It

* I heard, later, that the poor little fellow had been stabbed to death in some feud or other.

was a hopeless situation and should never have been allowed to develop. In the emergency of the World War it became appalling. Fully a month before we left the city Herr Dr. Cohen of the Deutscher Hilfsverein, one of the most admirable Jewish educational and philanthropic institutions in the city, told me that the Jewish Relief Committee was feeding some 7000 Jews daily in the soup kitchens. They would not have been able to do this had it not been for the American Jewish Relief Fund which was, indeed, manna sent from heaven in their distress. At the Evelina Rothschild School, another excellently conducted school for orphan Jewish children, they were able to give the poor little things but one meal a day. When we visited the school Miss L——, the matron, was talking to the children on the war. She asked them what it was that we were all longing for, expecting them to answer "peace." But at once they replied, "Our Messiah." Their minds were full of Israel's hope, for they were practicing their songs for the Ḥannukah festival which commemorates the great deliverance from Antiochus Epiphanes wrought by Judas Maccabaeus. Miss L—— told us of her experience in attempting to dole out bread to the Moghrebins, Jews from Northwest Africa, who lived down by the Wailing Wall. They are a savage lot at best and famine had reduced them to the level of beasts. She was obliged to stand at an open window and throw bread out to them. When she had given away all her supply they tried to force their way into the room where she was for more, and actually had to be *whipped* back by the commandant of the city who was with her.

One of the most pathetic sights was at our own Consulate. Whenever one visited it, morning, noon or night, the waiting room was sure to be filled with timid-eyed old Jews. They had come over from America in order to be buried at Jerusalem. The first thing they do on arrival is to buy a burial plot on the Mount of Olives. This is as near as they can get to the sight of the ancient temple, for the Mohammedans have preëmpted the ground directly by the temple wall. Both Mohammedans and Jews believe that the Judgment scene is to take place in the Kidron Valley. The government was, of course, drafting all the Jews into the army and these poor old men were trying to claim exemption as American citizens. But only too often their papers were defective and our kindly Consul could do nothing for them.

THE disasters which overtook the fellaheen and the Jews were also to be visited upon the great ecclesiastical orders in Jerusalem.

I well remember a visit we paid to the beautiful crusading Church of St. Anne's. This church was tenderly and reverently cared for by the White Fathers. Connected with it is the best museum of antiquities in Jerusalem. One pleasant, balmy morning we wandered through the cool gray aisles of the ancient sanctuary. No one, apparently, was about. We descended into the crypt and there in the quiet dimness was a White Father, sitting alone, keeping vigil over the reputed birthplace of the Virgin. It all seemed very subdued and peaceful and secure. Since we had plenty of time, as we supposed, we did not attempt to see the museum on that visit. A few days later we went again to inspect it. Now all was changed. War had been declared the day before. The White Fathers were fluttering around their once peaceful close like so many white doves disturbed by the approach of an enemy. They feared that St. Anne's would be seized. Establishments such as this would make excellent quarters for the Turkish troops.

When we, rather thoughtlessly, asked permission to see the museum, we were told it was impossible. The curator was covered with cobwebs and we shrewdly suspected that the treasures were being hidden away in some safe crypt.

Their fears and precautions were justified. We had scarcely returned home when it was announced that St. Anne's was in Moslem hands and later it was turned into barracks. Then came the news that the Convent of the Frères des Écoles Chrétiennes had been seized. We had spent a morning there, also, only a short time before, examining the ruins of the Tower of Goliath, possibly the great tower of Psephinus built by Herod Agrippa. One of the kindly brothers had taken us up to the roof to show us the truly magnificent view which was to be had from this point, perhaps the highest in the city. He pointed out the place where he thought Sennacherib had encamped and the little mosque just by the convent wall which was built to commemorate the spot where Saladin effected his entrance into the city. But now another storm was gathering against the capital and the Christian Brothers were to be caught within its sweep. They were shortly evicted from the shelter of their convent.

The same fate was ultimately visited upon the learned Dominicans of St. Stephen's. I chanced to be at the Convent when Père La Grange and his colleagues were making preparations against their expected exile. The Dominicans have the best modern library in Jerusalem and many valuable antiquities. They seemed to be more concerned for these than for their own safety.* Well they might be. We saw what could happen to such collections one day when we visited the Turkish museum. This was comprised of the collections which Bliss, Sellin and McKenzie had been obliged to turn over to the Turkish Government. Much of the material was boxed up, but it had been so often packed and repacked that it was hopelessly jumbled, while the unpacked articles were lying about the dingy little room gathering cobwebs. It is to be feared that the scientific value of these precious collec-

---

* I saw one of the Fathers carrying off the very heretical *Encyclopedia Biblica* in order to hide it from destruction.

tions has been largely destroyed. As for the Dominicans themselves, they were soon to be prisoners in their own convent.

The Russian Hospice was one of the first buildings to be taken over and the military commandant established his headquarters there. It was in these quarters that the ladies of our party joined in the activities of the newly established Jerusalem branch of the Red Crescent Society and learned to make socks and bandages for the Turkish soldiers. There is, or rather was, a Russian convent in the Gorge of the Wady Fara about six miles from Jerusalem. This wady is one of the wildest of the kind in the neighborhood. The convent itself is located high up on a stupendous cliff in an ancient cave, formerly a hermit's cell and later, I understand, a robbers' den. When we visited it, it had just been pillaged by the natives of the neighboring village of Hismeh. Its walls were riddled with bullets, its ikons pulled down, the tinsel flowers that adorned them scattered over the floor. A solitary guard was set over the desolation after the ruin had been wrought—the usual Turkish way! The world has been sated with nameless horrors since those early days of the war and I realize the little I saw is insignificant by comparison. Yet somehow that wrecked Russian convent in its environment of grim and savage crags, remote from the haunts of men, has always seemed to me a fit symbol of the madness and mercilessness of the World War.

But what was to happen to beautiful St. George's? The cathedral was near our home and we had become greatly interested in its fate and in the fate of our friends of the chapter who still remained in Jerusalem. We had been accustomed to attend afternoon service there. It was fine to see the brave attempt which Canon Hitchens and Mr. Reynolds, the headmaster of the cathedral school, made to carry on the stately services of the Church of England amidst their country's enemies. For a time the boy choir of the school was maintained. But we have been present at a service carried through in all its details, with lections, sermon, responses and anthems, when only four other persons besides ourselves sat in the great nave of the church. The choir was later obliged to be disbanded but Canon Hitchens still preached on. Later still, the Turks dug a great hole before a side altar where they claimed to have heard guns were secreted,* and we had to sit beside this pit and pray with increased fervor, *Good Lord deliver us.* To avoid further vandalism we undertook to dismantle the church ourselves and pack away such of the furnishings as could be packed. Finally we retired to a little side chapel for the services. Not once until the very end were they discontinued. The dignity, solemnity, I think I may truly say the quiet exaltation of those services when just a handful of us were gathered in the great cathedral or in the little chapel, none of us knowing what a day might bring forth, will never be forgotten by those who participated in them. The majestic calm of the things unseen and eternal seemed to challenge the turmoil of the present.

But what was to happen to all these very peaceable belligerents of the various ecclesiastical orders whose sheltering convents and churches had been seized over their heads? A hastily written note from Mr. Reynolds received December 10 seemed to decide the question. "Please inform the Consul at once," it read, "that we have been ordered to leave Jerusalem for Urfa this afternoon. I am imprisoned in the school building."

Just a few minutes before the card came I had met Canon Hitchens entering the cathedral close quite innocent of his doom. I hastened over to our Consul, Dr. Glazebrook, the friend of everyone in need in Jerusalem, Jew or Gentile, Latin, Greek, Protestant or unbeliever. To my astonishment the Canon was already there. He had passed in at the front

---

* They had mistaken the consecration of a canon at this altar for the making and concealing of artillery (cannon) there.

gate of the close, learned that he was to be regarded as a prisoner, immediately leaped over a back wall, and declining an invitation to tea(!) from a Mohammedan Effendi who had seen him in this rather strenuous and uncanonical exercise, had hastened over to the Consulate for advice. While we were discussing ways and means in came the other prisoner, Mr. Reynolds. He had been dispatched by the police to discover the whereabouts of the Canon! But in spite of the fact that the situation had this touch of *opéra bouffe* about it, it was serious enough. Urfa sounded a long way off and very wintry. The journey would have to be made in inclement weather which was now setting in. The lovely weather of the autumn had given place to rains that had broken all records for fifty-two years. There would be no consular protection for the prisoners from the probable exactions of the Turkish guards. There were also ugly rumors, which afterward proved to be authentic, that Djemal Pasha, at that time the Military Governor of Damascus, had threatened to shoot the English prisoners if any unfortified seacoast towns were bombarded. It seemed as if our friends were in a very precarious situation.

Dr. and Mrs. Glazebrook were just sitting down to dinner when the two gentlemen came in, and Mrs. Glazebrook invited them to dine with us. To the eye, it seemed like a cozy little party. But the good cheer of it only threw the actual situation into a darker background. It was impossible for our Consul to keep them and they were compelled to leave the shelter of the Consulate. Friends assisted them to pack their effects and then we all had tea together in the dismantled study of the Canon—a function which I am sure an Englishman would not omit or fail even to enjoy if his execution were impending within the hour—and waited for the gendarmes. But they did not come. Our Consul had secured an order temporarily suspending banishment. This was the beginning of a fortnight's cat-and-mouse play with the English ecclesiastics and the other religious orders, most trying to the nerves.

I had all my life been taught to believe in the unchanging East. It is a myth. The lightning-like rapidity with which the scenes were shifted in the next two weeks was quite beyond my experience. Counterorder followed order in quick succession. But at last it *did* seem as if things had come to a climax. One afternoon we saw between thirty and forty carriages drawn up at the gate of the Dominican convent. There was to be no fooling this time. Northward they were to go. One Father was in the last stages of consumption; another had a broken leg. But all were to be bundled off and obliged to stand the long, hard journey as best they could. They were not to start till after dark. That evening Canon Hitchens and Mr. Reynolds, who had been imprisoned in the Dominican convent and whose fates were still hanging in the balance, had secured a parole and were dining at the Colony. It was a bleak, windy night and the rain was falling. After dinner we gathered in the great reception room of the Colony which looks out on the Nablous road. It was bright and cheerful inside, but the thoughts of all were upon the Dominicans. Presently we heard the rumble of carriage wheels. It was too dark to see them pass, but for upwards of half an hour we listened with scarcely a word spoken among us as carriage after carriage jolted past in the darkness carrying the Dominicans to an unknown fate. As I watched the set faces of our two English friends while these doleful sounds came up to us out of the night, the horror of war, of which I was witnessing only the relatively trivial by-products, came over me, the utter helplessness of the thousands upon thousands of innocent, harmless people who had been caught in this awful maelstrom of civilization and were being sucked down into its disastrous vortex.*

* We learned afterward that the Dominicans were ultimately freed through the intervention of the Pope.

Meanwhile our Consul was leaving no stone unturned to save the English. Besides our friends of St. George's there was a group of splendid men and women, principally of the Church Missionary Society and Scotch missions, who had been driven in from their stations in Hebron, Gaza and Nablous. Their headquarters were in the Olivet House where good Mr. Hinsman must have housed them free of charge, for the money they had in the banks was confiscated almost immediately. For two weeks their bags lay packed in the hallway of the hotel ready to start for Damascus, Urfa, or home. They never knew a day ahead what their fate was to be. It was a trying ordeal which finally ended as we shall see in a really dramatic climax. Yet it should be said in justice to the Turkish authorities that while the fate of the English was being decided they were allowed to go about the city with perfect freedom and not once were they subjected to any insult or hostile demonstration.

As the holidays approached, the situation in Jerusalem became more and more tense. Evidences of the big campaign against Egypt which the Turks were planning to launch multiplied on every hand. Out of our window which looked toward the slopes of Scopus to the north of the city we used to watch the Red Crescent brigade at their daily maneuvers or soldiers practicing trench digging. One day we saw a vast shining mountain of tin raised up just outside the Damascus Gate. It proved to be made of Standard Oil cans. We were told that seventeen thousand of them had been collected for the march through the desert. Another day we attempted to visit Solomon's stone quarries only to be driven out as soon as we entered by an unspeakable stench. The vast cavern was full of camels which had been herded there to keep them out of the heavy rains. An occasional automobile with dashing officers came racing around the old walls of the city. One turned turtle just outside our doorway, to the great surprise of everybody. A civilization accustomed to the Palestinian ass did not know what to make of this roaring fiery dragon. A rumor finally grew to something like definiteness that the advance guard of the expedition under Djemal Pasha himself would shortly arrive and that the Holy Flag was to be brought to the city in token that the Holy War had begun. Everybody was uneasy, including the Mohammedan population themselves. They were mostly Arabs and they feared the coming of the Turkish soldiery almost as much as the Christians did. I have described elsewhere* the two remarkable scenes at the entrance of Djemal Pasha and at the coming of the flag and must pass over the details here, in order to speak of a third scene in which I happened to participate. Those who took part in it are not likely to forget it till their dying day.

The Holy Flag had come to Jerusalem on December 20. It was on that evening that Mr. Gelat, the dragoman of the American Consulate, hurried over to inform us of orders which had just come that all nonbelligerent foreigners who wished to leave the country must do so by the twenty-eighth of the month or stay until the war was over. A few days before the order had been that no foreigner could leave. When we heard we couldn't leave we were anxious to go. Now that we learned we *must* leave we wished to stay. Our hope all along had been to attend the midnight mass on Christmas Eve in Bethlehem. But an Italian steamer was due at Jaffa the next day, the twenty-first, and we could not afford to take risks. Instead, we spent a good part of the night packing for our flight into Egypt. But the next day it was blowing heavily and word came from Jaffa that no steamer could take on passengers. This gave us a breathing space and time to think over the meaning of what we had been passing through. It was a unique, a memorable experience in which we had been permitted to share. We had seen great historical

* In the *Christian Herald*, May 18, 1922.

events transpiring in the city of the Prophets, the Apostles and the Lord. We had seen the city itself facing with a grave and solemn air the new crisis in its strange eventful history. Perhaps it was not inappropriate after all—or rather was there not a mystical necessity operating in the fact—that the World War had involved the world city in its devastating sweep? Could Jerusalem exempt itself from the agony of mankind and remain true to its tragic past or to its prophetic future?

We walked about in a dazed sort of way waiting for news of another steamer. Word soon came that one was expected in the early morning of the twenty-sixth. We were obliged to leave the twenty-fourth to make sure of catching it. Christmas was to be spent at Jaffa instead of at Jerusalem or Bethany. It was a disappointment. We said good-by with genuine regret to the warm friends we had made at the Colony and who had done so much in the past weeks to make our stay pleasant and profitable in spite of the anxieties of the time. At the station we found a terrible jam, for at the last moment commands had come to let the religious orders, including the English, leave the country. Dr. and Mrs. Glazebrook were there to see us off, though it was fortunately not the last time we were to see them. Old Major F. was also there to wave us farewell. He was a retired English officer who loved Jerusalem and all it stood for. He was in charge of Gordon's Calvary, a really beautiful spot which Chinese Gordon had once suggested was the place of Christ's burial and which an English society has carefully explored and preserved. He had shown us about the place one quiet afternoon, with a contagious enthusiasm for the genuineness of this very fine rock tomb which it was hard to resist. When the permit finally came for the English to leave, the Major would not take advantage of it. He was firmly persuaded that this war was Armageddon, and he wished to be in Jerusalem at the great day of revelation. So there he stood on the platform cheerfully waving us of lesser faith a final, friendly good-by.

That evening a crowd of us refugees found ourselves located at Hardegg's Jerusalem Hotel in Jaffa. Mr. Hardegg was a German citizen but at that time he was acting as our vice-consular agent. The English had lodged some complaints with our Consul for allowing a citizen of one of the enemy countries to continue discharging his functions as a United States agent at such a time, but before the next two days were over they had changed their minds about him. I had some difficulties of my own about which I went to seek his advice. As I left he remarked: "This is Christmas Eve; these are my country's enemies in my hotel; but I am going to have a Christmas party and invite them to it." And so after dinner we gathered together, as many of us as could crowd into the private apartments of the Hardegg family. A Christmas tree was standing there with its twinkling candles. Grouped about it were our English friends of St. George's, with a number of the other English and Scotch missionaries, a party of Franciscan friars in their dark brown robes, and a variegated collection of Americans. There was to be a little Christmas interlude, written for the occasion by the sister-in-law of Mr. Hardegg, and performed by the children of the family. First, a young boy came out with helmet and sword and recited what war had done in the world. He was followed by another boy who represented *Kultur* (the world has laughed at Kultur much since then, yet these people had a faith in it which was touching). Then a young girl appeared who sang the praises of peace, and last of all a tiny *mädchen* in white, who represented the angel of the Christ child supreme over all. The German child stood just in front of a Franciscan and Canon Sterling, a fine type of a Scotchman, as she lisped her verses. There was no war between the monk, the missionary and the little maid. In spite of the sharp differences in our religious beliefs, in spite of the still bitterer political differences which then divided us, all of us felt for the moment, at least, the supreme and unifying power of the Christ child; and after the interlude it was natural for German chorals and English carols to be sung in turn by the enemies gathered together around the Christmas tree in Mr. Hardegg's Jerusalem Hotel! We subsequently read of the strange longing for reconciliation and the desire to express good will which took possession of the troops on either side of no man's land that first Christmas of the war, but I believe the story has never elsewhere been told of the first war Christmas in Jaffa. We had failed to hear the midnight mass at Bethlehem, but we had worshiped at a new birth of the Christ spirit which was far more beautiful.

Christmas Day itself, it seemed, would never end. No one had slept much the night before. Would the steamer come at the appointed time? Would we be allowed to go on board if she did come? Orders had been changed so suddenly and so often already that nobody had any assurance that a permit to leave would last for twenty-four hours. The elders tried to forget their anxieties by amusing the children of the party. It was a perfect day after the previous storms and Canon Hitchens and Mr. Reynolds took the children down to the seashore to skip stones in the unruffled blue Mediterranean. Later in the day, a few toys were purchased in a dingy little Jaffa shop and a Christmas party was held at which Santa Claus himself appeared.

But the English became so anxious that finally Dr. Glazebrook was telegraphed for. His coming brought a feeling of great relief and the Christmas dinner which Mr. Hardegg had patched up was eaten with considerable gusto by those of us who had not succumbed to splitting nervous headaches.

The next morning the Italian steamer *Firenzi* was reported in the offing. The Montgomerys and ourselves were the first to arrive at the customhouse, and before we realized it we were all on the narrow dock standing before the Kai-makam of Jaffa. For weeks he had spread terror through the city, and rumors of his deeds had reached Jerusalem. He was a fat, coarse-looking man, with a smile which was anything but reassuring. He pretended to read our passports, cocked a side-long eye at us, stroked the cheek of our small boy and said *tayib* (good), and before we knew it we found ourselves being rowed out to the *Firenzi* over the gentle swells, freed at last of all anxiety as to ourselves.

But what of our friends? We reached the *Firenzi* about nine o'clock in the morning. At first all seemed to be going well. Boatload after boatload of refugees was coming on board. Jews, monks and nuns, the Franciscans, the Sisters of Zion, Sisters of St. Vincent and St. Paul, Sisters of the Re-paratrice, poor Carmelite nuns who had buried themselves in a living death in their convent on the Mount of Olives and were now awakened to a cruel resurrection, with veils pushed back, and rudely jostled by the crowd on the ship's decks—eight hundred of them altogether. Among them came some of the English ladies with bad news. The Englishmen had got down to the dock but in spite of their permits to leave had been ordered back to their hotel by the sly Governor of Jaffa. In the afternoon Cook's agent came on board to take their baggage back. They had twice tried to get through the customhouse and twice been ordered back, and some of them had been roughly handled. It was a difficult situation for the English ladies, already on board the steamer. Should they rejoin their husbands or stay on board?

It was at this juncture that the wisdom of telegraphing for Dr. Glazebrook appeared. Our Consul at Jerusalem was a Virginian, an ex-army officer. He was a gentleman of the old school, in whom courtliness and kindliness were blended in rare degree. His unfailing tact and courtesy and native diplomacy had achieved in the preceding weeks what the

American businessman type of consul could not possibly have accomplished. His stately courtesy pleased the Oriental and his evident desire to be fair won the Turk's confidence.

I shall never forget a meeting I witnessed between him and the sheikh of the Bene Sachr tribe—the son of Virginia and the son of the desert. It was interesting to see how each at once recognized in the other the gentleman he was himself. They were on good terms immediately, though neither could understand a word of what the other said. But when our Consul thought any wrong or meanness was being done, his chivalrous indignation would mount high. At the Christmas dinner he had been toasted with rousing cheers by all present for the good work he had done. But now all his efforts seemed to be in vain. He was the official protector of the English. Their papers were in order; but he had suffered the mortification of twice seeing the English file dejectedly past him, their papers ignored by the obstinate man with the sidelong eyes and the unpleasant smile. It was then, as we afterward learned, that he told the Kaimakam of Jaffa quietly but firmly that he proposed to sit on that dock until the English were released, and he actually did take a chair and seat himself in a way to suggest that he was a fixture.

Then an interesting thing happened. Our cruiser, the *Tennessee*, had been expected for several days from Beirut. All day long we had been watching for it eagerly. About four in the afternoon, smoke was seen on the horizon and presently our warship, flying our flag (and what a beautiful flag it is), steamed into the offing. The Consul saw that smoke and so did the Kaimakam, who called to Dr. Glazebrook that for *his* sake he would let the English go! In the late afternoon we saw a boat putting out from shore loaded to the gunwale. As it came nearer we watched eagerly to see if it held the English. It did, and a great cheer went up from the decks of the steamer. Shortly afterward Dr. Glazebrook himself came alongside in a little dory to bid us Godspeed. The fine old soldier had won his fight, and an even louder cheer bore tribute to his victory.

As we steamed away for Egypt the sun was setting and the sea and sky were swimming in color. To the east, however, the Judaean hills were beginning to edge their dark shadows into the glory. Up there within the gathering gloom lay the ancient city, austere, resolved, waiting for the woe that was to come. On the afterdeck of the *Firenzi* the Sisters of St. Vincent and St. Paul in their blue dresses and great white-winged bonnets were singing the vesper hymn.

HOW SOME IDLERS IN EGYPT MET AN ASSYRO-CONGREGATIONALIST ON THE NILE

IN the ordinary season Egypt is visited only by English lords and American millionaires. They dine and wine at "Shepheard's," or sail up and down the Nile in lazy, luxurious dahabiyehs, waited on by handsome dragomen in gorgeous robes. In January, 1915, all this was changed. The dahabiyehs with folded wings brooded sadly on their happy past as they lay moored under the palm trees of the Gezirah Gardens at Cairo. The dragomen haunted "Shepheard's" in vain, though the band still played there for the soldiers of the Anzac, and a few stray snake charmers displayed their skill before the wondering Tommies. At Luxor the great Winter Palace Hotel was closed and its corridors reeked with camphor in which the bedding had been packed. The ancient Pharaohs slept in peace in their tombs or in the airier spaciousness of the National Museum. The modern Pharaohs had departed. Egypt was now open to the fellaheen and to us, their kindred, from Ohio. It was a unique experience thus to have a thousand miles of pleasure-ground, usually walled around with huge barriers of baksheesh and impossibly high hotel bills, suddenly made accessible to a pocketbook lined with piasters instead of with pounds. We accepted the new situation with a large-hearted responsiveness. We had intended to stay but three days in Luxor and to be contented with a very modest pension. We ended by choosing for ourselves two beautiful corner rooms out of many idle suites in the Luxor hotel, the most desirable khan in Upper Egypt, and remaining for three weeks immersed in roses and with 10,521 donkey boys (our youngster counted them one morning for his arithmetic lesson) seated outside the hotel gate to do us service. We outstayed everybody else at the Luxor, the occasional English officer on a week-end furlough from Suez and the occasional missionary working his or her way up from the Sudan. The servants, who by this time had made up their minds to an off year in baksheesh, took an unselfish interest in us as the only season guests they had. Dressed in flowing white trousers with red sashes and red slippers, they waited upon us deferentially as we sat sometimes quite alone in the great dining room that opened on the rose and palm garden. Nothing was said or done to dispel the happy illusion which our surroundings suggested, that we were millionaires traveling incognito in wartime. As we had just been under a considerable nervous strain for some weeks during the excitements of the war at Jerusalem, we allowed ourselves to sink down into the redolent verdure and uninterrupted irresponsibility of our environment without compunction.

In those three weeks we did in a leisurely way almost everything there is to be done at Luxor. We explored the temples of Karnak and Luxor and learned to distinguish knowingly between bud-capitals and papyrus-capitals. We could tell a hypostyle hall from a pylon without serious difficulty and spot a cartouche of Thothmes III or Rameses II on sight. We dived into the mysteries of the Egyptian religion till we could identify Hathor and her cow and Horus and his falcon, and we became learned in the genealogies of Mut and Thoth, of Khonsu and Amen. We crossed the Nile and scampered over the green wheat fields that had, by this time, freed themselves from the inundation, on the most delightful little donkeys to be found between Constantinople and the Sudan. Lovely-Sweet, Cincinnati, California—I recall their melodious names and their gently rocking backs with never-failing gratitude. On these happy creatures we journeyed to the great sights of ancient Thebes. We visited the Memnon colossi and strained our ears (in vain) to catch the morning music that ancient emperors came to hear. We looked upon the giant statue of Rameses fallen in his fallen temple. We scorched, very literally scorched, up the death valley where the mightiest of the Pharaohs burrowed below the burning sands and hundreds of feet into the solid rock to hide their poor mummies from the rapacity of robbers in those suffocating wells of tombs. We worshiped again and yet again in Deir el Bahri, the most beautifully situated temple in all Egypt. It rises on noble terraces in a spacious bowl of the Libyan Mountains. Sheer above it tower mighty sandstone cliffs angry red and bronze, like the colors I have seen on autumn leaves when the first equinoctial gales twist them from their stems. The Holy of Holies stands on the highest terrace close against this stern and awful background; while in the foreground, which may be glimpsed through the open portal of the shrine, flow the soft green wheat fields and the yellow Nile.

All these things and many others we saw and enjoyed, but one thing we had not as yet accomplished, which all the other lords and millionaires invariably do. We had not taken a Nile trip in our private dahabiyeh. We resolved to make the experiment. Cook was running a weekly packet boat from Cairo to Assuan. On inquiry we found that nobody had traveled on it for six weeks. This seemed to answer our demand for a private dahabiyeh. It was a very ancient-looking craft, evidently dating from the Middle Empire. No provisions were furnished on board, but we understood that the engineer's cook would warm up anything we might bring with us, also that staterooms could be had on the upper deck where, if the boat sank after its career of several thousand years, we could still keep our heads above water. We laid in a stock of provisions for a couple of days—eggs, cold chicken, bread and butter, tea, jam, oranges, figs, and so forth, and purchased tickets for Assuit, two days down the river. The evening before we left Luxor we paid our last visit to Karnak. We climbed the mighty entrance pylon and watched the sun set over the Libyan Desert. To the west the Nile was molten gold below us. The mud-brick girdle wall of the temple, dull and lusterless by day, ran round us, a ribbon of old rose. Eastward the great gateway of Euergetes stood pink against a cobalt sky. With beating hearts we descended to pace for the last time and quite alone through the hall of Rameses II, the most stupendous hall ever erected by the hand of man. The shadows were deepening among the mighty columns and we were in the proper mood to meditate upon the sublimity of man's ideals and the tragedy of history, when our small boy fell and bumped his shin. Suddenly through Rameses' hall resounded terrific howls. They were as high as the aspiring central columns and had a volume like their mighty girth. It was our farewell to Karnak.

At the boat landing the next day all our friends were present to see us off, the Mohammeds, the 'Alis, the Khalils, who had driven our donkeys, sold us manufactured scarabs and translated thousands of yards of hieroglyphs for us during the past month. Bukri', the dervish, was also there, in company with whom and a dozen others of his guild I had danced and howled on several nights in a back alley of Luxor under the light of the moon in honor of Mohammed's birthday. All smiled an affectionate farewell as the last largess from our royal bounty was dispensed, and now we were off in our own dahabiyeh, the *Queen Hatasoo*, named after the celebrated princess in whose reign its keel was laid. Down below there were, to be sure, a number of natives squatting about or saying their prayers, while the chickens picked around in the sugar cane with which the shallow hold was filled. But the natives could not be classed as tourists. They were the ballast of the *Hatasoo*, while above there were just the five of us, ourselves, the Greek engineer and the Assyro-Congregationalist. The last named filled the offices of captain and purser and was a most affable and courteous little man. He could speak English, fortunately, and was always ready to try it

out, though he never intruded. I asked him in Oriental fashion whence he came. He said, "I am an Assyrian." "You
mean a Syrian," I suggested by way of correction. "No," he
answered proudly, "an Assyrian." I looked with interest on
this descendant of Sennacherib and Ashurbanipal.* He did
not resemble in any way the reliefs one sees of these gentry
in the British Museum, and I was glad he did not. The last
time, I recollected, that the Assyrians had found their way
that far up the Nile—about 667 B.C.—hundred-gated
Thebes had reeled and fallen before them. I was glad that
my friend's grandfather had lived so long ago. But I was
still further relieved when he added, "I am also a Congregationalist." I had never chanced to run across such a combination before, an Assyrian and a Congregationalist! I warmed
up to him at once. Archaeological interest and the joy of
ecclesiastical kinship were alike satisfied. He told me his history. He had graduated from our mission school at Mardin
in Central Turkey but, after the terrible Armenian massacres
of 1895, had succeeded in escaping to Egypt. But his stories
of his student days at Mardin were what interested me most.
Dr. Gates, now President of Robert College, had been his
teacher and Dr. Gates, as it seemed, was opposed to smoking. But the imperious blood of his Ninevite ancestors ran
too strong in the veins of my new friend to submit to this
curbing of his liberty. "We boys," he said, "used to run away
and hide in caves and smoke; it was very wicked, but we
could not help it."

Was I dreaming, I thought to myself, as I listened to him?
Was this muddy stream really the Nile or only our Plumb
Creek at the flood? Was it a descendant of the conquerors of
Babylon and Thebes, of Elam and Ararat who was speaking

* In reality certain branches of the Nestorians apply the name Assyrian to
themselves. I have ventured to ignore this rude fact as not being germane
to my purpose.

to me, or some Oberlin freshman confessing a martyrdom to his faith in St. Nicotine?

A glance about me dispelled the illusion. The cook, with the meticulous* *un*cleanliness suitable to an Oriental whose art is successful in proportion to its defiance of the laws of sanitation, was spreading our table on the deck and disposing our jam and chicken. We were approaching Keneh. Over there on the western bank beyond the bending palms, though out of sight from our steamer, we knew the beautiful temple of Dendera stood, sacred to Hathor, the Egyptian Aphrodite. The sun was setting over the Libyan Desert and at the very instant that it set, the full moon rose over the Arabian Desert. In Egypt the color is not simply in the sky or in the far-off mountain; it is glowing and palpitating all around you. You are bathed in it as in a delicate vapor. Keneh, the deserts, the great sandstone ridge just across the river, the Nile, our boat, ourselves were all dissolving in a luminous cloud of color. We ate our supper in a kind of hush except for one strange sound, strange yet curiously familiar, too. The Assyro-Congregationalist sat a little way apart from us and breathed gently into his flute. Had his ancient faith mastered him in this magical hour? Was this a hymn to Ishtar or Hathor or Aphrodite that he was evoking from his flute? We listened to catch the wild Oriental note of bygone times. But it was of the future, not of the past, that the music sounded. The Congregationalist had triumphed over the Assyrian. He was playing "The Sweet By and By."

* I have eagerly watched for an opportunity to edge this modish word into the above sketch and I flatter myself I have discovered just the place for it.

PART IV
FAREWELLS

JONAH

I

FORTY odd years ago it was my good fortune to live a summer idyll in the village of Ilsenburg. The little town hides itself away in a great fold of the Harz Mountains. From the blue distance the Brocken looks down upon it, and through its street the Prinzessin Ilse dances and sings. Up above, on the side of the hill, stands the little castle-church of Ilsenburg. It is a very ancient structure, rude, amorphous; but in the crannied walls of its tower the wild flowers bloom, and from the great bell overhead a mellow thunder rolls across the valley, with all the mystery and sadness yet assurance of age-long history in its solemn tones. Within, the church is as unpretentious as it is without, save for the wooden angel above the pulpit, with a trumpet to its lips, and the curiously decorated paneled screen of the choir loft. This is adorned with scenes from the life of Jonah. In one of the panels the prophet issues with dignity and composure from the belly of the whale and gently wafts into space, clad in a beautiful, blue, unwrinkled robe, and with a seraphic smile on his face as if he were enjoying a semi-transfiguration.

The loggia of the Herr Pastor's family, of which, for the time being, I was a member, was hung high up upon the wall, and from it an excellent view of this astounding episode was obtainable. In those days my German was inadequate to follow all the details of the excellent sermons of the good Herr Pastor, and when my attention flagged, my eyes wandered. When I failed to understand the sermon, I occupied myself with the whale. The experience was a kind of parable of the history of Jonah in the Christian Church. From the beginning a perverse fate has followed this book. When St. Jerome translated the Old Testament for the first time from the original Hebrew into Latin, he ventured to substitute, in the third chapter of Jonah, the word *hedera* (ivy) for *cucurbita* (gourd) which had become familiar to the Church in the Old Itala Version. St. Augustine wrote in protest against this dangerous innovation. It has occasioned, he said, a disturbance among the people (*Tumultus in Vulgo*). Present critics still dispute as to the exact nature of the plant. Some opine that it is the *ricinus communis* (castor-oil plant); others that it is the *cucurbita lagnaria* (bottle-gourd)! In the Sistine Chapel, Michael Angelo has painted the Prophet Jonah. The thing that impresses artists in this picture, as I once heard a critic explain, is the marvelous technique displayed in painting a man leaning back upon a wall that hangs over the observer. The ordinary tourist, engrossed in this technical achievement, is likely to miss the little children who stand behind the prophet with hands upraised in horror and appeal. The treatment accorded by the Christian Church to one of the most profound and beautiful documents in the history of religious literature illustrates human nature's fatally debased appetite for husks when it might feed on heavenly manna. Today the mention of Jonah provokes either a fierce discussion among the superstitious over the gullet capacity of Mediterranean sharks or among the emancipated a supercilious smile. The men of Nineveh shall rise up in the judgment with this generation and shall condemn it, for *they* repented at the preaching of Jonah. Our attention wanders from the sermon and is absorbed by the whale.

II

THE book is intended to be a sermon. Its position in the Old Testament is evidence of this. It stands among the prophetical books, not among the historical books. It does not occupy this position because Jonah himself is a prophet; in that case the narratives of Elijah and Elisha would also be placed among the prophets. It stands where it does because the book itself is a prophecy, that is, a sermon. It is not written in an historical interest. If it were, we would expect more information about the prophet's life. Where did he land after his strange sea voyage? How did he accomplish his long and tedious journey to Nineveh? Who was the great king of Nineveh who repented at the word of a foreign prophet? What became of the reform movement in the Assyrian capital which was begun by Jonah? What became of Jonah himself? The author leaves him sitting in a little tent on the east side of the city. If the book were written in an historical interest, it should at least end with "to be continued." As a matter of fact, there is recounted to us simply one episode in the prophet's life, the details of which are so arranged as to teach just one supreme lesson. But what is the lesson? If the book is a sermon, what is its text?

It was probably written long after the fall of Nineveh, in the period of Jewish history which followed the Babylonian Exile. At that time there were two great tendencies striving for the mastery in Judaism, the one nationalistic and exclusive, with an almost fanatical hatred of the nations, quite explicable under the circumstances; the other, universalistic, with a great love for mankind and a solemn feeling of responsibility toward man welling up in the Jewish consciousness. The author of the Book of Jonah is an advocate of the latter view. His tract is a protest against religious intolerance and perverted nationalism, against the idea that an individual or a nation can have a copyright on God or exist for itself alone. But, unlike many protesters, our author is no intolerant champion of tolerance. He does not shriek liberty and love. A delicate feeling for beauty and a sense of humor save him. His work betrays a man of refinement and largeness of heart. He is steeped in the culture of his own people. He is familiar with the finest examples of the national literature. Indeed, much of the subtler meaning of the book is lost upon those who are not intimately acquainted with the Old Testament. By a single word or phrase he often refers to incidents or teachings in the literature of his nation with which his readers would be familiar, and thus he weaves around his story the poetry of treasured associations which are largely unfamiliar to the modern reader. Alas, that what may be called the biblical culture of the English-speaking world is so rapidly disappearing! The literary loss, to say nothing of the spiritual, is enormous.

III

THE author illustrates the lesson which he desires to teach by three pictures. In the first are drawn the figures of *The Fugitive Prophet and the Pious Seamen* (Chapter I and Chapter II, the first and last verses).* Jonah heard the command of God to go to Nineveh, *"that great city."* Great in its wickedness! Wicked it was, as Sodom, as the phrasing of 1.2 reminds the reader. But Jonah rebelled against the command. Why, we are not told as yet. Instead, he went as far away from Nineveh as he could get. Nineveh lay far to the east. Jonah would go to Tarshish (Tartessus) in Spain, far to the west. Thus he sought to escape "from the presence of the Lord." Silly Jonah!

> Whither shall I go from thy spirit
> Or whither shall I flee from thy presence?
> If I ascend up into heaven, Thou art there;
> If I take the wings of the morning,
> And dwell in the uttermost parts of the sea,
> Even there shall thy hand seize me,
> And thy right hand lay hold on me.

* The prayer in Chapter II can scarcely be original. It is a prayer of thanksgiving for deliverance from drowning (probably symbolic of deliverance from trouble) and it does not at all agree with the situation in which Jonah is supposed to have uttered it. The incongruity was long ago recognized by that acute interpreter, John Calvin.

"It is not by our feet or by change of place that we either turn from Thee or return to Thee," Augustine once said. God defies geography. Jonah cannot escape Him by "going West." Jonah should have remembered the motto of his great predecessor, Elijah: "The Lord in whose presence I stand." But he did not do so, and blithely journeyed down the Palestinian hills and across the Philistine plain to Jaffa. There, by a happy coincidence, he found a ship just setting out for Tartessus. The Lord seemed to be making the primrose path easy for him. He immediately embarked in order to escape "from the presence of the Lord." But Jonah was an honorable man, a very honest passenger; he paid his fare!

Hardly had they got well under way when a great storm arose and the ship threatened to founder. The sailors, undoubtedly Phoenician and therefore heathen, did their best under the circumstances. They jettisoned the cargo and earnestly prayed to the gods for deliverance. But what had become of the honest passenger who had paid his fare? Search being made, he was found in the innermost part of the ship, in "a deep sleep," a sleep as profound as a trance. The prophet slept, numb, insensible to all that was going on about him.

For the Lord hath poured upon you [Israel] the spirit of deep sleep,
And hath closed your eyes,
And your heads hath he covered (Isaiah 29.10).

The captain of the ship was shocked at this sluggishness of his passenger. He approached the prostrate figure, roused him and urged him to pray. The prophet of the Lord must be reminded by the heathen sailor of his duty to pray! Meanwhile the storm was increasing in fury. The anger of the gods must be behind the spindrift. It was proposed to cast lots in order to discover who on board had provoked the divine wrath. The lot fell upon the sleepy-eyed passenger. "What is your business," they asked, "whence come you,

from what land, of what people?" Questions pressed thick
and fast. Jonah's reply was most unexpected. "I am a Hebrew," he said, "and the Lord God of heaven do I fear, who
made the sea and the dry land." A noble profession of the
noble faith of Judaism. But in what a ridiculous position it
placed the prophet! If God made the sea as well as the dry
land, how could Jonah expect to escape Him by going to
sea? Jonah is one of those unlovely persons "whose life
laughs through and spits at their creed." The sailors were
much impressed by Jonah's answer. Here was a man whose
god was a god of the sea, but one who had evidently provoked his god, for the lot had fallen upon him. What was to
be done? The sea was ever increasing in its fury. They
turned to their strange passenger for advice. The advice they
got was as strange as the man who gave it. "Take me up,"
he said, "and hurl me into the sea, and the sea will quiet
down; for I know that it is on my account that this great
tempest has come upon you." In this singular reply our author has subtly conveyed the controlling thought of Hebrew
prophecy. Israel was the prophet-nation, but it had been
largely insensible to its privileges and responsibilities. It was
in a spiritual torpor, as Jonah had been. But its deeper
thinkers had foreseen the end. There was to be national disaster. The suffering of the Exile was to come upon Judah as
a punishment for the nation's blindness and its failure to
realize its mission. Just as the spiritual torpor of the prophet-
nation is symbolized by the deep sleep of Jonah, so the prophetic anticipation of the necessity and certainty of national
ruin is expressed in the command: Take me up and hurl me
into the sea. It was not due to the cruelty of the heathen that
Judah was taken captive; it was due to its own sin. The lot
had fallen upon Jonah.

The purpose of the writer to reiterate the prophetic teaching that the people's misfortunes were due to their own sins

and not to the sins of other nations is also clearly seen in the
kindly way in which the heathen sailors are characterized.
They did not wish to destroy Jonah; they did their best to
rescue him. They fairly dug their oars into the sea in their
endeavor to save the ship and land their passenger. But all
to no purpose. At last, when no other course was left open to
them, they prayed for forgiveness to Jonah's God, and that
He would not lay innocent blood to their charge: "For
Thou, O Lord, according as Thou hast pleased, so Thou hast
done." Then they lifted up the prophet and hurled him into
the sea, and immediately the sea ceased from its raging. On
landing, the heathen sailors, overcome by awe at what had
happened, piously offered sacrifices and paid their vows.

Meanwhile, Jonah was swallowed by a great fish, but
after three days he prayed to the Lord. The Lord heard his
prayer and the fish spewed Jonah out upon the seashore. This
episode seems grotesque to us, but no one would have been
more astonished than our author at the perverse fate which
has dogged his tract, due to this incidental allusion to the
great fish. The subsequent tragic misunderstanding of the
significance of this allusion would have pained him sorely,
but it would also have provoked from him, being the kind
of man he was, a smile, even though a rueful one, at his own
expense. The fact is, our author made use of the fish incident
because he knew its symbolic meaning would be at once understood by his readers. If we may judge from a passage now
found attached to the collection of Jeremiah's prophecies,
the symbol of the sea monster for the Babylonian Exile (a
symbol ultimately derived from Babylonian mythology)
was a favorite one among the people. At Jeremiah 51.34 and
44 the nation, Judah, is made to speak as follows: "Nebu-
chadnezzar, the king of Babylon, hath devoured me, he
hath crushed me, he hath made me an empty vessel, he hath,
like a sea-monster, swallowed me up, he hath filled his maw

with my delicacies; he hath cast me out." And immediately afterward the Lord says: "I will execute judgment upon Bel and Babylon, and I will bring forth out of his mouth that which he hath swallowed up." The intention of the author of the Book of Jonah was to compare, in the current fashion, the prophet swallowed by the fish for his rebellion to the nation engulfed in the Exile for its apostasy.

IV

In Chapter III the second picture is drawn for us, entitled: *The Preaching Prophet and the Praying People*, or *The Repentance of Nineveh and the Repentance of God.*

Again the command of the Lord came to Jonah to go to Nineveh, *that great city*, this time great, as was about to be disclosed, in its repentance. On this occasion Jonah did not try to evade his duty, though he evidently performed it with no good grace. He entered Nineveh, as would be natural in coming from Palestine, at some western gate. The city was a vast one, three days' journey in diameter. But he had scarcely traversed a third of the distance, proclaiming as he went that Nineveh would be destroyed, when Nineveh repented. The Assyrians actually believed the Hebrew prophet's word. They proclaimed a fast, they clothed themselves in sackcloth. The great king himself arose from his royal throne, laid aside his robes of majesty and put on the garments of mourning. A decree was published to make the fast universal (even the cattle were to be included) and to pray mightily to God, if haply he might repent and Nineveh perish not. Nineveh a repentant city? That was as incredible a thought to many of the earliest readers of this tract as the fish episode is to us. Nineveh, the capital of the most brutal, militaristic monarchy of antiquity, which had for centuries belched forth its armies like volcanic lava flow over the doomed cities and countrysides of Syria and Palestine—was this city to repent and escape the judgment of God?

Thy shepherds sleep, O Assyrian King, thy nobles slumber;
Thy people are scattered upon the mountains with none to gather
   them.
No cure to thy hurt; grievous thy wound.
All that hear a report of thee clap their hands;
For over whom hath not thy wickedness passed continually?

This exultant close of Nahum's magnificent hymn of hate
far more fittingly expressed the proper attitude toward
Nineveh, from the popular point of view, than the sentimental idealization of "the bloody city, full of lies, full of
rapine," found in the third chapter of Jonah.

But is it a sentimental idealization? Has not our author
suggested here, in his own inimitable way, the same fundamental truth of which a modern writer caught a glimpse
when he described man as "incurably religious"? Repentance
is possible even for Nineveh. Without this faith in the final
response of the human heart to spiritual appeal, the greatest
incentive to a life of sacrifice would be lost. A noble stoicism
might indeed remain, but the tragedy of futility would be
stamped upon some of the most beautiful and glorious activities of men. The author of Jonah believes no soul is beyond the pale. He would not scruple, as Peter did in his vision at Joppa, to feed on the squirming contents of the
lowered sheet. When one of his fellow countrymen in a later
age recounted to a mob a vision in which he heard the Lord's
voice say to him: "Depart, for I will send thee far hence
unto the gentiles," our author would not have been found
among those who gave Paul audience "unto this word" and
then "lifted up their voices and said: Away with such a fellow from the earth, for it is not fit that he should live." On
the contrary, he placed himself in line with the joyous lovers
of mankind and the confident believers in mankind, who, because of this love and faith, have had creative power. He
sided with the Son of Man who came to seek and to save that
which was lost.

The ready repentance of Nineveh was promptly answered by the repentance of God. "God saw their works, that they turned from their evil way, and God repented of the evil which he had proposed to do unto them, and did it not." Long before this Ezekiel had said: "Have I any pleasure in the death of the wicked, saith the Lord, and not that he should turn from his ways and live?" But Ezekiel had in mind the sinning Jew. The author of Jonah says that God's attitude toward the sinning Ninevite is just the same.

V

WHAT effect had all this upon Jonah? This is revealed in the last picture, a genre picture, and a very singular one. In the foreground are grouped a sulky man, a gourd, one hundred and twenty thousand babies (the canvas is a spacious one), and much cattle. Surely a heterogeneous collection of objects. Only a genius could combine them into a harmonious whole.

Jonah is the first figure to attract, or shall we say to repel, the attention. He is very angry because God's love has extended to Nineveh. "Alas, Lord," he complains, "is this not just what I said to myself when I was in my own country? Therefore I fled the former time to Tarshish." In his anger he now lets slip the ugly reason for his earlier flight. "For I know," he continues, "that Thou art a God of compassion, long suffering and abundant in loving kindness and one who repenteth of evil." Jonah knew this because in a great and solemn hour, according to the national tradition, the Lord had thus described himself to Moses, Jonah's great forerunner in the prophetic office. But was this high mystery, revealed to Israel upon Mount Sinai, to be profaned by being communicated to a heathen city? Were these dogs of Assyrians to enter the Holy of Holies of Israel's religion into which the High Priest alone could enter, and that but once a year, where stood the Mercy Seat? Jonah is outraged at the thought and bursts forth: "O Lord, take away my life, for it is better for me to die than to live." It seems to escape his attention that this was just the prayer Elijah offered, but in how different a mood! Elijah prayed to die because his preaching to save his people seemed to be in vain; Jonah prays to die because his preaching *has* saved the people. Elijah despaired because he seemed to fight a losing fight in behalf of the rights of God over His own people; Jonah despairs because he is fighting a losing fight against the rights of God over manki d.

To all this ill-nature God responds with no stern rebuke, but only with a gentle sarcasm: "Doest thou well to be angry?" Jonah, like a spoiled child, refuses to answer. He knows he is in the wrong but he will not give in. Having entered the city from the west, he now continues on his way through it till he passes out at a gate on the opposite side and sits down on the east of the city to see what will happen next. Meanwhile he builds a little shack to make himself as comfortable as possible while he waits to see whether some thunderbolt of God may not even yet blast the city with its population of a million men!

At first God appears inclined to humor Jonah. He prepares a gourd (remember, gentle reader, that wise critics still dispute as to its proper botanical classification) which quickly grows and spreads its broad leaves over the shack. It is pleasant to sit thus in a little shack with a cool shade protecting him. Jonah rejoices in the gourd. Surely the Lord is considerate to make his prophet so comfortable. But the next day God sends a worm which smites the gourd and it withers. And when the sun is up the sirocco begins to blow, and Jonah swoons at the fell touch of it. Again he prays to die, "for it is better for me to die," he whimpers, "than to live." These were the very words he used before. But at first he wished to die because Nineveh was *not* destroyed; now he wishes to die because the gourd *was* destroyed. Then God repeats his question, gently yet with some insistence: "Doest thou well to be angry for the gourd?" "Yes," replies the prophet fiercely, "I do well to be deadly angry." God's answer to this outburst is the text of the sermon, placed here at the close, where its full import can now be understood: "And the Lord said: Thou didst have pity for a gourd, over which thou didst not labor and which thou didst not tend, which in a night grew up and in a night perished. And I, shall I not have compassion upon Nineveh, *that great city* [great in its wickedness, but great in its repentance, too; above all, great in its experience of God's unbounded love], in which are one hundred and twenty thousand human beings too young to tell their right hand from their left, and much cattle?"

Jonah was sorry for a mere gourd, God for a great city. Jonah was sorry for a weed, an insubstantial and ephemeral thing; God pitied an empire's capital, a vast and complicated thing. Jonah grieved for the gourd, not for its own sake, nor because the death of the simplest living thing should cause him pain, but because the gourd had ceased to minister to his own selfish enjoyment; God grieved for Nineveh *for its own sake.* The helplessness of the little children and the "much cattle" appealed to him. "Thou lovest all that is," sings Wisdom, "and hast no hate for those things which thou hast created. Nor hast thou prepared anything with dislike. For how could anything exist if Thou didst not permit it? Thou sparest all, for it is Thine, O Lord, who rejoicest in every living thing." He spareth all for it is His. The helplessness of mankind appeals to him, the poor little babe, the "much cattle." Are not most of mankind children, "infants crying in the night"? Are not most of mankind much cattle? Lost sheep, the Prophet of Nazareth calls them.

These things I have thought upon for over forty years, since I lived that summer idyll in Ilsenburg, studying on

Sundays the figure of Jonah ejected from the whale when I
could not understand the sermon, or listening at sunset to the
bell of the old church, mellow with mystery and sadness,
yet with confidence also, born of its experience through the
centuries in calling men to thoughts upon the unseen world.
A few years ago I visited Ilsenburg and its castle-church
again. The life that I had once lived there was gone, never
to return. The age to which it belonged was gone, forever
gone. But the wooden angel over the pulpit with trumpet to
its lips was still publishing silently the *Evangelium*, and
Jonah was still in his ascension on the panel of the choir
screen. I have wondered whether in this new and bitter time
there is not more need than ever before of the gentle humor,
the sense of beauty, the spirit of tolerance, the profound pity
which breathe from this ancient tract.

SOME PROBLEMS OF LIBERAL PROTES-
TANTISM IN HISTORICAL PERSPECTIVE*

A S I come, at this hour, to the close of my teaching service in our Seminary I have found it extremely difficult to select a subject suitable to the occasion.
Thinking over the forty odd years in which I have been
teaching the Old Testament, I find that my interest in it has
not been archaeological. It has not even been historical, fas-
cinating as the history of Israel and of Israel's religion is
(and I have never been more alive to its fascination than I
am today). In all these years of study my chief preoccupa-
tion has been with the relationship of Israel's religion to the
Christian religion and to the burning problems of our own
day. I have therefore chosen, as indicating this special interest of mine, the subject: Some Problems of Liberal Protestantism—in Historical Perspective—with special emphasis
upon the last clause. I propose to look first at the origin of
the religion which we profess as a reform movement within
Judaism, then to look briefly at its development in its Ancient Catholic and Roman Catholic phases, and finally to
consider some of its main trends since the Protestant Reformation and the problems to which these latest developments
give rise.

It is with some misgiving that the following analysis of
the crisis in Protestantism is offered to the public. I am well
aware of the fact that there is scarcely a sentence in my argument which would not be disputed by somebody or other. I
am also conscious of the dangers of generalization in dealing
with great historical movements; for it leads almost inevitably to systematization and oversimplification. But just as

* Valedictory Address at retirement, delivered at the Commencement of
the Graduate School of Theology, May, 1934.

a generalized view of Egypt's wonderland from an airplane
has led to the discovery of the outlines of many buried cities
which the excavator, dealing with a multitude of details,
had failed to recognize, so a bird's-eye view of a great historical movement may serve to disclose its more important
trends, of which even a very careful scrutiny, if limited to a
study of details, may lose sight. What follows is, indeed, the
result of much detailed study over a long period of years.
But an attempt to document my generalizations would require a lengthy monograph in the mazes of which one could
easily lose his sense of direction. I have hoped, however, that
the bird's-eye view here given of the development of Judaism and Christianity, culminating in the present crises of our
own day, may serve to distinguish more sharply the great
trends of Christianity, particularly in the Protestant form of
it. The necessity of brevity of expression in an article which
attempts to cover so wide a field has compelled a resort to a
form of presentation hardly distinguishable from a classroom syllabus. For this I beg the reader's indulgence.

I

In the Exile, Judah won a sublime faith and developed a
noble ideal. The faith was monotheism; the ideal was holiness—"Be ye holy for I am holy"—a people completely
consecrated to one supreme God, whose life both collectively
and individually was to be regulated down to the most trivial
detail with reference to God. What a noble, what a daring
ideal! It was wrought out principally by Ezekiel and the
authors of the Priests' Code. "Hear, O Israel, the Lord our
God is one," Jahweh, the creator of the universe and ruler
of human history—in this great synthesis of II Isaiah monotheism reached its culminating formulation.

But how were this faith and this ideal to be best preserved
and adapted to the life of the people? This was to be accomplished through the Torah (the Law), the mass of the laws

saved out of the wreckage of the Exile and later worked over in the interest of monotheism and holiness. The result was a complete change in the life of the nation. The nation, Israel, of pre-Exilic times becomes the sect, the Jews, of post-Exilic times. The kingdom becomes the congregation. The theologians of Judaism were Ezekiel and II Isaiah. The organizers of Judaism were Nehemiah and Ezra. The last two laid the foundations for the transformation of the nation into a church by the imposition of the Law as the constitutive principle of the Jewish community life, and by the separation of the congregation (the holy seed) from the surrounding nations. Very contradictory tendencies soon began to develop out of these premises.

The first is the emphasis upon universalism as against nationalism. Monotheism logically denationalizes the idea of God, and the great thought would naturally arise that the God of the whole earth is to be worshiped by the whole earth (universalism). It is no accident that the Book of Jonah, the most universalistic tract in the Old Testament, came out of the age of developed monotheism.

Again, monotheism emphasizes individualism in religion as against nationalism. In earlier days religion was the concern of the individual only as he was a member of the nation. Eighth-century prophecy did not address the individual soul, as our modern evangelists do, but only the nation or the citizen in the nation. "Prepare to meet thy God, O Israel," warned Amos. But on the monotheistic conception of God the relationship to Him came to be determined by choice, not by place of birth or national connection. This means a new emphasis upon the individual which, in turn, becomes one of the most powerful factors in spiritualizing religion. According to Jeremiah: "They shall no longer use the proverb, the Fathers have eaten sour grapes and the children's teeth are set on edge. But every one shall die for his own iniquity. Every man that eateth the sour grapes, his teeth shall be set on edge." Or as Ezekiel expresses it: "The soul that sinneth, it shall die." Into the immediate connection between individualism and the rise of the belief in the next life I cannot enter except to say that this belief among the Jews was not an achievement of the intellect but a spiritual experience and thus differed sharply from the Greek speculations on the nature of the soul.

When we turn to consider the consequences for religion which follow from the ideal of holiness, we find the tendencies of the monotheistic principle at times, though by no means always, directly counteracted.

The exclusiveness which is inherent in the idea of holiness may easily pass over into bigotry and fanaticism, the very opposite of the magnanimity of monotheism. The custom among Jews of drawing a sharp line of distinction between themselves and their neighbors in the interest of self-preservation might lead them to imagine that they had a copyright on God. Possessed of the pearl of greatest price, the Jew was in danger of becoming a religious miser. The Imprecatory Psalms and the Book of Esther are unfortunate examples of this tendency. There is nothing more dangerous in the history of religions than the identification of one's own hatreds with the justice of God.

There is another danger inherent in the original idea of holiness. It meant separation from ceremonial as well as from moral defilement. This danger may be better understood when we turn to consider the consequences to religion that may follow upon the idea of the Law as the constitutive principle of the national life.

While the Law was of the greatest value in conserving the faith of monotheism, the ideal of holiness, and, along with these, the unity of the national life, this must not blind us to certain of its theoretical defects.

The first defect is the Law's tendency, in its ceremonial form, to externalism. It must never be forgotten that the aim of the Law was to teach prophetic morality. But with the enveloping of prophetical morality in ceremonial the distinction between prophetical morality (i.e., righteousness) and ceremonial purity (i.e., cleanness) was in constant danger of being obliterated. In all fairness, however, it should be said that these abuses by no means always manifested themselves. The purified idea of God in monotheism and the development of the inner life through individualism often led under the Law to a piety that was beautiful and sincere. It was in the post-Exilic period that the profound conception of sin, the great spiritualizing doctrine of repentance, and the most intimate prayer life were developed in Judaism. Consider such a statement as this of Rabbi Kahana: "God says to Israel, I bade thee read thy prayers unto me in the Synagogue, but if thou canst not, then pray in thy house. If thou art unable to do this, pray where thou art in the field. If this be inconvenient to thee, pray on thy bed. And if thou canst not do even this, think of me in thy heart." Nevertheless, where there is an elaborate ceremonial, the original soul of it is apt to die out. Ceremonialism plays too easily into slothfulness of habit, and human nature in its weakness too often prefers the external in religion to the internal. It is easier to do than to be.

A second consequence which follows on the establishment of law is that religion becomes identified with law. Revelation comes as a command. The danger of this is familiar from the writings of Paul. Religion in the form of law has the great value of discipline, but, on the other hand, it may check and stunt the free moral life of the individual. "Religion becomes," to use the word of another, "simply right behavior before God [that is, it is resolved into an ethic] instead of being a communion of man with God in order to right behavior."

The further fact that the Law now became identified with the codex of the Law was even more disastrous. The religion of the spoken word of prophecy had not only become a religion of law but a religion of a law book. Religion can now be learned as a lesson. Isaiah pronounces his woe upon those whose fear of the Lord "is a commandment of men which has been learned by rote," and Kipling echoes the same warning in his famous line: "The God ye took from a printed book be with ye, Tomlinson."

Again, if bound too rigidly to a written document, religion becomes incapable of progress. It is interesting to notice that from the time the law book became the final binding authority, prophecy, which had kept religion from becoming stereotyped, began to wane. This is not simply a curious coincidence. When revelation was summed up in an authoritative way in a law book, what further need was there for prophetic teaching? All that was needed now was interpretation. This leads us to our next consideration.

With the change from the nationalistic to the ecclesiastical conception of the Jewish community, with the establishment of the codex of the Law as the written constitution of this community, and with the correlative passing of the prophet, two orders came more and more to the front, the priest and the scribe. The function of the priest was primarily to care for the cult. Into this it is unnecessary to go. The function of the scribe was to interpret the Law.

This power to interpret is all-important and gave to the scribes a superiority even over the priests. How did this come about? The Law as the authoritatively revealed will of God set down in a book was unchangeable. On the other hand, conditions did change. But how could a formally fixed law be adapted to changed conditions without sacrificing its character as an ultimate revelation? The scribes solved this problem by the introduction of the oral tradition, or the authoritative interpretation of Scripture supposed to be handed down through the scribes themselves from the time Moses gave the Law at Sinai. This is "the tradition of the elders" of the gospels or "the hedge about the Law" of the Talmud, and, though its burdens were great, it provided for Judaism its only chance for development. The way the final authority of our Constitution has become adapted to changing conditions through the interpretation of the Supreme Court offers a close analogy.

If we now turn to the New Testament and look at the beginnings of Christianity in the light of Judaism, we may be able to see more clearly what are some of the essentials of our religion and what are some of the problems which confront us.

II

(1) Christianity in its initial stage preserved monotheism but gave to it a richer interpretation through Jesus' experience of God as the heavenly Father. (2) It emphasized the ideal of love rather than the ideal of holiness. (3) It emphasized not submission to a law but attachment to a person, by means of which the ideal of love could be more easily attained. (4) It emphasized the ideal of the Kingdom of God rather than the ideal of the church.

In all these points the original difference between Judaism and Christianity is one of emphasis and proportion rather than of essence. Yet the differences are, nonetheless, of very great importance.

To begin with the second point, it is true that the ideal of love is not wanting in Judaism nor the ideal of holiness in early Christianity. But I believe it is fair to say that the emphasis was changed and that Christianity, through the powerful qualification of the ideal of holiness by the ideal of love, was able to accomplish all for righteousness that Judaism did and to escape, in a measure, the dangers which were always present in the earlier ideal.

We have seen how the ideal of holiness in its exclusiveness tended to counteract the universalism of monotheism. There is nothing in the ideal of love to counteract universalism but everything to stimulate it. All middle walls of partition are now broken down. Exclusiveness, theoretically at least, is a thing of the past. Bigotry and fanaticism, though often enough manifested in the Christian Church, are absolutely alien to its spirit. It is not an accident that almost immediately the Christian propaganda began to push out into the gentile world.

Again, in the realm of practical ethics the new emphasis is of the greatest significance. Holiness is inherently negative and defensive; love is inherently positive and aggressive. Holiness, in order to secure itself, must exclude the world; love, in order to secure itself, must win the world. To adopt the military jargon of the day, holiness follows the old strategy of the defensive, love follows the new strategy of the offensive defensive. The one guards itself against defeat; the other guards itself by victory.

In the next place, the Christian principle of love finds its inspiration in attachment to a person. In Judaism the agency to effect holiness was the law; in Christianity the agent to effect love was a person. From this point of view the central significance of the person of Jesus, even apart from the dogmas as to his peculiar nature, can be understood.

We have seen how, through the frequent identification of holiness with ceremonial purity, the door was open to externalism in religion. Love, unlike holiness, is never ceremonial. It belongs to the inward in religion, not to the outward. Paul was only carrying out the principle of attachment to a person when he taught that the law in its historic sense was no longer binding. This agency to effect holiness had served its turn. Through attachment to a person not only ceremonialism but legalism is sloughed off.

Further, the confusion of ceremonial purity with righteousness, which the ideal of holiness often encouraged, is avoided. At this point the ethical clarity of Jesus' view admitted of no compromise. "There is nothing from without the man that, going into him, can defile him; but the things which proceed out of a man are those which defile him." Here Christianity attached itself directly to the prophetic movement, particularly to the teachings of Jeremiah, and deepened the idea of inwardness both in religion and in ethics.

Because Christianity rejects the idea of law and substitutes an attachment to a person, it also succeeds in avoiding the resolution of religion simply into morals. It emphasizes morality but not legality, a distinction that is often overlooked with disastrous consequences. Unfortunately, at this point the Christian Church is continually breaking down and turning the gospel back again into law, a fault that reformers are especially liable to.

Again, because Christianity substitutes attachment to a person for submission to a law, it follows that it substitutes attachment to a person for attachment to a law book. At this point confusion has often arisen, especially in Protestantism. Christianity is undoubtedly a book religion but not in the sense in which this statement was understood by the post-Reformation theologians. The great parallel movement of Humanism (that is, the literary revival of the sixteenth century), the completer synthesis of which with the Reformation movement we have been witnessing during the last century and a half, is teaching us a truer conception of the Bible. Christianity is a book religion in so far as it is a historical religion, and the Bible books are regarded as the authentic documents to inform us concerning its genesis and historical meaning, but no further. This conclusion the history of the Canon leaves no possible room to doubt. Religion in order to live must be personal, but there is a legalistic way of looking at the Bible as a kind of law code that ignores the personal elements which entered into its composition. Against this legalistic conception of the Bible the essence of Christianity protests. In essence Christianity is far more closely related to the spoken word of prophecy than it is to the Law deposited in a codex, and modern criticism which has made prophecy the starting point of its investigations and reconstructions is much more in touch with the real spirit of the gospel than is the traditional view which has been curiously inclined to emphasize the Law.

Lastly, Jesus emphasized the idea of the Kingdom rather than of the church, that is, of an ecclesiastically organized group. Jesus did not consciously or deliberately found a church. This negative fact is of great importance. It frees in principle the idea of a church when it did develop from any authoritatively constituted polity. Neither priest, as the official administrator of the cult, nor scribe, as the official interpreter of the church's teachings, belongs to the essence of Christianity. In this respect there is a sharp difference between Jesus and Judaism on the one hand and between Jesus and the later Christian development on the other. Judaism and the later church laid greatest emphasis upon ecclesiastical polity. Jesus did not. His absorption in the idea of the Kingdom of God implies a total disregard of all external organization. And that is the important thing. I shall return to this subject again.

III

AND now we come to a turning point in the development we have been tracing. While thus far we have considered Christianity as a reformed movement within Judaism and while at the first the Christian communities were most flexible in their organization, they soon began to take on the form of a church. This was due to three new factors of immense significance: (*a*) the development of the sacramental system probably under the influence, in part at least, of the mystery religions, (*b*) the development of Christology based upon faith in the death, resurrection, and session of Jesus (not primarily upon his teachings) and carried through by means of

Greek metaphysics combined with a spiritualizing interpretation of the Bible, especially the Old Testament, and (*c*) the development of the apostolic tradition.

The final result of this development was the vast and complex structure of the Church of Rome—the church of the seven sacraments, of the christological and trinitarian creeds, and of the apostolic tradition. In the first two of these forms the church differentiated itself completely from the synagogue. In the third it resembled Judaism in form but not in substance. The apostolic tradition assumed two forms as in Judaism: (*a*) the written tradition (our Canon of Scripture) and (*b*) the unwritten tradition, supposed to be handed down from Christ through the succession of bishops who were enabled by means of it to interpret the Scripture, just as in Judaism the unwritten tradition of the interpretation of the written Law was handed down through the succession of scribes from Sinai. But there was one fundamental difference in the two theories. Those whose office it was, on the Christian theory, to interpret the Scripture and so to impart truth to the believer were the same persons whose office it was to impart grace to the believer through the sacraments and thus to reconcile man to God. Power is the most corrupting influence to which human nature is exposed, and it was this double power—to impart final truth and saving grace—which the church through her ministers possessed that led to the desperate moral situation just prior to the Reformation.

The two things in this great structural development of the church that were most readily recognized by the reformers as alien to the original simplicity of the gospel were the magical element in the seven sacraments, particularly in penance, and the oral tradition which was used to support the sacramental system. Protestantism reduced the seven sacraments to two and rejected the oral tradition. This meant a tremendous reduction of the complexity of Catholicism. But the end was not yet. Another step was taken by the Protestant reformers, the full significance of which is after four hundred years still unrecognized by the majority of Protestants, ministers included. Hitherto there had been no scientific method of interpreting Scripture. The spiritualizing or allegorizing method of interpretation had been the one regularly followed. But this left the real meaning of Scripture entirely uncertain. The Roman Church took advantage of this difficulty in order to introduce the oral tradition by which the meaning of the written tradition (the Bible) was determined, at least in theory. But when the oral tradition was abandoned by the reformers and the Scripture only was left as the sole principle of authority, a way had to be found to ascertain its meaning with some measure of certainty; for an obscure authority would be quite unusable in the contest with Rome. The reformers were accordingly led to set up the grammatico-historical method of exegesis, a scientific principle of interpretation, in order to make the Bible usable as the sole principle of authority.

The interest in adopting the new principle of interpretation was, undoubtedly, a dogmatic one, but, once introduced, it came more and more to assert its own rights as a scientific principle. Applied rigidly to the Bible, it provoked the great inspiration controversies of the seventeenth century over textual criticism and in the nineteenth century over historical criticism, and the result is a momentous change in the theory of the Bible. It is no longer a dogmatic authority but becomes only a historical authority.

But if our views of the Bible itself have been so completely changed by the application to it of the Reformation principle of exegesis, we cannot expect the creeds to remain untouched which, as we have seen, were formulated on the basis of the pre-Reformation, unscientific methods of interpreting Scripture combined with Greek metaphysics. All this means a still further reduction and simplification of our religion. It is rap-

idly assuming, whether we like it or not, an undogmatic
form. But have we not lost something that is priceless in this
long process of the disintegration of dogma? What is Catholic dogma in its essence but the expression in a series of magnificent symbols of a belief in the transcendental in life? As
such has it not appealed to some of the keenest intellects, the
greatest artists, the sublimest poets, the most daring mystics
of the last two thousand years? Has this marvelous cultural
development come to an end? With the decay of dogma, of
the principle of ecclesiastical authority, the great ultimates
of religion come swinging slowly and solemnly into view
above the tempestuous billows of human life. I shall content
myself with referring to just one of the deeper problems
which confront the church, more particularly the liberal Protestant wing of it.

IV

As less and less stress has been laid upon dogma in our liberal
Protestantism, more and more stress has been laid upon the
ethical element in our religion. This is the meaning of the
many back-to-Jesus movements in the last generation. The
ethical teachings of Jesus rather than his death, resurrection,
and session at the right hand of God have chiefly occupied
the thought of liberal theology. Is this, however, not all to
the good—to be relieved of the burden of dogma by paying
the price of an intensified ethical life? But is it intensified?
There is the rub. In the latest phases of liberalism this ethical
teaching has assumed a primarily sociological character. The
practical result has been that liberalism has become more and
more engrossed in social reform, and in order to carry through
social reform the church has felt itself compelled again and
again to enter politics and thus expose itself to the insidious
dangers of rationalization and externalization. Religion tends
again to become simply "right behavior" instead of "communion with God in order to right behavior." From what

was originally an undogmatic movement liberalism is now well on the way to evaporating into a secularist (humanist) ethical movement.

It is this danger which is giving great concern to many who have been in times past supporters of the liberal movement. Are we quite certain that a rather crude sociology is an adequate substitute for a matured dogmatic? In nothing is this ethical rationalization more conspicuous than in the modernist treatment of Jesus' conception of the Kingdom of God; and here I return to catch up the thread that was temporarily dropped. This idea of the Kingdom was taken over by Jesus from Judaism and in the main was a strongly apocalyptical idea. The phrase "Kingdom of God" conveys to us a misleading meaning. It suggests a sociological or political structure. The proper translation is "God's sovereignty." It is God's rule, not his realm, that is thought of in the use of this phrase. God's sovereignty is only finally realized outside the sphere of time and space. The idea is a thoroughly supernaturalist one. In agreement with this is the almost total lack of interest Jesus displayed in social problems—a fact that is most uncomfortable for modern liberalism. Accordingly, liberalism seeks to turn this supernaturalist, apocalyptic idea into a sociological one. In doing so it has allied itself with the idea of progress, a conception inherited not from the gospels but from the rationalistic French philosophy of the eighteenth century.

It would seem that at this point liberalism has made as complete a break with the teachings of Jesus as it has with the dogmatic constructions of the ancient Catholic Church. Is there any way to bridge over this gulf between the present and the past, any way to preserve a true continuity with the past, any way to hold to the transcendental, which dogma symbolizes, while rejecting the dogmatic forms? This leads us back to consider the first point of difference mentioned above between Christianity and Judaism: Christianity preserved monotheism but gave to it a richer meaning through Jesus' experience of God as heavenly Father. In doing this it secured all the great spiritual advantages of Jewish monotheism, namely, individualism, universalism, faith in a future life; but all these are now realized with an intensity never known before because they are freed from the restrictions imposed by the ideal of holiness.

It is true, again, that Jesus borrowed the idea of God as Father from Judaism, but among the Jews this idea was mediated to the individual through the nation. God was Father first of Israel, the nation, and then of the individual Israelite. But in Jesus' view God is Father first and last of the individual. Here the peculiar God-consciousness of Jesus is a determinative factor in the Christian religion.

This doctrine of the fatherhood of God in his direct relationship to the individual is the source of what I believe to be the most distinctive thing in Jesus' teaching—his individualism. It is the relationship of the individual soul to its heavenly Father that is the primary fact with him. "What shall it profit a man if he gain the whole world and lose his own soul?" (*Psyche* is used in the double sense of soul and life.) Here Jesus intensifies the teachings of Jeremiah and Ezekiel. This particular and primary interest of Jesus gives to religion an inwardness which has never before been attained. This means that he insists upon the righteousness of the pure in heart, that inner righteousness which reflects the sovereignty of God in the heart of man.

The contrast of this interest of Jesus in the inner life of the individual with his seeming lack of interest in the organization of society is most significant. It means that in Jesus' view the individual is the religious unit, his relationship with God the primary concern; and ethics now secures its firm basis in religion. Communion with God in order to right behavior! We may reject the conception of an apocalyptical Kingdom of God, but the conception of its righteousness we can reject only at our peril, that inner righteousness of the heart expressly opposed to the externalized rules of conduct which Jesus often saw around him.

Jesus' individualistic ethics, as Schweitzer points out, is not shattered when his eschatology is denied. This latter belongs to Jesus' intellectual endowment, and in this he was a child of his age. We are not bound by this intellectual inheritance of Jesus. "Not the tie of mind with mind, but of will with will" is the all-important thing, as Schweitzer insists. He continues: "If Jesus appeared to us to-day, he would not think in terms of late Jewish apocalyptic." This does not mean, however, that he would change the essential character of his ethics. "But with respect to all philosophical and theological, national and social ethics which express the modern Law he would continue to teach: Except your righteousness exceed that of the scribes and Pharisees ye cannot enter into the kingdom of Heaven."

Here is transcendence in a new form, the transcendence of the self through the inner righteousness of self-denial and self-surrender—the religion of the Cross in a very true sense. Dogma has imposed upon the intellect a burden too great to be borne. That dogma liberalism has consciously or unconsciously discarded. But the ethical demands of Jesus make an even greater demand upon the will, and who without God's help is sufficient for these things? The great practical problem before our Protestant churches today is how to maintain the inwardness of religion and the freedom of the soul, as taught by Jesus, in the midst of the externalism of even necessary social reform. Without the profound inwardness of Jesus' individualistic religion all reform will sooner or later become legalistic in character and lose its vitality.

It is disconcerting to find that the drift in our liberal churches is distinctly away from the emphasis of Jesus and back to eighth-century prophecy with its emphasis upon the social group and social morality. If only a synthesis could be effected between the profound emphasis of Jesus upon the inner life and the fervent interest of eighth-century prophecy in social justice! Just at present we seem to be putting our greatest emphasis upon the second element in this synthesis. This I believe to be a mistake. The change in the individual's inner life must precede social reform. Our increasingly complicated legal technique for checking the corruptions of our business and political life, for example, will be little more than a challenge to lawyers to devise new ways to circumvent the law unless, at the same time, there is a restoration in our individual lives of the sense of honor and of the ideal of honesty.

This leads me to make one final suggestion. Individualism is just at present at a discount. It is connected with the discredited doctrine of laissez faire in our economic life, with the resistance of wilful minorities in our political life, and with the undisciplined subjectivism of our cultural life in almost all its phases. And so the world in its blindness is seeking to correct these admitted evils by substituting a greater evil—the totalitarian state. Tennyson already in 1842 chanted the song, "The individual withers and the world is more and more." What he sang in optimism I quote in fear. The world has largely got rid of the infallible church and now, with a fatuousness beyond belief, is putting in its place the infallible state.

The final sovereignty of the state, which is the essence of totalitarianism, joined in unholy alliance with supreme physical force furnished by the black magic of science means international anarchy and war, and within the state the complete triumph of the outward over the inward. The free life of the individual must no longer be free. He must be coördinated. His deepest, innermost convictions must be surrendered. The liberty of the individual which civilization has won with such outpouring of blood in past generations is again endangered. Conscience itself is assailed. Anti-Christ was formerly found incarnated in the infallible church. It is now found in an even more terrible form in the totalitarian state, the apotheosis of the tyrannously external. At such a time as this the religious individualism of Jesus and his doctrine of inwardness may be the final means to fortify the human soul in its supreme struggle to preserve itself from desecration.

SHREDS AND PATCHES

Commencement Address, Oberlin College, June, 1931

Young Men and Women of the Graduating Class:

IT would be mock humility on my part as well as gross ingratitude if I failed to express to you my deep sense of the signal honor you have done me in inviting me to give this address. I shall cherish the memory of it always. Yet I confess to a disconcerting suspicion that after all I am only a kind of Humpty Dumpty set up on a wall and in danger of a very shattering fall. I would feel much more at ease if I could take advantage of my temporary mural situation to pay off the old scores I have against my pagan friends in the Faculty of Arts and Sciences, and smite these Philistines, as Samson did of old, with the jawbone of an ass! The presence in force of trustees and alumni is also a beckoning invitation to instruct them in the significance of faculties in higher education. Such an opportunity has never come to me before and is not likely to occur again. I turn from it with regret. But I wish your Commencement Day to pass without any untoward incidents. Besides, this address belongs to *you*. There lies the difficulty and also the reason why I would like to escape into these other delightful by-path meadows of discussion. For what have I to say to you? I was born in 1865, the prehistoric era of Mid-Victorianism, eleven years before the Johns Hopkins University set up its altars to that dreadful god, Research. In those eocene days it was still a pleasure to go to college. My childhood was passed when civilization was just beginning to step on the gas. I remember the first time I went sixty miles an hour on a railroad train, bouncing along the then unsubstantial trackage of the New York Central, our car filled with dust, our eyes with cinders, our minds with awe, as my father and I, watch in hand, marked the mileposts speeding by, one every minute. I have tried to keep up with the procession ever since, but in vain. With such early conditioning (the word is intended to indicate that I have read Mr. Watson) it has been well-nigh impossible for me to adjust myself to the new environment which you of the postwar generation accept as a matter of course. I still find more pleasure in the everlasting hills as observed on a hike than when they are on the move and jumbled up together as seen from a speeding automobile. I still shudder at attaining high altitudes and stratospheres with nothing under me (I never was inclined to metaphysics) as one does in an airplane. As for the radio, I simply do not know what etiquette would require if Mlle. Lily Pons should, figuratively speaking, enter my house as she did that of a friend of mine recently, leaning, as it were, on the arm of M. WBQX (a Polish gentleman if I may judge from his vowel-less name) and hymning in recitative and aria the praises of the Simmons deep-sleep mattress. I must also sadly own that I prefer Trollope to Mr. Hemingway or Mr. Aldous Huxley, neither of whom I have read, and would, with more pleasure dine out with Emerson, Lowell, Hawthorne, and Longfellow, if that were still possible, than with Mr. Dreiser or Mr. Sinclair Lewis, whose novel forms of repartee would undoubtedly put me at a disadvantage.

You see, there is an almost impassible gulf fixed between you of the present era and myself of the old Stone Age. Can we in any way get together?

Fortunately, I remember that we have *one* experience in common. I, also, once had a commencement even in that untutored era of my youth, and, which is more to the point, I had to give a speech on that memorable occasion just as I have to do today. But, *horribile dictu*, I forgot it when in the middle of it. I can still see the startled, loving look of my mother as for several agonizing moments I stood silent as

Cortez on a peak in Darien while all things swam *out* of my ken. Father and mother had provided a bunch of lovely roses to give me when I should finish. The question was would I *ever* finish, or stand there eternally chained to the pulpit platform as Prometheus to his rock. I forget the speech now as I did then, except for one unfinished sentence which runs: "I hate that hard cold scientific spirit which—." Evidently I had something very evil to say of science. But it has properly avenged itself upon me, for it has made my life miserable down to the present date. And this suggests to me an idea. Dare I give you a few shreds of autobiography which may faintly indicate the adjustments one must make who has spent sixty-five years in such an epoch as the present one, and may I attach to these shreds some patches of comment and advice?

And first, a few words about the kind of home I was brought up in. It was not a Puritan home but one, from the modernist point of view, just as bad—from mine just as good—a Scotch-Irish, covenanting home. It is the fashion at present to point the finger of scorn at these earlier homes as places where fear rather than love ruled. That was not true of my home. Yet undoubtedly there was discipline in it. I had to come in before dark on soft summer evenings when my playmates were out of doors throwing their hats in the air and chanting "Bat, bat, fly under my hat and I'll give you a piece of bacon," and I did not like to be interrupted in that lyric revelry. On Sunday I was not permitted to walk outside our yard unless I accompanied father on his pastoral calls upon the sick. My shoes always had to be blacked Saturday night. It was in connection with shoes that I received from father some elementary principles in morals. We blacked our shoes together and I was always interested to see what pains he took to polish the unobserved heels. "My boy," he would say to me, "the Greeks always finished the backs of their statues as carefully as they did the fronts."

Father believed that true art, even in blacking shoes, must be sincere. He also enjoined upon me always to put left shoe on first. The reason given was that right foot could take care of itself better than left foot; therefore first consideration should be given to left foot. These are undoubtedly rather whimsical illustrations of the integrity and chivalry of my father's character, pleasant ripples on the surface of an inner life-current that ran clear and deep. I am of the opinion that a truly refined character manifests itself in the little things of daily life as well as in life's great emergencies. And so, even yet, when, in my senescent absent-mindedness, I happen to put on right shoe first, I religiously take it off again and put on left shoe in memory of my father. To me, though over thirty years have passed since he died, this little bit of family ritual still is sacred.

Another slight incident indicative of my father's character I cherish in my memory. I was home from college on vacation and was walking with him again on one of his pastoral rounds as I had done when a boy. We had come into a poor section of the town and were making for a certain tenement house when I caught sight of a little girl not yet in her 'teens standing at the window and waving to father with the sweetest smile of expectation you could wish to see. I remember thinking to myself how much that smile told of previous gentle comradeship shared by my father with that little child.

My home was one in which love was blended with discipline. It was also one in which, on the whole, literary rather than scientific interests prevailed. Father, of course, guided my reading. On Sundays *Pilgrim's Progress* was my solace. I read it over and over again, and whatever ability I may have to write plain English is largely due to John Bunyan. On a certain birthday before I was in my 'teens father gave me *Twenty Thousand Leagues under the Sea* and Hawthorne's *Wonderbook and Tanglewood Tales*. The first was profusely illustrated and devoured immediately. The second had not a picture in it and was postponed to a more convenient season. At last at father's special request I took it up, though reluctantly. It was a cold winter day and a fire was burning brightly in the back parlor. I lay down before it on a rug and turned to the story of The Gorgon's Head. Suddenly I was flying with Perseus in his magic slippers over the wonderland of Greece and watching its marble palaces and temples gleaming in the moonlight. It was an epoch in my mental life and the thrill of it is not dead within me yet. I am no poet. I do not pretend to have the intense imagination of Wordsworth. And yet as I look back upon my early home I think I am enabled to understand something, at least, of what he meant when he penned those marvelous lines:

> Fair seed-time had my soul and I grew up
> Fostered alike by beauty and by fear.

Just here may I venture to introduce my first little patch. Most of you young people will, in the course of time, be married and have children committed to your care. Your homes will, in outward form, be very different from my childhood home, but I could wish no better wish for you and your children than that your homes should be informed with the same spirit of purity and gentle and refining love as mine was. As I look back upon it, I can see some defects in its training, not due to the unwisdom of my parents but to the times in which they lived. But at least I was not exposed to two pernicious influences that now threaten our children. The doctrine of self-expression had not yet begun to run riot from the cradle to the grave. And the sensationalism of the movie had not yet arrived to corrupt the imagination and morals of children. I am amazed and profoundly disturbed at the indifference of parents to this last subject. Eye-gate gives more ready access to the citadel of man's soul than ear-gate, as John Bunyan long ago pointed out in his *Holy War*. Social workers are becoming seriously alarmed at this new menace.

A few years ago "the Child-welfare Committee of the League of Nations analysed some two hundred and fifty films and found in them 97 murders, 51 cases of adultery, 19 seductions, 22 abductions, and 45 suicides. Among the principal characters in these pictures were 176 thieves, 25 prostitutes, 35 drunkards, etc." When we remember that suggestibility and imitation are two of the dominant traits of children, the appalling influence of the movies becomes apparent. We would be horrified if one of our children fell into a garbage can, but we seem to be unmoved when they are smeared with the moral garbage of our civilization.

Wherever there is a strong family feeling as there was in my boyhood home, a passion for the past, to use Tennyson's phrase, is apt to be engendered. The home is the natural mediator between the past and the present. My father was a War Republican and an Old-School Presbyterian. As I deeply loved and reverenced him, it was natural for me to grow up both politically and religiously a conservative. And I am glad I did not begin my life in rebellion. If I had done so, I would have possibly missed one of the most beautiful and helpful experiences that can befall a boy, perfect companionship with his father. I never questioned anything in the Bible except on one memorable occasion. We had arrived in our family prayers at the Book of Proverbs, and to my amazement I heard father solemnly read: "As a jewel of gold in a swine's snout so is a fair woman without discretion." I could not believe my ears. Was the Holy Bible really as funny as that? I had a sudden attack of the giggles, and family worship for that day was completely disorganized. The *New York Tribune* was the family *political* Bible, but I don't remember finding anything funny in *that* paper to disturb my inherited reverence.

I went to college utterly immature and I came out the same way. I never really knew what it was all about. I learned lessons instead of mastering subjects and did it by the painful effort of mechanically memorizing them. I *did* rebel against the scientific courses (the genesis of my commencement speech), I suppose because I associated them with mathematics which was and still is a horror to me. I do not know even to this day just what an I.Q. is. My linguistic training tells me that quotient for which Q stands is the Latin for "how many times." But how many times what—that I could not discover. It still stands for the X in life which I have always been fumbling for but never firmly grasped. I rarely read the daily papers in college except after the Yale-Princeton game, and then usually with distress of mind. I remained a conservative through my college course.

After graduation I studied at Union Theological Seminary. Most of my particular friends there were tainted with liberalism which had been seeping into the Presbyterian Church from German biblical criticism. I did my best throughout my three years at Union to uphold the strictly orthodox position, though not with entire success, for when I finally came before the Washington Presbytery to be examined for my license to preach, there was one point on which I could not satisfy the examiners. I could not bring myself positively to affirm that there was no error in the original autographs of Scripture. As nobody had ever seen these documents for several thousand years, such an affirmation seemed even to me to go beyond the evidence. My license was held up for two years in order to permit me to go to Germany for further study and learn the error of my ways. Germany was not precisely the place to go for that purpose. In Berlin I came under the influence of one of the greatest scholars and teachers of the nineteenth century, Adolf Harnack. From him I unconsciously imbibed something of the hard, cold, scientific spirit which I had deprecated in college because it was associated in my mind with mathematics, and challenged in the Seminary because it was allied with the German criticism of the Bible. But now it was neither hard nor cold but glowing with the imaginative insight and enthusiasm of a really great personality. How glad I am that the discussion-group method had not yet supplanted the lecture system in those days, and that I had the chance to feel the power and mastery of Harnack rather than to have my own ignorance enlarged by the ignorance of my fellow students. Yet in spite of Harnack I was not deterred at that time from the attempt to reconcile every difficulty in the Book of Genesis which critics had alleged as evidence of its non-Mosaic origin. I still have, yellowing in my study, some hundred or more closely written pages of well-named foolscap paper in which I defended the traditional views of the Bible. I returned home still a conservative.

The following eleven years were spent at Lane Seminary. I arrived on the ground with two lectures in my pocket, one on the Virgin Birth and one on the genealogies in Matthew and Luke. By judicious manipulation I made them last five or six hours. Probably I could have attenuated them still further if there had been a discussion group. I shudder yet to think of how I had to live from hand to mouth the remainder of that first year. With all my might I fought to retain the implicit faith in which I had been reared. The problem of the absolute and final authority of Scripture with which I was so concerned may seem very trivial and unreal to you, but it was not so to young men of those days who wished to enter the Christian ministry but hesitated to enter through the doorway of intellectual insincerity. If you wish to know what anxiety some of us had, read that old best seller in its day, Mrs. Humphrey Ward's *Robert Elsmere*.

But all this time Harnack was yeasting in my subconsciousness. When I began actually to teach the Bible and face the facts on every page of it, the accumulating evidence weathered away my powers of resistance. I just grew tired out with attempting over and over again to reconcile two contradictory statements by assuming a *tertium quid* through which they might hypothetically be brought into agreement. In this situation I thought it my duty to the truth as I was beginning to see it to set down for my classes in one, two, three order the *pros* for the liberal views and then, in order to satisfy my obligations to the institution which was employing me, to formulate in the same order the *cons*, without expressing my own views. It was a ticklish sort of tightrope walking at best, and one day after more than usual difficulty in preserving my balance a very rude student asked me without warning, "Well, Professor, what do you think about it?" I hemmed and hawed and finally sweated out some sort of evasive reply. Upon which he remarked with even more barbarous bluntness: "I guess I can tell what you think by the tone of your voice." The tone of my voice—that was Harnack emerging out of the subconscious. I had to throw up the sponge. The hard, cold, scientific spirit which I had repudiated in my commencement speech had, in the form of historical criticism, won the day. My days at Lane and in the Church of my Fathers were numbered.

I have calculated that it took me upwards of ten years to effect this religious change of base. It was a serious loss of time, professionally, for most of my fellow students had accepted the liberal positions with but little struggle and had forged far ahead of me. In fact, I have never quite caught up with some of them yet. This has stung me at times. Did it pay, I have often asked myself—this attempt to test and test again every step of the way I had come so far as I was able? I think it did. In any case, it seemed to me that I owed it to my parents not lightly to abandon the intellectual form of the religion in which I had been brought up. It was consecrated to me by their beautiful and simple lives. Moreover, this authoritarian religion of theirs from which I was in a measure separating myself was consecrated by a great and ancient tradition and had accomplished much for the purification and ennoblement of life. I have already pointed out,

and here I come to my second little patch, that if one is bound
by cords of love to one's home, the value of tradition, of continuity, will probably come to be recognized. To cut oneself
off from one's home, from the past, is to cut a great taproot
of life. Nietzsche held that "it was" is the great tyrant over
life. It may at times become so but by no means always. As
life goes on, isolation, accentuated by the thought of that
supreme hour which awaits us all, becomes a very solemn
thing. By contrast, to feel oneself a part of some larger whole
is a great solace and support. The immemorial past gives
body, substantiality, richness to the present. Mere contem-
poraneity which seems to characterize so much of life today,
particularly religious life, has too little perspective, is too
thin, becomes too easily unbalanced and distracted. Our
people at the present time seem to be busily engaged in hack-
ing away most of our inherited habits, customs and beliefs. In
consequence we are one of the most unstable civilizations in
the world—wonderfully flexible, it is true, of great potentialities, but quite as likely, if things continue in their present
course, to disintegrate as to consolidate. Therefore I make
no apology for my long, laborious attempt to retain the religion of my fathers in its completely integrated, logical
form. I believe the attempt was good for my soul.

> All my days I'll go the softlier, sadlier,
> For that dream's sake.

My call to Oberlin came in the nick of time, when every
door at Lane seemed to be closing against me. I was, as I
have intimated elsewhere, the last of the "Lane rebels" to
come here. That was in 1904. There followed what for me
was a golden age. I entered with zest into the privileges of
my new citizenship in this republic of letters. No longer was
I obliged painfully to explain away the differences in the
Bible. I was now at liberty to inquire into their significance.
The true meaning of the great prophetic movement in Israel's

history began to dawn on me, a movement paralleled in importance for subsequent generations only by the movement of Greek philosophy. And then in the midst of interesting studies and pleasant friendships came the Great War, and with it a new struggle for me. As I look back upon my life I am astonished to realize how many wars have touched it. I was born the year in which the Civil War closed. My father's family was abolitionist and ardently supported the Federal cause. I was brought up on an idealistic view of that war. Nothing was heard in *our* family about its economic causes. It was a war for *freedom and the Union*, and as such was consecrated in my father's eyes and mine. Yet there was an experience in my boyhood which should have made me question more than I did the ideality of any war. In 1883 my parents and I spent several weeks in Columbia, South Carolina. Though they had certain claims to recognition there, we were scarcely spoken to during our entire stay by any save those about the hotel who waited on us. I learned the reason why as I went horseback riding with my father around the countryside and saw the chimneys of the old manor houses rising gaunt and desolate from their blackened foundations. They had been burned, wantonly burned, by our own troops on Sherman's march to the sea. Once while we stood before a ruined fireplace at the base of one of these chimneys father quoted sadly Longfellow's lines:

> In that mansion used to be
> Free-hearted hospitality;
> The great fire up the chimney roared,
> And strangers feasted at the board.

Many years afterward, when we fed daily on atrocity stories, that scene came back to me, with the lesson that if nations accept the premise of war they must not squeal at its dreadful consequences. Atrocities are a part of war which will never be eliminated. I dimly remember in 1871 looking

with awe at pictures in *Harper's Weekly* of dead soldiers in
the Franco-Prussian War. Later came the Cuban War, the
Boer War, the Russo-Japanese and Balkan Wars in omi-
nously quick succession. I took them all for granted except
in the case of the Cuban War. That my father and I opposed,
and I had my first taste of the hysteria which attacks people
in wartime, the idealization of their own national egoisms
and the defamation of their national enemies.

Into my experiences during the Great War it is not my
purpose to enter. It is of no use to reopen old wounds. I will
only say this much. Whatever historical sense I had developed in the criticism of biblical documents protested
against the idea that it was possible for us here and now
quite so accurately to anticipate the discriminations of the
Day of Judgment as it was popularly supposed could be
done. My telescope simply would not focus on the picture of
all the Allied sheep innocently nestling down in the green
pastures on the right side of the Throne, while all the hun-
nish goats were being herded to the edge of the bottomless
pit on its sinister side. I was, I suppose, put down as pro-
goat, though I was doing my best to keep in the middle of
the road and to avoid a diet either of grass or brimstone. I do
not believe that those who threw themselves with honest
convictions into the war and experienced its exaltation can
ever realize the strain and agony of mind the rest of us endured who could not follow them. I well remember how a
good friend of mine said to me in the midst of the fury of it
all: "How can you believe you are in the right and all the
rest of the world wrong?" Well, how could I? I knew I was
not cut out to play the heroic role of an *Athenasius contra
mundum*. I needed to be at least six inches taller than I am
to do that successfully. I lay awake the most of the following night, wrestling with my friend's question. Next morning I arose very jaded and still perverse.

But the war compelled me, if I were to have any peace of

mind, to attempt to justify my position to myself, and this
led me to pay more attention than I had ever done before to
the social and political problems of the times. Hitherto my
interest had been almost exclusively theological and ecclesiastical. I had always lived a sheltered life. Now I began to
face life in the raw. In the war I fully realized for the first
time the fearful passions that can boil up out of the heart of
man, the savage cruelties, the treacheries, the lies, the un-
reason. It shook me terribly, and the postwar developments
contributed still further to the dissipation of my earlier com-
placence. I entered on a struggle parallel in some measure to
my previous theological struggle and I am still in it. I honestly believe, on the basis of a study of current journalism
during the past dozen years, that those who felt compelled
to look at the war with a somewhat critical eye were enabled
more quickly than the majority to sense the terrible dangers
of postwar conditions, for example, the madness of the Versailles Treaty, which was only a new declaration of war
against the Central Powers under another form and is today
a cancerous growth in the organic law of Europe; the madness of the Palmer raids in this country, an expression of the
most dangerous form of lawlessness, namely, the lawlessness
of law, a danger still gnawing at our civil liberties; the
emergence again of that sinister phenomenon, Ku-Kluxism,
whose fever has abated for the moment but whose germs, I
fear, are in our blood; the intoxication of our country with
newly acquired, almost illimitable power, resulting in a dis-
eased nationalism and the rapidly expanding Fascist doctrine of the absolute authority of the state, even over the
conscience of the individual, as seen in the 5-4 decision of the
Supreme Court to deny naturalization to alien pacifists; our
money-madness when we suddenly found ourselves the richest nation of the earth not only today but of all time, a madness that has corrupted our business and political life as perhaps never before in our history (witness that Federal ad-

ministration the memory of which we would like to forget if Marion would only permit us to do so); our sex-madness (I borrow the characterization from Professor Dewey) that finds its logical culmination in the suppurating spectacle at present staged in Reno; our current, crudely formulated sophistical philosophy of ethics which recently denied from this very platform any distinction between good and bad and triumphantly proclaimed the nonexistence of conscience because it is not as tangible as a chicken gizzard!

What is the result of this wild debauch during the past dozen years? A hangover of world dimensions, a splitting cosmic *katzenjammer*. And into this situation it has devolved upon me, born a Mid-Victorian, with my own secure anchorage in the authoritarian religion into which I was baptized loosened by the north winds of the hard, cold, scientific spirit to which I finally had to yield—into this situation, I say, it devolves upon me to introduce you of the Graduating Class of 1931. Can the blind lead the blind? Will not both fall into the ditch? I confess I am baffled by it all. I cannot provide for you a thoroughly worked-out pattern according to which the tangled threads of life may be woven into some order. I can only stitch on to what has already been sewed together a few further concluding patches of suggestion.

But before I proceed to these I wish to insert, even at the risk of losing the thread of my discourse, an illustration of one of the problems just referred to, the conscription of the conscience by the state. I do this because Oberlin is traditionally interested in this question and it is one which is likely to have increasing public attention in the years to come.

Scene (it is an actual one*). A Federal courtroom in Louisiana; Rev. T. F. King, pastor of the Methodist Church in Lake Arthur, La., is applying for naturalization.

* *See* "The Pacifist Bogey," by Dorothy Dunbar Bromley, *Harper's Magazine*, October, 1930.

Judge. What did you do during the World War?

Ans. I served for three years in the British Army, and spent about fifteen months overseas in Salonika.

Judge. Supposing the United States engaged in a war that you considered was wrong, what would be your attitude?

Ans. I would consider it my duty to protect and defend Democracy.

Judge. But supposing, to take a concrete case, California wanted more territory, and decided to seize some in Mexico, and everyone was drafted for some form of service, would you object or be loyal?

Ans. I do not believe the United States would engage in such a war.

Judge. I do not want any conditions. Under such circumstances, a war of aggression, would you object?

Ans. In all probability I would. I would first have to consider my duty to God and to humanity.

Judge. In other words, you cannot subscribe under any and every condition to the doctrine, "My country right or wrong, but my country"?

Ans. No. (In other words Mr. King refuses the pinch of incense to Caesar.)

Judge. Then you cannot be admitted. What we want are citizens who are prepared to say, "My country right or wrong, but my country."

This would seem to be placing the acceptance of the political philosophy till recently championed by the *Chicago Tribune* above that of James Madison and Thomas Jefferson as a condition of naturalization in the United States. Unfortunately, by its 5-4 decision in the MacIntosh case, which involves the same principle as the King case, the Supreme Court of the United States has put its imprimatur on the legal propriety of this terrible scene. Once before, in the history of the country, the Supreme Court, in the Dred

Scott case, set its legalism against the growing conscience of mankind on the subject of chattel slavery. Today, by this decision, it sets its legalism by a majority of one vote against the growing conscience of the world on the subject of war. In 1857 its decision was challenged from an Oberlin platform. Will our Oberlin family give its moral support to this decision in 1931 or withhold it? Will it or will it not seek the repeal of the Congressional law thus precariously interpreted by the Court? For my part I do not believe that great moral issues were ever decided by a majority of one in an opinion based upon a doubtful technical point of law. May I also remind you that Chief Justice Hughes wrote the dissenting opinion with which Justices Holmes, Brandeis and Stone concurred.

I turn to my brief concluding patches. In the first place, you have two assets which I think are extremely important at such a time as this. One of these is your splendid physical endowment. Not for many generations has graduating youth been so favored in this respect as you are. Your country's prosperity during your childhood and adolescence has presented you with this great gift of abounding health, especially as compared with the undernourished youth of Europe.

Good health is a great insurance against morbid, one-sided views of life, a great aid to the clear thinking which you will have to do if you would escape disaster. Your second asset is, if I understand you, your hatred of bunk. That is altogether to the good. The world has been engaging, especially in our land, in a bull bunk-market for sometime past. Deflation is sorely needed. But these two assets by themselves will not save you. They have their own dangers. A fine physical endowment may be the cause of one's downfall. The pleasures of the senses may become overmastering and may lead youth to turn its back upon what Wordsworth so finely calls "organic pleasure," the pleasure that becomes a part of one's

growth, that lasts through life and properly informs it with
the spirit of unsoiled joy. And again, the hatred of bunk
may easily turn to cynicism, a very shriveled and juiceless
imitation of the sweet fruit of sincerity. Cynicism too easily
becomes a pose and thus lapses into bunk again, or solidifies
into a hard-boiled view of life that will rob it of all its finer
possibilities. No, something else in addition to robust health
and a high-spirited hatred of insincerity is necessary in the
face of the problems and confusions of the present. And here
I come back to my father again. You may have noticed my
frequent references to him. These were purposed. He turned
away when a young man from what I have always understood were brilliant prospects. He did so out of a sense of
duty and devotion to *his* Father. The result was a life of
comparative obscurity, though he was loved by all who knew
him. But never in his life did he have the opportunity to
speak to such an audience as this. I cannot begin to tell the
debt of gratitude I owe him, and therefore it has been a peculiar satisfaction for me to feel that he is joined with me in
speaking to you this day. And now to the point I have been
aiming at. When I was looking over my father's papers and
sermons after his death I found certain verses quoted from
Matthew Arnold (an "Eminent Victorian," by the way)
with which I should have been familiar but was not. I looked
up the passage and found that it was taken from "Obermann
Once More." The verses in a somewhat expanded context
are these:

> In his cool hall with haggard eyes
>   The noble Roman lay;
> He drove abroad, in furious guise,
>   Along the Appian way.
>
> He made a feast, drank fierce and fast,
>   And crowned his hair with flowers;
> No easier nor no quicker passed
>   The impracticable hours.

The brooding East with awe beheld
   Her impious younger world.
The Roman tempest swelled and swelled,
   And on her head was hurled.

The East bowed low before the blast
   In patient, deep disdain;
She let the legions thunder past,
   And plunged in thought again.

So well she mused, a morning broke
   Across her spirit gray;
A conquering, new-born joy awoke,
   And filled her life with day.

"Poor world," she cried, "so deep accurst,
   That runn'st from pole to pole,
To seek a draught to slake thy thirst—
   Go, seek it in thy soul!"

Go seek it in thy soul. That was the message of the Christian religion to the Roman world when, rich, luxurious, and materialized, it was plunging into ruin. That is the message which comes to us today who are richer, more luxurious, and possibly equally materialized. Reforms are necessary, tragically necessary, but reforms *alone* cannot save us. After all, they deal with the externals of life and cannot rise permanently above the level of our inner lives and ideals. When the individual citizen is living in his own soul a distraught and disorganized life, as is so largely the case at the present time, we cannot expect any ordered or unified collective life. What not only you of the Graduating Class but all of us need as we face this distracted age is to save our souls, recover our inner life. In order to achieve this self-discipline is more necessary than self-expression, the grace of renunciation than the tact of acquisitiveness, the insight of "selective consumption" than the crude power of mass production. It is significant that the two religions which have exerted the

greatest and most lasting impression upon the lives and imaginations of men, Christianity and Buddhism, have emphasized at least the first two of these qualities. Possibly that is
not accidental; possibly that is a hint of what human nature
really needs—a challenge to its moral and spiritual heroism.

THE ARBORETUM—NOVEMBER

In quiet dignity the year draws to its close,
On solemn winds the scent of Autumn blows,
A shadowed light falls from the brooding sky,
And Nature, hushed yet unafraid, confronts mortality.